In Busine

Student's book

Graham White and
Margaret Khidhayir

Nelson

Thomas Nelson and Sons Ltd
Nelson House Mayfield Road
Walton-on-Thames Surrey KT12 5PL UK

51 York Place
Edinburgh EH1 3JD UK

Thomas Nelson (Hong Kong) Ltd
Toppan Building 10/F
22A Westlands Road
Quarry Bay Hong Kong

First published by George G. Harrap and Co. Ltd 1983
(under ISBN 0-245-53803-8)

Second impression published by Thomas Nelson and Sons Ltd 1984
ISBN 0-17-444192-4
NPN 9 8
Printed in Hong Kong

Dedication

To Ann and Alexander
To Mahmoud, Karim, Danny and Natasha

Note All the characters and incidents in this book are entirely fictitious and bear no relation whatsoever to any known person or persons.

Key to symbols used

- reading
- pair work
- language
- listening
- language laboratory drills
- writing
- role play
- group work

Acknowledgements

The authors wish to thank the Principal of the Regent School Brighton, Susan Drake, and the teaching and administrative staff, Robert Blackadder, Kathy Deech, Marjatta Gordon, Vicki Lloyd, Gail Louw and Valerie Roantree for their help, advice and encouragement during the writing of this book.

The authors and publishers are grateful to the following for permission to reproduce the illustrations:

P Harrison for pages 2, 19 (*right* taken courtesy Panalpina Travel, Ludgate Hill, London EC4), 63, 78, 80, 99, 107, 139, 146, 148, 151, 169 and 187; Stephen F Morley for pages 5 (taken courtesy Executrade Centres at their Fleet Street complex), 10, 27, 86, 93, 97 and 116; RHP Group Publicity for page 4; Lufthansa for page 16; Thorn Lighting Ltd for page 21; Camera Press Ltd for pages 31 and 143 (photograph by Pascale Villiers Le Moy); the Brazilian Embassy for page 43; Port of Liverpool Authority for page 47; Robert Golden for page 49; Ford Motor Co Ltd for pages 54 and 56; Fran Miller for pages 55 and 154; Bell and Howell Ltd for page 121; the United Arab Emirates Embassy for page 129; Alan Hutchinson Library for page 131; Shell Photographic Library for page 133; Picker International for page 162; *Practical hi-fi* magazine for page 174.

London Transport Underground Map Registered User Number 83/036.
Extracts from the British Code of Advertising Practice (pages 179 and 180) are reproduced by kind permission of the Advertising Standards Authority. The Innovation for Industry competition (pages 166 and 167) was adapted with the kind permission of the *Observer*.

We should also like to thank William Quirke, Linda Freed, Gianfranco Chinellato, Teruaki Morifuji, and all those who helped as models.

Drawings by Russell Barnett
Cartoons by Nigel Paige

Contents

Syllabus

UNIT	FUNCTION	GRAMMAR STRUCTURE	TOPIC	ACTIVITY
1	asking and answering questions giving information routines and habits	simple present tense adverbs of frequency	company structure personal routines conferences	reading for information listening and note-taking group decision-making exercise
2	asking polite questions	indirect questions	conference agenda company performance letters of enquiry	pair work letter writing group activity
3	comparing and contrasting discussing advantages and disadvantages	simple comparisons intensifiers	air travel flight reservations offers and quotations	listening and note-taking role play group decision-making exercise
4	describing things and people measurements and calculations	prepositions	shapes, sizes, area, cost calculations	listening and drawing gap-filling exercise pair work calculation exercise
5	sequencing criticizing	simple past tense *should/shouldn't have done*	factory layout newspaper reports insurance	role play listening and reading for information letter writing
6	describing trends dealing with statistics	simple past tense present perfect tense	graphs and statistics marketing budget	listening and drawing a curve discussing statistics interpreting figures writing a company profile

UNIT	FUNCTION	GRAMMAR STRUCTURE	TOPIC	ACTIVITY
7	giving instructions and directions obligation and necessity	modals (*must/mustn't/ needn't/don't have to*)	directions export regulations operating instructions credit cards job descriptions	pair work listening and note-taking writing a job description
8	describing processes	passive voice	car production house building memoranda	listening and note-taking group decision-making and problem-solving exercise memo writing
9	Consolidation exercises	Revision of Units 1 to 8		
10	future plans and intentions anticipating reactions	simple future tense *going to* and present continuous tense for future conditional 1 + *may/ might/could*	travel plans newspaper article energy saving	listening and note-taking true/false reading exercise group discussion and decision-making exercise memo writing
11	reporting and passing on information	reported speech — statements and questions	travel to the USA telephone messages overseas sales visit	listening and note-taking jigsaw reading exercise discussion
12	personal opinions agreeing and disagreeing putting a point and interrupting in meetings	*should/shouldn't*	meetings public opinion surveys	listening and note-taking pair work presenting ideas to a group discussion on company policy
13	complaining explaining and apologizing promises and offers	simple future tense for promises and offers *shall* with offers	delivery of goods problems with an order noise pollution	listening and note-taking role play gap-filling exercise
14	interviewing techniques asking for clarification placing emphasis	questions adjective order	job advertisements and interviews	listening and note-taking role play pair work

UNIT	FUNCTION	GRAMMAR STRUCTURE	TOPIC	ACTIVITY
15	advising and suggesting	gerund and infinitive *that* clauses conditionals + *may/might*	investment shares, unit trusts and building societies	listening and note-taking information exchange reading for information decision-making exercise
16	comparing and contrasting evaluating alternatives expressing preferences	intensifiers superlatives adverbial expressions	renting accommodation quotations factory location	listening and note-taking telex writing decision-making exercise gap-filling exercise report writing
17	presentation techniques dealing with objections and queries referring to visual aids	inversion focussing passives	presenting a product visual aids order processing	listening and note-taking pair work presenting a point of view to a group and dealing with objections
18	Consolidation exercises	Revision of Units 9 to 17		
19	sequencing information evaluating information	revision of past tenses (simple past, present perfect, past perfect, past continuous) and passives	graphs and statistics entering a new market	gap-filling exercise listening and note-taking reading and note-taking vocabulary work group decision-making
20	requests and offers	modals simple futures indirect questions	phoning a travel agent negotiating an agreement with a foreign government medical care	controlled role play free role play letter writing listening and note-taking
21	certainty and uncertainty ability and achievement	*could/was able to* *must have/might have/can't have*	sales visits company fortunes senior executive's illness	gap-filling exercise letter writing logical problem-solving case study

UNIT	FUNCTION	GRAMMAR STRUCTURE	TOPIC	ACTIVITY
22	plans and intentions rumours probability	simple future tense conditional 2 future continuous tense	setting up a new production plant Government plans making a film about the company economic trends	listening and note-taking discussing content of a film group work
23	chairing a meeting agreeing and disagreeing talking about suitability	*enough/too/such/so* + adjective	discussion of a new product machine specifications 'Innovation for Industry' competition	listening and note-taking role play report writing evaluation meeting
24	giving reasons making recommendations	connectors	office reorganization examining reasons for a company's decline	listening and note-taking controlled practice on connectors case study
25	permission prohibition restrictions regrets recriminations	modals past perfect tense conditional 3	advertising regulations advertising drugs and cigarettes losing a contract problems of an advertising agency	listening and note-taking reading for information group discussion letter writing
26	making arrangements sorting out problems	gerund and infinitive reported speech	problem in the technical sales department	problem-solving activity listening and note-taking gerund/infinitive exercise
27	Consolidation exercises	Revision of Units 20 to 26		

1 The Executives' Conference (1)

There are 11 steps in Unit 1. You will:

- revise the present tenses
- practise asking and answering questions
- discuss company structure
- talk about personal routines and job responsibilities
- arrange a conference on marketing techniques

1 Company details

You are attending the annual Executives' Conference of the Swiss-owned multinational UMC (United Manufacturing Corporation). The organization has recently acquired two companies, Ambermold International and Fittenwell Pharmaceuticals. In order to be fully informed about all aspects of UMC's activities, you have asked your secretary to provide you with background information.

Work in pairs, one student reading an extract from Ambermold International's brochure, the other student reading an extract from Fittenwell Pharmaceutical's brochure. As you read, look out for the information required for the questionnaire on page 3.

Extract from the company brochure

FITTENWELL PHARMACEUTICALS

The Fittenwell Group of companies was established 15 years ago and has its headquarters in Switzerland overlooking Lake Geneva. There are three manufacturing companies in Switzerland (two in Zürich and one in Basel), sales companies in 20 countries and agents in a further 15. Following lengthy negotiations over the past three years, the Fittenwell Group was taken over by UMC in May of last year.

The Group manufactures and markets drugs and pharmaceutical preparations which are distributed on a world-wide basis through their network of subsidiaries and agents. A recent development has been the setting up of a manufacturing plant in Switzerland to produce hospital and laboratory equipment. This new venture is proving extremely successful and demand for Fittenwell's high quality and specialized equipment is growing rapidly. There is a possibility that additional subsidiaries will be created overseas for the assembly, marketing and distribution of this equipment.

The Fittenwell Group is already making a very positive contribution to UMC. Last year its turnover was 250 million Swiss francs and it is expected to rise by 8% this year. Altogether 5,500 people are employed by the Group and, despite worries about recession, the Directors are determined not to reduce the range of Fittenwell's activities in the foreseeable future.

Extract from the company brochure

Ambermold International

Ambermold International was founded 25 years ago by Godfrey Thomas (now Sir Godfrey Thomas) in Manchester as a one-man manufacturing company. The Group now comprises five companies throughout Europe and is represented worldwide by a comprehensive network of agents. The total number of employees on the payroll is now some 8,000.

This dramatic expansion was due in no small part to Godfrey Thomas's foresight in patenting his simple invention of a roller bearing system which reduced friction by nearly 50% and at the same time increased the system's working life by a similar amount. It is not possible here to go into too much technical detail, but we can say that Thomas's revolutionary invention relied on the use of a heavier than normal lubricating oil, stainless steel roller bearings accurate to 1/10,000 mm, and the sealing of the whole system under sterile conditions at a very high temperature.

Godfrey Thomas was, and is, a perfectionist who insists on the highest standards and the result is that the Ambermold Bearing System (or ABS as it came to be known) is now used in machinery all over the world. Annual turnover is currently in the region of £22 million.

UMC, the Swiss multinational, first showed interest in Ambermold International two and a half years ago and a take-over was finally agreed at the end of last year. Under the agreement signed by the two companies, Godfrey Thomas remains Managing Director of Ambermold International and Karl-Heinz Braunfels becomes Chairman. The take-over means that substantial funds will now be available for investment in new projects, especially the development of new products and the opening of a new plant abroad. Manchester is still the company's headquarters and the Swinton Lane plant in Manchester is the main manufacturing base, although there are small factories in Greenock, Scotland, and Port Talbot in South Wales, which are due to be modernized and automated over the next five years.

2 Exchanging information

You will now exchange information with your partner, but first make sure you know how to ask questions accurately. Look at the questionnaire and write down the questions you want to ask in full. Like this:

When was the company established?
Where are Ambermold's headquarters located?

Give your partner the information you have obtained, and ask him or her for information about the other company.

Finally, exchange information about each other's companies.

	Ambermold International	The Fittenwell Group	Your partner's company
Date company established	25 years ago		
Location of HQ		Geneva Switzerland	
Date of take-over by UMC			
Number of employees			
Main products			
Location of factories			
Annual turnover			
Number of companies in group			
Recent developments			
Future plans			

3 Vocabulary work

Look back at the two extracts in step 1. Below are some definitions. Can you find words or phrases in the extracts which mean the same?

Ambermold International

Paragraph 1:

in all parts of ....

established ....

consists of ....

Paragraph 2:

closing completely ....

new technical idea ....

pure and clean ....

Paragraph 3:

total value of sales ....

Paragraph 4:

money ....

eventually ....

Fittenwell Pharmaceuticals

Paragraph 1:

lasting a long time ....

Paragraph 2:

companies controlled by larger companies ....

place where scientific research is carried out ....

Paragraph 3:

period of low economic activity ....

variety ....

4 Keith Andrews

Listen to Keith Andrews talking about his job with Ambermold International. Note down information under these headings:

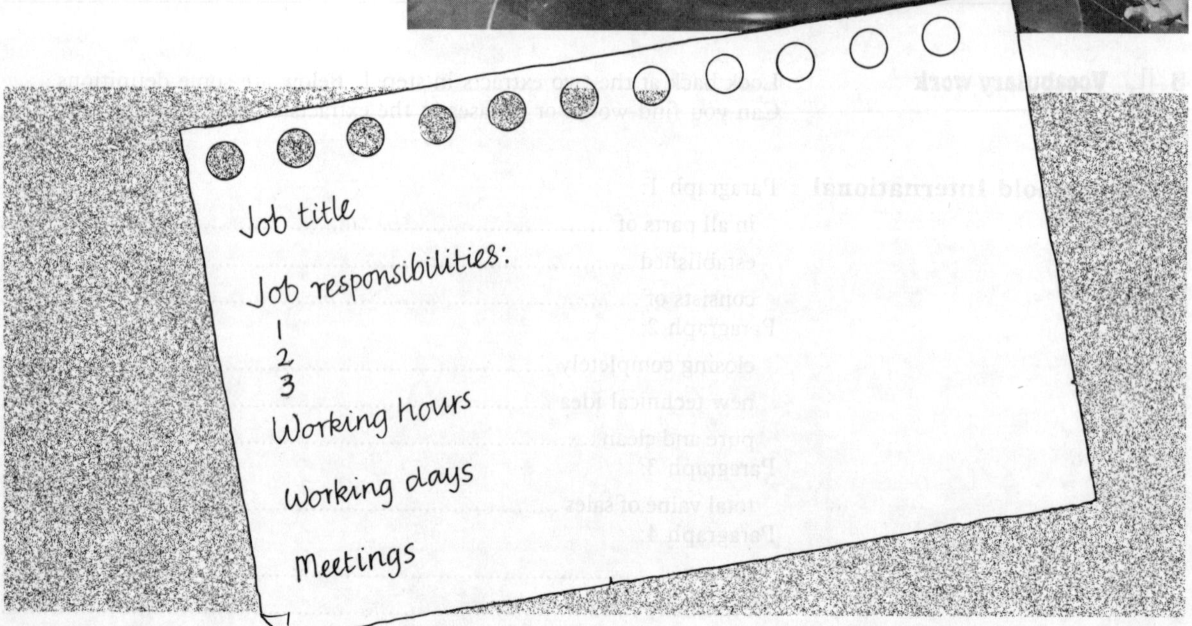

5 The simple present tense

When we are talking about facts, or events which happen regularly, we use the **simple present** tense. For example:

Mr Andrews works for Ambermold.
He attends meetings every week.
He starts work at 8.30, has lunch at 1.00 and goes home at 5.30.

We also use the simple present tense with words like *never, always, often, sometimes, occasionally, usually* and *seldom* to show the regularity with which we do something.
Don't forget that the negative form of the simple present is made with *doesn't* and *don't*, and that we use *do* and *does* to make questions.
For example:

He doesn't work on Sundays.
I don't speak Italian.
Do you smoke?
Does he live in France?

6 Questions

Answer these questions about Keith Andrews:

Who does he work for?
Does he work on Sundays?
What meetings does he attend?
What do they discuss at these meetings?
What is his first job responsibility?
How long does he have for lunch?

Make more questions about Mr Andrews. Work with a partner and practise asking and answering the questions.

7 At the Executives' Conference

Listen to two of the delegates who have just met for the first time. As you listen, note down the questions they ask each other.

8 Interviews

Now interview your partner about his job and working hours. You could also ask him about his spare-time interests and his hopes for the future.

Report back to the group the information you have found out.

9 Drill 1: And Ambermold?

You are trying to find out as much as possible about Ambermold. You already have some information about Ambermold's competitors. Use this as a basis for your questions.

I know there are seven companies in the Britsteel group.
How many companies are there in the Ambermold *group?*

I understand Sheffield Metals spend £12 million every year on new projects.
How much does Ambermold *spend every year on new projects?*

Notice that the word 'Ambermold' is emphasized. This is because facts about Ambermold are being contrasted with facts about other companies.

Repeat again:

How many companies are there in the Ambermold *group?*
How much does Ambermold *spend every year on new projects?*

Now you go on in the same way.

Drill 2: Do you . . .?

Somebody is asking you about your spare-time interests. Listen:

Do you like going to the cinema?
Yes, I often go to the cinema.

Do you ever have a meal in a restaurant?
Yes, I occasionally have a meal in a restaurant.

Do you enjoy going to the opera?
No, I never go to the opera.

Each time use the notes to help you make sentences which show how regularly you go to the cinema, opera, and so on. Don't forget that the adverb of frequency (for example, *often*, *sometimes*) comes immediately after the subject:

I often go . . .
I never visit . . .

Now you go on in the same way. The notes will help you. (Begin at number 3.)

1 often
2 occasionally
3 never
4 sometimes
5 never
6 often
7 hardly ever
8 nearly always

10 The Marketing Conference

A one-day Marketing Conference for all UMC Marketing Executives is to be held at the headquarters of Fittenwell Pharmaceuticals (UK) in six months' time. At the Executives' Conference a working party has been set up to plan this conference. Two groups have already met for preliminary discussions and the notes they have made are printed below and at the end of the Unit. Read through these notes and then hold a general meeting to make a final decision on the day's programme.

Provisional programme A

<u>Timetable:</u> 8.30 - 1.00 (Coffee 10.00 - 10.15)
Lunch
2.00 - 5.30 (Tea 3.30 - 3.45)
Drinks
Dinner 7.30

<u>Lecture</u> by Adrian Barford, Senior Lecturer in Business Studies at Manchester Polytechnic, "Marketing in the Eighties ... and into the Nineties". Followed by Question and Answer session.

<u>Workgroups</u> on the following topics (maximum 6 groups):

1. Presentation techniques
2. Marketing and psychology
3. Questionnaires
4. Publicity stunts
5. Training marketing and sales staff
6. The Far East as a potential market

<u>Film:</u> "UK Ltd - How can Britain sell herself more effectively?" (Produced by Federation of Accredited Marketing Executives.)
Interviews with marketing managers of successful British companies - tips on how to achieve dramatic increases in turnover with modern, aggressive marketing techniques.

11 Memo writing

Now that you have decided on a programme for the forthcoming one-day Marketing Conference to be held at Fittenwell (UK), write a memo to all Marketing Executives at UMC, giving them details of the programme.

Tapescript for step 4 *Tape section 1*

Hello, my name's Andrews, Keith Andrews. I'm Quality Control Manager here at Ambermold. Quality control is a very important part of any manufacturing process and here at Ambermold we have a team of 15 people who are responsible for making sure that the quality and reliability of the products are as high as possible.

As Quality Control Manager I have three basic areas of responsibility. First, I decide on the sampling rate of finished goods. It's not possible to check every single roller bearing system so I have to calculate what percentage should be checked. Secondly, I run tests on those bearings which we sample. I have to set up these tests and produce statistics to show the results clearly so that the design engineers can make any necessary alterations to the production process. But I don't actually carry out the tests myself. I deal with complaints from customers who've had problems with their bearings. I try to find out exactly what has gone wrong and then suggest the best way of overcoming the problem.

It's a very demanding job. I'm normally in the factory from 8.30 until 5.30 Monday to Friday with three quarters of an hour for lunch if I'm lucky. And one Saturday in three I'm on call if any of our customers has a sudden problem with one of our components. Once a month I attend meetings where we discuss technical problems; I report on trends in quality control, whether the defect rate has gone up or down, problems with customers, and so on. Every Thursday afternoon I have a short meeting with all the quality control staff when we discuss technical matters and sometimes working conditions, like tea-breaks etc. I never work on Sundays, thank goodness, although I may have to if the management introduce a seven day week production programme.

Tapescript for step 7 *Tape section 2*

PIET: Hallo, my name's Johanssen. And you're . . .?

GEORGE: I'm George Baxter. Where do you come from, Mr Johanssen?

PIET: Call me Piet, please. I come from Holland.

GEORGE: Oh, whereabouts in Holland?

PIET: Bergen-op-Zoom. It's in the south-west of the country on the coast. Where are you from?

GEORGE: I live in Cheadle.

PIET: Huh?

GEORGE: It's a suburb in the south of Manchester.

PIET: Ha! And which part of UMC do you work for?

GEORGE: Ambermold International.

PIET: Oh yes, you make ball bearings, don't you?

GEORGE: Roller bearings, actually. And who do you work for?

PIET: UMC Chemicals in Rotterdam. I'm a production manager for one of the sites there.

GEORGE: Oh are you? I'm a production engineer at Ambermold's Swinton Lane plant.

PIET: So why are you here at the Executives' Conference?

GEORGE: Well, mainly to give technical information about Ambermold's production, the latest developments and so on. I think they've arranged a workshop for production people to get together and discuss common problems.

PIET: Oh well, I hope to see you again there then. I'm going to be leading one of the workshops myself.

Information for step 10

Provisional programme B

TIMETABLE

9.00 - 12.30 (Coffee 10.15 - 10.45)
Lunch
2.00 - 5.00 (Tea 3.00 - 3.30)
Dinner

LECTURE by Gert Praunheim, Senior Marketing Manager of UMC, "MARKETING IN THE THIRD WORLD ... A NEW APPROACH?", followed by discussion.

WORKGROUPS on the following topics (maximum 6 groups):

1 Market survey and research
2 Direct mail shots
3 Producing a brochure
4 Organization of the marketing department
5 Presenting statistics
6 Following up enquiries

FILM: "BALLICO - A MARKETING CASE STUDY" - how a multi-national completely reorganized its marketing activities and achieved amazing success within a remarkably short time.

2 The Executives' Conference (2)

There are 7 steps in Unit 2. You will:

- find out how to ask polite questions
- exchange information about conferences
- write a letter of enquiry
- question the Board about their past performance and future plans

1 Arriving at the conference

Piet Johanssen of UMC Chemicals is talking to the receptionist at UMC Head Office in Zurich about the conference programme. Listen to their conversation and note down the information which the receptionist gives.

2 Could you tell me . . .?

When we are speaking to someone we don't know very well it is important to use polite forms, especially when asking questions. It's not enough to add the word 'please' to a question; we have to introduce the question with a polite phrase. There were several examples in the dialogue you have just listened to. Listen again and note them down.

Here are some other polite question phrases:

Would you mind telling me . . .
I'd like to know . . .
I wonder if you could tell me . . .
Can you tell me . . .

Completing these sentences is not always easy. Look at these two questions:

Where is Room B107? (*direct*)
Would you mind telling me where Room B107 is? (*polite*)

Notice that the word order changes in the second half of the sentence. We repeat the question word *where*, then comes the subject *Room B107* followed by the verb *is*.

If there is no question word we use *whether* or *if*. Like this:

Is Room B107 on the second floor? (direct)
Could you tell me if Room B107 is on the second floor? (polite)
I'd like to know whether Room B107 is on the second floor. (polite)

3 Asking for information

Now make these questions more polite by adding a suitable question phrase at the beginning. Don't forget to change the word order as necessary.

1 Where is the main Conference Hall?
2 How much is a single ticket to the airport?
3 Where can I buy a film for my camera?
4 How long does it take by taxi?
5 Who is that over there in the corner?
6 Do you work for Ambermold or Fittenwell?
7 Are telex facilities available in this building?

4 Conference agenda

Working in pairs, play the roles of conference delegate and receptionist. The delegate wants details of tomorrow's programme and must ask the receptionist (politely) for the information. The delegate's role-card is printed below. The receptionist's information is at the end of the Unit.

Delegate

You need information about the following events:
1 Publisher's exhibition of new books on marketing: Where? When?
2 Lecture: Who? Where? What time? What subject?
3 Workshop sessions: What subjects available? Where? When?
4 Video programme: What title? When? Where?
5 UMC Directors answer questions: What time? Where?
6 Discussion group: What times? What topic? Where?

5 Drill 1: Is it true?

A colleague has heard certain rumours about the Ambermold Managing Director. At the Executives' Conference you have a chance to find out if these rumours are true, when you meet a senior member of the Ambermold management team. For example, your colleague wants to know:

Is the Managing Director hoping to go to Brussels soon?

So you ask the Ambermold manager:

Is it true that the Managing Director is hoping to go to Brussels soon?

Has the Managing Director borrowed £15,000 from company funds?
Is it true that the Managing Director has borrowed £15,000 from company funds?

Now you go on in the same way. Listen to the question from your colleague and then ask for confirmation from the Ambermold manager.

Drill 2: Yes, it is true!

You now have the information you want, so you can tell your colleague if the rumours about the Managing Director are true or not. Like this:

So what did you find out while you were in Switzerland. Is it true about Brussels?
Yes, it is true that he's hoping to go to Brussels soon.

And the rumour about that large sum of money? Is that true?
No, it isn't true that he's borrowed £15,000 from company funds.

Now you go on in the same way.

Your information

Is he hoping to go to Brussels soon?	Yes
Has he borrowed £15,000 from company funds?	No
Is he planning a holiday from tomorrow?	No
Has he signed an agreement with Britsteel?	Yes
Is he having talks with the Saudi Arabian Government?	Yes
Has he decided to appoint a woman as Chief Accountant?	Yes
Is he going to announce a large export contract?	No
Is he buying another Rolls Royce?	No

6 Letter writing

First read this letter of enquiry. Underline the phrases which introduce polite questions.

Ambermold International

Swinton Lane
Manchester M95 7TZ

British Screws Ltd
Freshfield Estate
Walsall
West Midlands B43 5KT

24 May 19--

Dear Sir,

We refer to your recent advertisement in the 'Engineering Gazette' for heavy-duty nuts and bolts and would be pleased to receive detailed information including price-list.

In particular, could you let us know the maximum load-bearing capacity of your products and the range of sizes which are available. At the same time, could you tell us whether you consider that they are suitable for the construction of an automated production line.

As we are budgeting for a project to be carried out over the next 18 months, we need to know when your prices are likely to be increased.

Thank you for your help.

Yours faithfully,

G Baxter

GEORGE BAXTER
Production Engineer

Now write a similar letter of enquiry to Britsteel Ltd, Britsteel House, Oakland Road, Sheffield S3 4PJ. Use these notes to help you:

— refer to an advertisement in the *Iron and Steel Journal* for stainless steel casing units
— request catalogue and price list
— request specific information about sizes and weight
— ask about suitability of units for manufacture of roller bearing systems
— ask about discount facilities
— thank Britsteel in advance

Don't forget to use polite requests.

7 UMC Directors in the hot seat

Tomorrow afternoon at 2 pm UMC Directors will answer questions on topics of general interest in the Main Conference Hall. They can be asked about their past performance, their thoughts on the present economic situation, their plans and hopes for the future, or on similar topics.

You are meeting to decide what questions to put to the management team. Try to reach agreement on a list of about ten questions.

Then divide into two groups (Conference Delegates and UMC Directors) and re-enact the question and answer session. The UMC Directors will find some information which may be useful at the end of the Unit.

Tapescript for step 1

Tape section 4

PIET: Excuse me, could you tell me what time we have to be here tomorrow morning?

RECEPTIONIST: Well, the conference hall opens at 8.30 but the first event isn't until 9.15.

PIET: And what is that?

RECEPTIONIST: Just a moment. I'll have a look. Yes, it's a discussion about research budgeting.

PIET: Ah! That's OK. I don't have to go to that. Do you happen to know when the production managers' meeting is?

RECEPTIONIST: Yes, it's at 10.30 in Room B107.

PIET: B107 . . . thanks very much. Is it true that the workshop session on marketing techniques has been cancelled?

RECEPTIONIST: Yes, that's right – there weren't enough people interested.

PIET: Oh, I see. Oh, and could you tell me the telex number of UMC Sweden?

RECEPTIONIST: Yes, I'll have to ring Central Information . . . Hallo? Yes it's UMC Sweden I want, no, not their telephone number, I just wanted to know what their telex number is . . . Yes I've got that. Thanks a lot . . . Right, it's S217364.

PIET: Thanks very much.

Receptionist's information for step 4

	MAIN CONFERENCE HALL	ROOM B107	ROOM A208
9.00	Lecture: Mr J Smythe -'Corporate Management'		-
10.00		Workshop Session -'Decision-Making and the Microprocessor'	Workshop Session -'Standardizing Internal Communications'
11.00	Publishers' Exhibition of New Books on Marketing		
12.00			
13.00	L U N C H		
14.00	UMC Directors Answer Questions - All Invited	Video + Discussion UMC Training Film	Discussion Group -'Public Relations How to Improve UMC's Image'
15.00			
16.00			
17.00			

UMC Directors' information for step 7

Increase in profit before tax this year: 7½%
  Increase in turnover: 9.3%
Target increase in profit before tax next year: 5%
  Increase in turnover: 7%
New companies taken over in last year:
  Ambermold (roller bearings)
  Manchester HQ
    Turnover: £22 million
  Fittenwell Pharmaceuticals
    Switzerland HQ represented worldwide
    Turnover: 250 million Swiss francs
Take-over next year:
  Aluminium Producers (W Germany)
  Chemical Works (Italy)
New factories opening over next three years:
  Engineering Co (Columbia)
  Bottle Making Plant (Central Africa)
  Engineering Co (Venezuela) producing oil industry equipment
Factory closures:
  Auto Components (France) Factory
  Manufacturer of Reinforced Glass
New UMC Director:
  James Alexander, formerly of Grindlays Merchant Bank, City of London, to be Financial Controller of UMC.

3 More or less

There are 10 steps in Unit 3. You will:

- revise simple comparisons
- learn how to use intensifiers (for example, *a lot*, *much*)
- find out how to discuss advantages and disadvantages
- discuss offers to supply goods

1 Flight details

George Baxter is Senior Production Manager at Ambermold Manchester and often has to fly to cities in Europe to deal with production problems at Ambermold's subsidiaries.

A branch of the German subsidiary has recently been opened near Frankfurt, and George will have to visit the plant regularly over the next six months to help set up the production line.

He has asked his secretary to get as much information as possible about flights to Frankfurt, so that he can telephone his German colleagues and make arrangements.

Study the information carefully. You will refer to it later in the Unit.

Airline	Departure		Total flying time	Transfer	Return fare	Special conditions
	Day	Time				
British Skyways	Daily	08.15	2 hrs 20 mins	None	£98	Open ticket. Telephone 24 hours in advance to reserve place.
Hawkwind Airlines	Daily	10.30 16.45	2 hrs	None	£98	Open ticket. Telephone 24 hours in advance to reserve place.
Condor Airways	Daily	09.25	3 hrs	Heathrow	£64.50	Ticket must be purchased one month in advance.
Inland Airways	Daily	09.25	3 hrs 30 mins	Heathrow	£59	Ticket must be purchased two weeks in advance.
Overseas Airways	Tuesday Friday	17.00	3 hrs 15 mins	None	£53.50	Ticket must be purchased 48 hours in advance.

Return flight			
Inland Airways British Skyways Hawkwind Airlines	Open	Overseas Airways Condor Airways	Within 2 weeks Within 1 week

2 Comparing

It's easy to compare things in English. We say:

The 09.25 flight is slower than the 08.15 flight.
Flying British Skyways is more expensive than flying Overseas Airways.

Or:

The 09.25 flight is not as fast as the 08.15 flight.
Flying British Skyways is not as cheap as flying Overseas Airways.

But to show how wide the difference is between the two things we are comparing, we often use extra words called 'intensifiers'. If there is a big difference, we might use *a lot*, *a great deal*, or *much*. For example:

The Hawkwind Airlines flight is a lot more expensive than the Overseas Airways flight.
Flying Inland Airways is a great deal cheaper than flying Hawkwind Airlines.
Hawkwind Airlines fly much more frequently than Overseas Airways.

If we want to show that the difference is small, we can use *a bit*, or *a little*. For example:

Condor Airways is a bit quicker than Overseas Airways.
Overseas Airways is a little cheaper than Inland Airways.

When we are comparing, we often have to balance advantages against disadvantages. Here are some ways of pointing out disadvantages:

British Skyways are faster than Condor. The only trouble is, they're rather expensive.

Inland Airways are cheaper than Hawkwind. The only problem is, you have to change.
Inland Airways leaves earlier than Hawkwind. The only thing is, it takes a long time to get there.

3 Contrasting

Compare the following pairs of services. Use the words and phrases in step 2.

1	British Skyways and Overseas Airways	(frequency)
2	Hawkwind Airlines and Condor Airways	(flying time)
3	Condor Airways and Overseas Airways	(cost)
4	Inland Airways and Overseas Airways	(departure time)
5	Hawkwind Airlines and Inland Airways	(flying time)

Now discuss the advantages and disadvantages of the following pairs of services. Write down your sentences first.

1 British Skyways and Overseas Airways
2 Condor Airways and Inland Airways
3 Hawkwind Airlines and Overseas Airways
4 Hawkwind Airlines and Inland Airways
5 British Skyways and Hawkwind Airlines

4 Which flight?

Now look at George Baxter's diary for the period January to April. Work out which flights will be most suitable for each of the journeys. The notes will help you to decide.

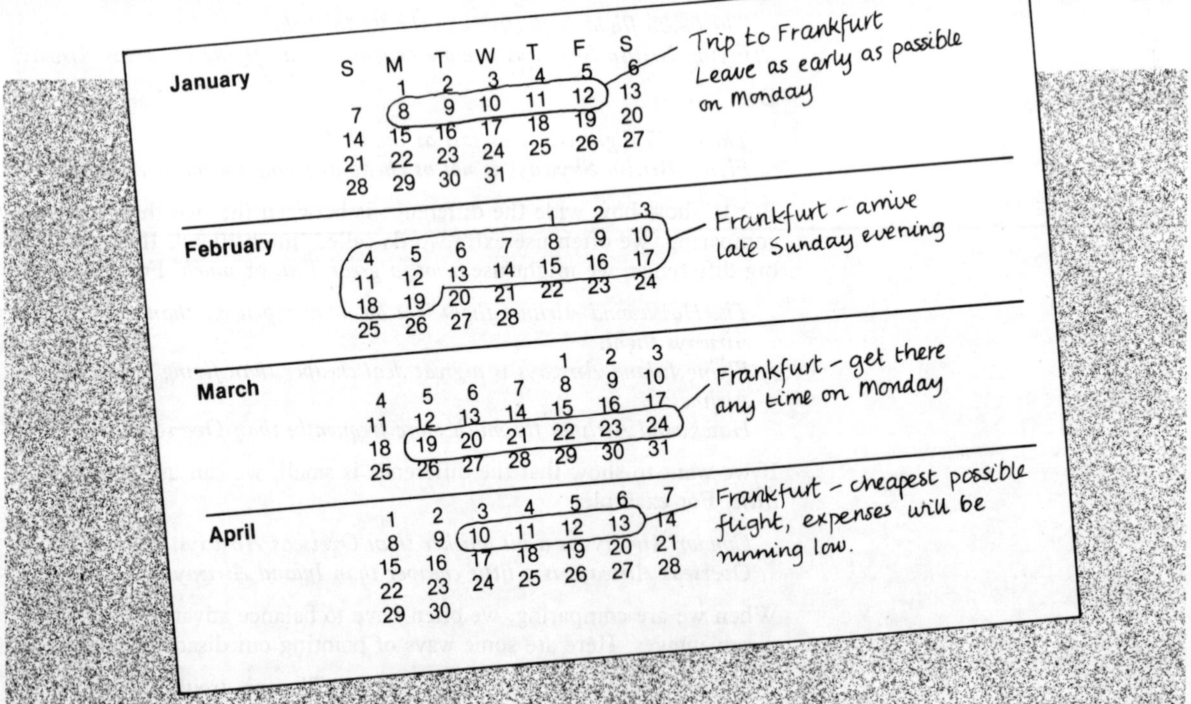

5 Seat reservations

George Baxter telephones Global Travel to reserve a seat on a flight to Frankfurt. Listen to the conversation and note down the information under these headings:

Departure date: ....

Time: ....

Airline: ....

Flight: ....

Ticket: ....

Check-in time: ....

Check-in place: ....

6 Calling the travel agent

Now work in pairs and reserve by telephone a seat on one of the other flights George Baxter will be taking. Some of these phrases might be useful:

GEORGE BAXTER: I'd like to reserve a seat on a flight to Frankfurt, please.
The flight's the one leaving at . . .

GLOBAL TOURS: When are you flying?
Could I have the airline and flight number?
Hold the line and I'll check for you.

7 Prepositions

Make sure that you know the prepositions we use when we are talking about travel arrangements. Try to fill in the blanks in this paragraph.

I'm flying . . . . . Frankfurt . . . . . British Airways flight number BA743. It leaves Manchester . . . . . 10.30 . . . . . Friday 9 February and arrives . . . . . Frankfurt . . . . . 12.55 local time. I have to check in . . . . . the international departure terminal at least one hour . . . . . the aircraft is due to take off.

8 Drill 1: Frankfurt is better . . .

Listen to George Baxter and Christine Weber talking about their home cities.

Manchester is a very expensive city, the most expensive in northern England.
Yes, but Frankfurt is much more expensive.

On the other hand, it's a nice place to live.
Yes, but Frankfurt is much nicer.

Each time Christine Weber says that Frankfurt is very different from Manchester, she says it is *much nicer* or *much more expensive.*

Now you go on in the same way. Imagine you are Christine Weber. Listen to what George Baxter has to say about Manchester and then say how Frankfurt is different.

Drill 2: Yes, but . . .

Your colleague is pointing out the advantages of travelling by different airlines. But you know that there are disadvantages. Tell your colleague about them. Like this:

Skyways offer a very frequent service.
Yes, but on the other hand, their flights are rather expensive.

Hawkwind Airlines have the fastest flights.
Yes, but on the other hand, their flights are rather infrequent.

Now you go on in the same way. The notes will help you. (Begin at number 3.)

1 Skyways .... expensive
2 Hawkwind Airlines .... infrequent
3 Inland Airways .... long
4 Skyways .... early in the morning
5 Overseas Airways .... late in the afternoon
6 Hawkwind Airlines .... expensive
7 Overseas Airways .... infrequent
8 Inland Airways .... long

9 Choosing a supplier

Your department has been asked to order all the equipment needed for refitting Production Hall B at the Swinton Lane plant. You have asked three firms for quotations for supplying fluorescent tubes to light this area.

You have received letters from two of the firms and you have spoken on the phone to someone from the third firm.

First listen to the phone call to Office Supplies and write down the information under these headings:

	Office Supplies	Candor Lighting	Brilight
Brand name			
Price per item			
Discount			
Delivery period			
Payment terms			
Guarantee			

Now work with your partner and read the letters from Candor Lighting (below) and Brilight (at the end of the Unit). Write down the information under the same headings.

QUOTATION

CANDOR LIGHTING
BRILLIANCE HOUSE
ERDINGTON ROAD
BIRMINGHAM 12

Our Ref	Your Ref
CL 3421	AMB/4093M

Ambermold International
Swinton Lane
Manchester

22 April 19--

Dear Sirs,

We are glad to submit the quotation for which you ask. Please do not hesitate to approach us again if we have in any way misunderstood your instructions.

This estimate is given subject to our Standard Conditions for ~~all work done and~~ goods supplied, a copy of which is set out on the back of this letter. Accordingly these Conditions shall be deemed to be embodied in any contract based on or arising out of this quotation unless otherwise agreed in writing.

Yours faithfully,

for CANDOR LIGHTING

DESCRIPTION/SPECIFICATION

Candor Special Fluortube   Cat. No. CSF 1359-79
Price per item £4.20 + VAT
Normal working life 3,500 hours.

We are able to offer discount to customers placing orders worth more than a total of £150 in any one month. Discount rate = 5%

Allow up to two weeks for delivery.

Delivery	Carriage	Terms of Payment
buyer's address	lorry	net within 60 days

Finally, try to reach a group decision on which company should be asked to supply the tubes. You need to purchase 55 lamps altogether.

10 Letter writing

Now that you have decided which company should supply the fluorescent tubes, write a short letter to place the order.

Don't forget to include the following points:

— thanks for the offer received
— the exact brand name of the tubes
— the number of tubes you require
— the price, less any discount
— delivery address
— request for prompt delivery

Tapescript for step 5

Tape section 6

TELEPHONIST: Global Travel. Good morning.
GEORGE BAXTER: Oh, good morning. I'd like to reserve a seat on a flight to Frankfurt, please.
TELEPHONIST: Hold the line and I'll put you through to reservations.
SALESGIRL: Reservations.
GEORGE BAXTER: Oh yes, good morning. I want to reserve a seat on a flight to Frankfurt, please.
SALESGIRL: When are you flying?
GEORGE BAXTER: Monday, the 19th of March.
SALESGIRL: Yes. And could I have the airline and flight number?
GEORGE BAXTER: It's British Caledonian. The flight's the one leaving at 8.15 am.
SALESGIRL: From Manchester?
GEORGE BAXTER: Yes.
SALESGIRL: That's flight BCL241. What's the number of your ticket?
GEORGE BAXTER: JB 248320.
SALESGIRL: And your name?
GEORGE BAXTER: Baxter. B-A-X-T-E-R. The initials are GM.
SALESGIRL: Hold the line and I'll check for you . . . Yes, that'll be alright, Mr Baxter. Check in before 7.30 am at the International Departures Desk on Monday the 19th of March.
GEORGE BAXTER: Ah! Thank you very much. Goodbye.
SALESGIRL: Goodbye.

Tapescript for step 9

Tape section 8

TELEPHONIST: Office Supplies. Good afternoon.
AMBERMOLD: Good afternoon. Sales Department, please.
OFFICE SUPPLIES: Sales. Can I help you?
AMBERMOLD: Yes, this is Ambermold Manchester here. We're having fluorescent lighting installed at our Swinton Lane plant and we wondered if you could quote us for 150 watt tubes.
OFFICE SUPPLIES: I see. Hold on a minute and I'll get the stocklist. Hallo? Yes. What length would the tubes be?
AMBERMOLD: Oh, the standard size. About one metre.
OFFICE SUPPLIES: Yes, I know. Well, our Mazoda tubes would be what you're looking for. They have a guaranteed life of 2,750 hours.
AMBERMOLD: Oh, that sounds fine. How much do they cost?
OFFICE SUPPLIES: £4.00 per tube plus VAT, but we offer a discount of 10% on orders of over 50 tubes.
AMBERMOLD: Fine. What about payment and delivery?

OFFICE SUPPLIES: We have a delivery period of approximately two weeks. And payment, well it's against invoice within 30 days unless you arrange to have an account with us.

AMBERMOLD: Ah, OK. Thanks very much. I'll have to discuss the matter with my manager and then if we decide to place the order with you, I'll let you know. Thank you again. Goodbye.

OFFICE SUPPLIES: Goodbye.

Information for step 9

BRILIGHT

LIGHTING SPECIALISTS

BRILIGHT HOUSE
HOMEFARM ROAD
LONDON NW11
01-743 1946

Purchasing Department
Ambermold International
Swinton Lane
MANCHESTER

24 April 19--

Dear Sirs,

Re: Inquiry - Fluorescent Tubes

Thank you for your letter of 17 April inquiring about fluorescent tubes for the new lighting installation in your Manchester plant.

We confirm that we are able to supply BRILIGHT 150 watt tubes at a price of £3.75 each, plus Value Added Tax. Each BRILIGHT tube is guaranteed to have a working life of 3,000 hours.

You should allow approximately 28 days for delivery. Please note that we are unable to offer discount facilities on lighting orders and that our invoice falls due 25 days after receipt.

Please do not hesitate to contact us if you require any further information.

Yours faithfully,

G.M. Brown

G.M. Brown
Sales Department

4 All shapes and sizes

There are 7 steps in Unit 4. You will learn how to:

- describe things and people
- measure and calculate in English

1 Listen and draw

Listen to these descriptions. Can you draw a simple diagram of the things being described? What is the total area of each of them?

2 What's it like?

Here are some ways to describe shapes, sizes and dimensions, and relative positions of objects, as well as the materials they are made of.

Shapes

This is a square.	It's square.
This is a rectangle.	It's rectangular.
This is a circle.	It's circular.
This is a triangle.	It's triangular.

Sizes

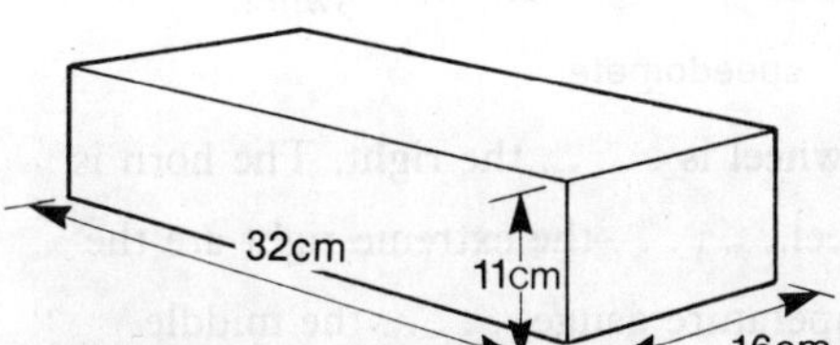

It measures 32 cm by 16 cm by 11 cm.
It's 32 cm long, 16 cm wide and 11 cm high.

It's about 30 cm long.	It's quite long.
It's approximately 15 cm wide.	It's fairly wide.
It's just over 10 cm high.	It's not very high.

Positions

The window is opposite the door.
The TV is in the corner.
The sofa is next to the TV on the right-hand side.
The armchair is near the door on the left.
The table is under the window.
The stool is in front of the bookcase.

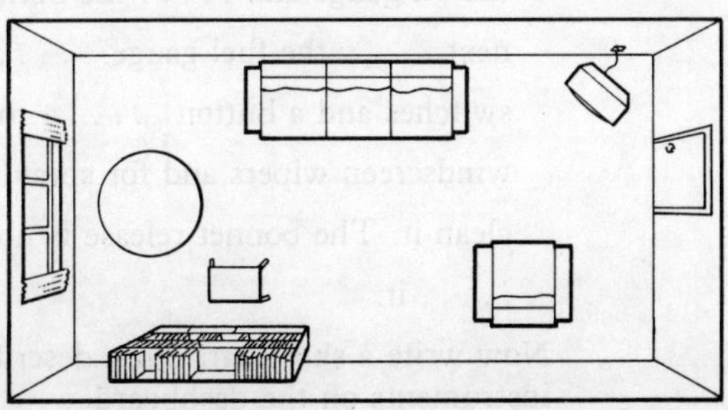

Room

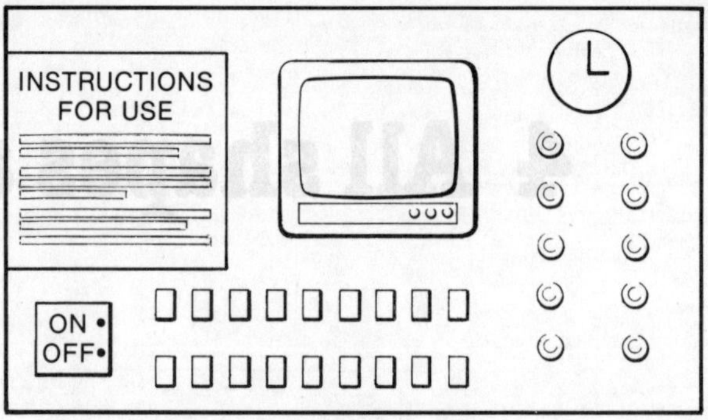

Control panel

The main ON/OFF switch is in the bottom left-hand corner.
The clock is in the top right-hand corner.
There are two vertical rows of lights under the clock.
There are two horizontal rows of switches along the bottom.
The clock is above the lights.
The video screen is in the middle.
The instructions are on the left-hand side next to the video screen.

Materials

It's made of wood.
metal.
plastic.
glass.

It's made mostly of metal, the rest is plastic.
It's a mixture of wool and man-made fibres.
It's an alloy of copper and tin.

3 Prepositions

Look at this diagram of the dashboard of a British car and then fill in the prepositions missing from the paragraph.

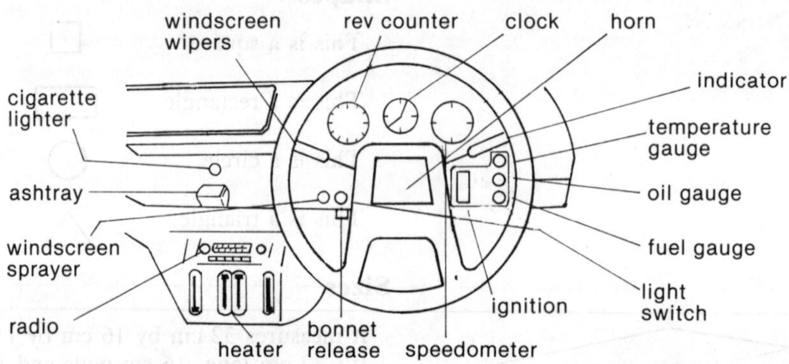

. . . . . British cars, the steering wheel is . . . . . the right. The horn is . . . . . the middle . . . . the wheel. . . . . . the extreme right are the gauges: . . . . . the top is the temperature gauge, ... the middle the oil gauge and . . . . . the bottom the fuel gauge. The ignition is next . . . . . the fuel gauge. . . . . . the steering wheel are two switches and a button . . . . . a row. These are . . . . . lights, windscreen wipers and for spraying the windscreen . . . . . water to clean it. The bonnet release is not . . . . the dashboard itself, it is . . . . . it.

Now write a short paragraph describing the positions of the other instruments on the dashboard.

4 What does he look like?

Look at the picture and then read the description of the man's appearance.

Well, he's of medium height, about 1 m 70 cm, he's got black hair cut fairly short. He sometimes wears glasses, but only for reading. At work he usually wears a suit, either dark blue or grey, with a blue or white shirt and a tie. He always has black shoes. When it's raining he wears a raincoat and carries a large black umbrella.

What is he like?

Look at this picture and read the description of the man's character.

He's very nice. I've always found him very helpful. And he's quite funny. He's always telling jokes and making people laugh. But he's got his serious side as well. Sometimes he's very quiet and seems rather sad.

Now write two paragraphs describing the character of the first man and the appearance of the second man.

5 Describing

a) Working in pairs describe a room, or a machine or an everyday object, so that your partner can draw it.

b) Then describe someone who you both know, from the point of view of appearance and of character, and see if your partner can guess who it is.

6 Drill 1: How big . . .?

Look at the drawings of two packages. You must give approximate information about their dimensions and weight. Like this:

How wide is package A?
It's just under 30 cm wide.

And how long is it?
It's exactly 40 cm long.

And how much does it weigh?
It's just over 1,000 gms in weight.

Now you go on in the same way.

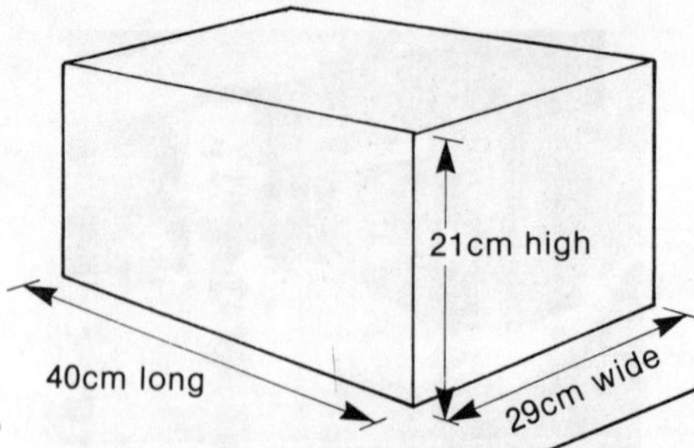

Package A: weight 1,025 gm

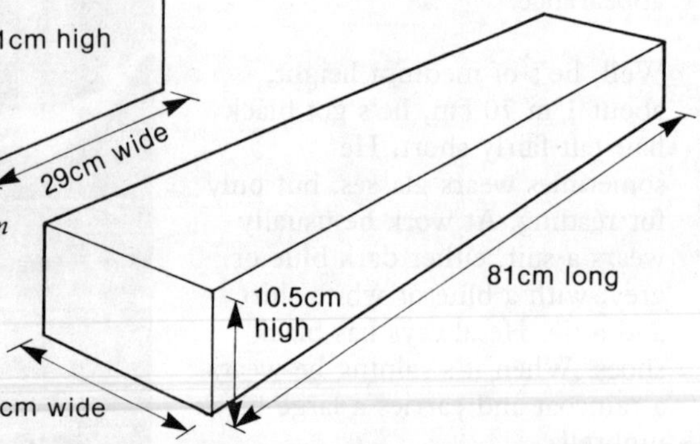

Package B: weight 695 gm

Drill 2: No . . .

You're talking to somebody who has all the wrong information about the design of the control panel for a new machine. Give her the correct information. Like this. Listen:

The light switches are on the left, aren't they?
No, they're on the right.

Oh yes. And the master switch is in the top right-hand corner, isn't it?
No, it's in the bottom left-hand corner.

Now you go on in the same way.

7 Work it out!

Here is a diagram of a section of profiled aluminium.

There is a similar diagram at the end of the Unit.

(measurements in cm)

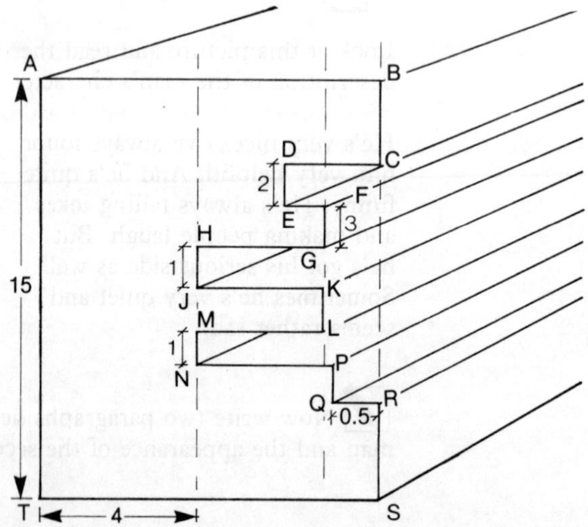

a) Work in pairs. One of you should use the diagram shown here, the other should turn to the end of the Unit. Find out from your partner all the information you can about the profile's dimensions. You should now have enough information to work out all its dimensions.

b) Can you calculate the total area of the section? Work in pairs and try to do all your calculations in English. The easiest way is to divide the section into rectangles first.

c) If the piece is to be two metres long, what is the total volume of aluminium needed? Give your answer in cubic metres.

d) If a cubic metre of aluminium costs £28.50, what is the cost of the aluminium needed to make this piece?

Tapescript for step 1

Tape section 9

A: I'm going to describe a room to you. It's rectangular, 6 metres long by 4.5 metres wide. The door is in the middle of one of the shorter walls. As you come in, there's a TV in the corner on your right and a bookcase along the right-hand wall. There's a large window opposite the door in the middle of the wall, with a small table under it. There's a big round table in front of the bookcase with four chairs round it and a large armchair in the far left-hand corner. Finally there are two small windows in the long wall on the left-hand side.

B: Can you guess what this is? It's square and it measures about 8 cm by 8 cm. It's made of white plastic. Near each corner there is a small metal screw and in the middle there's a rectangular hole measuring 1½ cm by 2½ cm. In this hole there's a movable piece of plastic.

C: This is the control panel of one of our new machines. It's rectangular, the horizontal's longer than the vertical. It measures approximately 50 cm by 35 cm. Along the top there are ten small lights, evenly spaced and underneath each one there's a switch. On the right-hand side there are two needle display units, one above the other; the needles move according to the amount of electricity passing through the machine. The ON/OFF master switch is in the bottom left-hand corner. In the middle of the console there's a large square video unit with three knobs along the bottom. The console is made mostly of metal; the rest is glass and plastic.

Second diagram for step 7

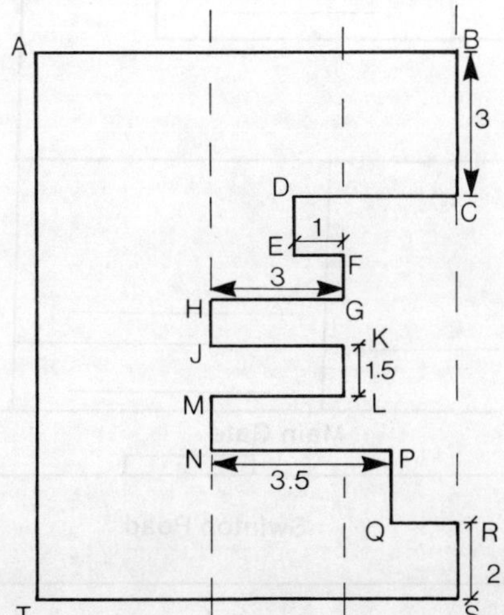

5 Disaster at Swinton Road

There are 11 steps in Unit 5. You will:

- revise the past tenses
- learn how to describe a sequence of events in the past
- find out how to criticize someone's past actions
- discuss a problem about insurance

1 Factory layout

Peter Jackson, Managing Director of Ambermold Manchester, is talking about the company he runs. Fill in the names of the various departments at the Swinton Road plant on the map below.

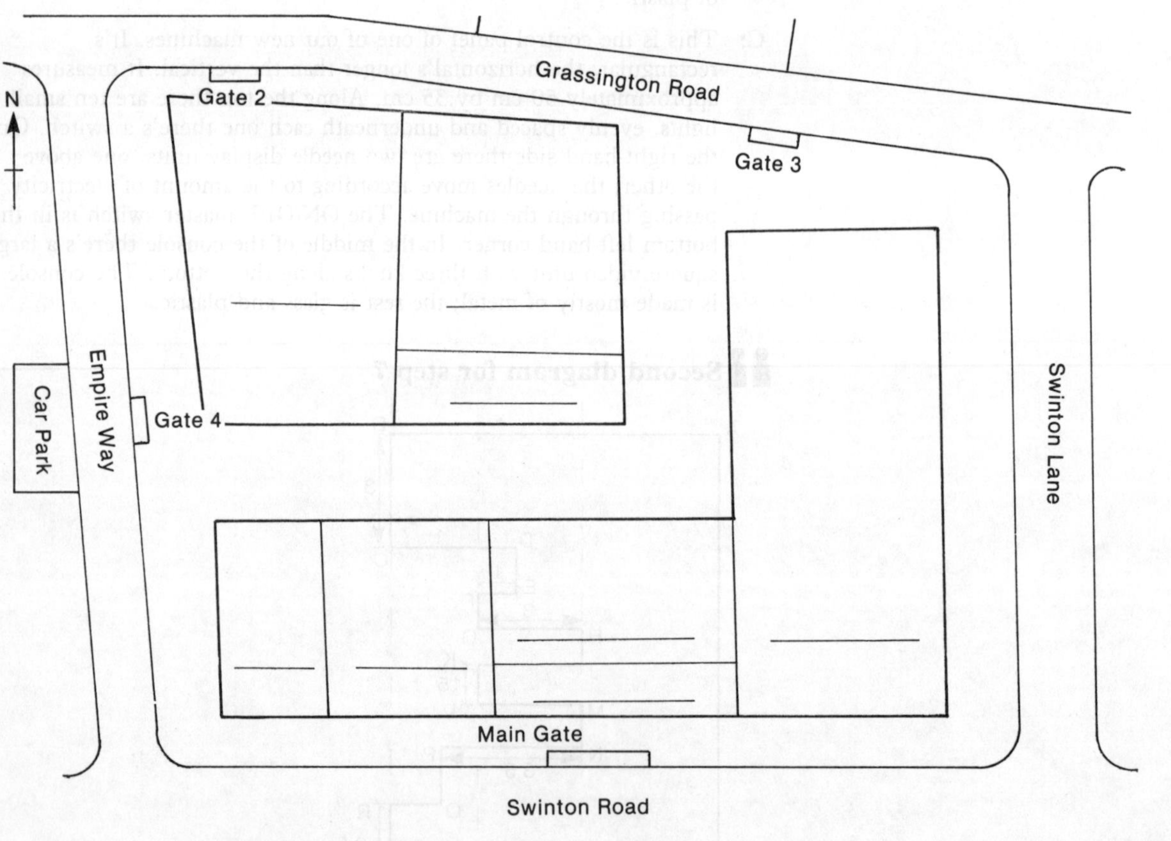

2 The phone rings . . . Late one Thursday evening Peter Jackson receives an urgent telephone call from a colleague

3 Press report The following day the *Manchester Evening Post* publishes the dramatic news about Ambermold on its front page.

Fire destroys local factory

Damage estimated at £1 million

FIRE SWEPT THROUGH Ambermold's plant in Swinton Road late last night wreaking havoc and causing damage of 'at least £1 million', according to Mr Peter Jackson, Managing Director of the well-known roller-bearing company. Surveying the smouldering ruins of what was yesterday the busy office and warehouse complex, he commented sadly: "The real tragedy is that we only completed our computerisation programme a week ago. It'll mean starting right from the beginning again."

The southern half of the warehouse and the data processing department suffered extensive damage and the reception area is also affected, although not seriously.

Smoke and flames

The fire was discovered by Mrs Olga Nutting, 54, of Broadwood Close, Swinton, at about 11.25 p.m. She told our special reporter: "I was walking along Swinton Lane with my dog, when I heard crackling and smelled burning. I thought it was kids playing around until I suddenly saw smoke and flames coming out of the roof. I went straight home and phoned the fire brigade." Mrs Nutting's quick thinking saved the factory from complete destruction, according to the Chief Fire Officer for the Manchester

Continued on back page

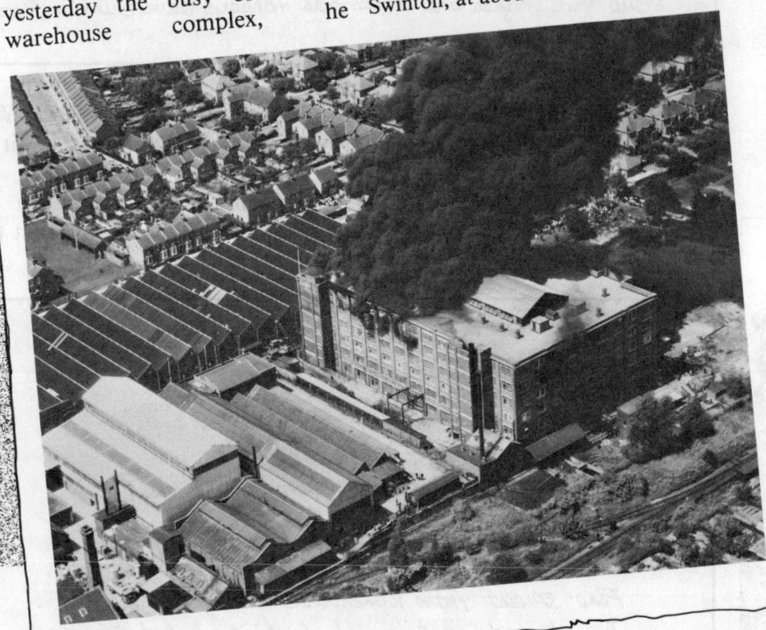

Now mark on your map the area affected by the fire. Put a cross where you think Mrs Nutting was when she first saw the fire.

4 The simple past tense and sequencing

When we are narrating a sequence of past events at a given time in the past, we use the **simple past** tense to talk about what happened.

The fire broke out at 10.20 pm.
We informed the police immediately.
Mr Smith arrived within ten minutes.

The events of the narrative itself can be linked in a number of ways.

The first thing that happened was . . .
After that . . .
The next thing was . . .
Then . . .
Finally . . .
In the end . . .

5 Paragraph writing

Look at these notes from the police record file. Put them in order and then write a paragraph using the simple past tense and the linking phrases shown above.

P. Jackson & B. Owen arrive at Swinton Road
Fire brigade leave fire station
Constable Jones phones B. Owen (Ambermold)
Telephone call to fire brigade (Mrs Nutting)
Fire brigade extinguish fire
Fire brigade arrive at factory
Start of fire
Mrs Nutting goes out for walk with dog
Mrs Nutting sees smoke and flames
B. Owen speaks to P. Jackson on telephone
Evening Post reporter interviews Inspector Cox
Police, fire brigade and Ambermold managers leave Swinton Road

6 Questions to ask

Imagine you are the reporter from the *Manchester Evening Post*. You have made notes (below) to remind you of the questions you want to ask Inspector Cox.

Write out these questions in full. Don't forget to use *did* when necessary. Be careful: not all the questions need the simple past tense.

Breakout of fire – when?
Mrs Nutting saw fire – what time?
Mrs Nutting left house – when?
Managing Director of Ambermold – name?
Fire destroyed part of factory – which part?
Fire brigade arrived – what time?
Fire spread from warehouse – why?
Fire brigade extinguished fire – what time?
Mrs Nutting – address?

7 You didn't . . .

When we criticize someone we can point out their mistakes by saying either what they didn't do or what they should have done.

You didn't lock the door.
You didn't phone the police immediately.
You left the warehouse unattended.
You should have locked the door.
You should have phoned the police immediately.
You shouldn't have left the warehouse unattended.

Notice that positive and negative are normally reversed, when changing from the simple past tense to the *should have* form.

8 You should have . . .

Change these sentences into the *should have* form. Don't forget to change positive to negative and vice versa.

1 You didn't lock the door.
2 You didn't call the fire brigade.
3 You left paper on the warehouse floor.
4 You didn't inform Mr Jackson about the fire.
5 You didn't check the fire extinguisher.
6 You didn't close the main door.
7 You left the key in the door.
8 You didn't notice the smoke coming from the roof.

9 Drill 1: No, it didn't . . .

You are the reporter from the *Manchester Evening Post*. Your boss, the Editor, has all the wrong information about the fire in Swinton Road. You must correct him. Listen:

The fire started in the morning, didn't it?
No, it didn't. It started in the evening.

Mrs Nutting was out with her cat, wasn't she?
No, she wasn't. She was out with her dog.

Stress the words 'evening' and 'dog', to show which part of your boss's information was incorrect. Now you go on in the same way.

Drill 2: Yes, I realize . . .

You are Peter Jackson, the Managing Director of Ambermold. You are talking to a representative of the insurance company, after the disastrous fire at the Swinton Lane plant. Listen:

You know, Mr Jackson, the fire door wasn't locked.
Yes, I realize the fire door should have been locked.

And private cars were parked outside. That's against the regulations, you know.
Yes, I realize private cars shouldn't have been parked outside.

Now you go on in the same way.

10 Meeting the insurers

Representatives of the insurance company have now investigated the circumstances of the fire and have asked for a meeting with Ambermold managers to discuss the matter. It is this meeting which you are going to re-enact.

In small groups divide into two teams (Ambermold and Insurance Company) and prepare your arguments. The notes will help you.

Insurance company Your notes are at the end of the Unit.

Ambermold You want full settlement of your claim. Details supplied by your Service Department are given below. Decide which parts of the claim are the most important and where you are prepared to compromise. Agree on an absolute minimum amount, below which you cannot accept settlement.

Ambermold International

Swinton Lane
Manchester M95 7TZ

REPORT ON DAMAGE TO BUILDINGS AND EQUIPMENT CAUSED BY FIRE ON 13 JULY 19-- AT AMBERMOLD MANCHESTER, SWINTON ROAD.

WAREHOUSE	ESTIMATED VALUE
Stocks destroyed	£ 12,500
Stocks damaged	£ 17,250
Damage to walls/ceilings/floor	£ 33,000
Damage to heating & lighting systems	£ 10,500
TOTAL	£ 73,250

DATA PROCESSING DEPARTMENT	
Computer terminals	£ 12,000
VDUs	£ 9,750
Records	£ 2,000
Office equipment	£ 1,800
Damage to walls, carpets etc.	£ 750
	£ 26,300

We therefore recommend that a claim for £ 99,550 be submitted to Underwriters for their consideration.

Service Department

Here are some more documents which Ambermold management will need for the discussion with the insurance company.

SWIFTEX FIRE PREVENTION LTD.

All extinguishers and sprinkler systems checked and found in good order:

25/3	All correct JW	14/1	All OK JW
30/6	No problems JW	15/5	" JW
19/9	" JW	10/8	No. 2 repaired JW
20/12	all in order MP	12/11	No. 2 repaired again JW
3/4	" MP	30/2	No. 7 installed MP
7/7	no. 1 repaired MP	25/5	no problems MP.
18/10	sprinkler tested MP		

N.B. Please advise SWIFTEX immediately of any leakage or malfunction.

Invicta Insurance Company

Droylesden Road
MANCHESTER
M12 3QW

. . . . . and we are pleased to confirm that the above mentioned premises, having been duly inspected, are now fully covered under this Company's COMPREHENSIVE, ALL RISKS and FIRE Policy No. 808736/81.

Please note that any claims under this policy must be notified within thirty days by letter . . . . .

Manchester Constabulary
Police House
Piccadilly
Manchester 1

. . . and it is therefore suggested that Gate 3 situated in Grassington Road, Swinton should remain locked between the hours of 7 pm and 7 am to avoid the possibility of another break-in . . .

11 Letter writing

Write a letter from the insurance company to Ambermold explaining why this claim cannot be accepted in full. Use the information on the map at the end of the Unit as a basis for the letter. End by suggesting a compromise settlement. Note how to set out the letter. The first part has been done for you.

Invicta Insurance Company

Droylesden Road
Manchester
M12 3QW

Mr P Jackson
Ambermold Manchester
Swinton Road
MANCHESTER

20 September........

Dear Mr Jackson,

I am writing in connection with the claim you submitted to us following the fire at your factory two months ago. I am afraid that we are unable to accept this claim in full for the following reasons:

Firstly..
....
....
....
....
....
....
....

Please contact me as soon as possible to let me know if you are prepared to accept settlement as I have suggested above.

Yours sincerely,

G.M. BROWN (Manager – Claims Department)

Tapescript for step 1

Tape section 11

. . . and now I'd like to tell you something about our Swinton Road plant. As you know, it was opened in 1968 and we have just completed a modernization programme, including an up-to-date computerized accounts and stock control system.

There are two main blocks at the plant. As you enter the Main Gate, which is in Swinton Road, the administration and warehouse complex is immediately in front of you. On the extreme left is the canteen, then comes the administration (that's where my office is). The reception area is next, with the data processing department behind and on the right, the largest area, is the warehouse where all the finished goods are stored.

The other block consists of two factories, A and B. (Factory A is on the left and Factory B on the right, and there's a store for all the equipment which is in front of Factory B.)

The car park is on the other side of Empire Way opposite Gate 4.

The factory itself is most interesting. Perhaps you would like to hear about some of the new robot-controlled equipment which we have recently installed and which we are sure . . .

Tapescript for step 2

Tape section 12

MRS JACKSON: Hallo. 773402.

MR OWEN: Hallo. Bill Owen here. Could I speak to your husband please, Mrs Jackson? It's rather urgent.

MRS JACKSON: Yes, of course. Hold the line and I'll get him.

MR JACKSON: Hallo Bill. What's happened?

MR OWEN: The worst I'm afraid, Peter. There's been a fire at the factory. The police have just phoned me.

MR JACKSON: Oh no!

MR OWEN: Yes.

MR JACKSON: What's the damage? Is it still burning? I'll get over there right away.

MR OWEN: Hold on a minute. The fire's more or less out now, so there's no immediate hurry.

MR JACKSON: But where was it? What happened?

MR OWEN: Well, it started in the warehouse, as far as they can tell. A woman was out walking her dog at about half past eleven and saw flames coming out of the roof, so she telephoned the fire brigade. It's a good job she did. Otherwise the whole place would have burned down.

MR JACKSON: Is it just the warehouse then?

MR OWEN: No. It spread quite quickly to the offices. All the computer room, most of the terminals and the VDUs have been destroyed.

MR JACKSON: Oh my God! How did you hear all this then?

MR OWEN: Well, as I said, the police have just phoned me. I was just sitting watching the television when they rang. I couldn't think who it was.

MR JACKSON: Well, we'd better go and see what's going on, even though I don't suppose there's much we can do at this time of night. I'll meet you at the Main Gate in about ten minutes.

MR OWEN: OK. See you then. Goodbye.

MR JACKSON: Yes. Goodbye.

Insurance company information for step 10

Look at the map below. You will see that your investigator has discovered that Ambermold did not do everything they could to prevent the fire. Use this information to support your argument that Ambermold are asking far too much money in settlement.

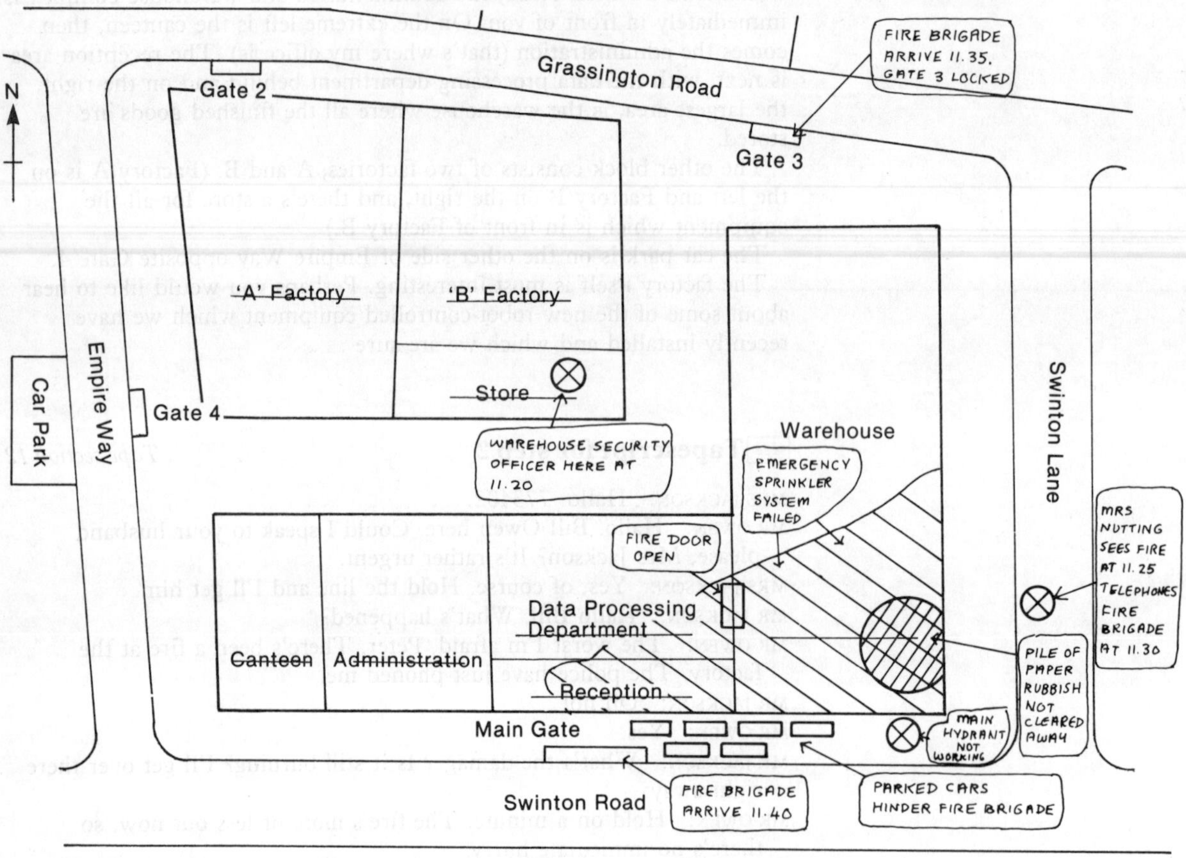

6 Facts and figures

There are 12 steps in Unit 6. You will:

- look at the language of graphs and statistics
- learn how to use the simple past and present perfect tenses

1 The sales graph

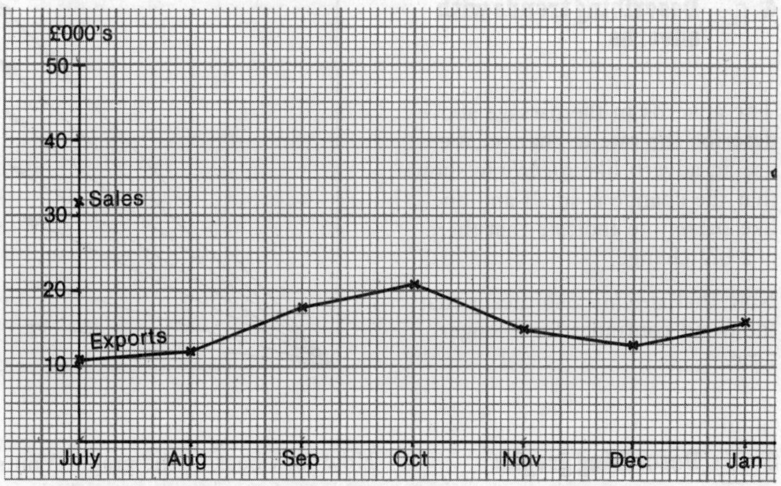

Listen to the Managing Director of Ambermold Manchester giving details of overall sales of his company's products during the second half of last year. Put a cross on the graph to indicate the level of sales each month. The first one has been done for you. Finally, join all the crosses together to plot the overall sales curve, as in the export curve below it.

2 Describing trends

Here are some of the verbs we use to indicate upward and downward trends.

go up	*go down*
rise	*fall*
increase	*drop*
recover	*decrease*

Notice also the use of the prepositions *from, to* and *by*:

Sales went up from 25,000 to 30,000, in other words they increased by 5,000.

Now write a paragraph describing what happened to sales during the period July – January.

3 The chairman's report

Sometimes we want to give information about trends without mentioning figures. Using adverbs is one way of doing this. Read this extract from a press release which gives the same information about Ambermold's sales record as you heard on tape. Underline all the adverbs.

> and the chairman agreed to this proposal.
>
> **Steady progress in difficult times**
>
> The Chairman went on to say that the second half had not been easy. At the beginning of July sales had been at a reasonable level. They rose slightly during that month and in the following month went up quite substantially. Unfortunately the momentum was not maintained and sales fell sharply in September. They continued to fall slightly in October to reach a low point for the period at the end of that month. During the remaining two months sales rose slowly, but steadily, and at the end of the period they were at about the same level as at the beginning.

4 Describing trends with adverbs

The adverbs in the passage above describe the rate of change. We use an adverb like *slightly* to show that the change is small and one like *sharply* to indicate that there is a big change.

Note that *steadily* also means that the trend continues for a longer time.

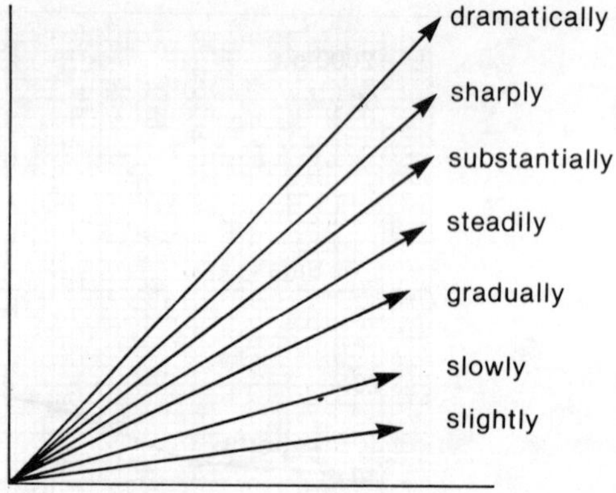

5 Describing graphs

Now look back at the graph. You should now be able to describe the exports curve in two ways: (i) by giving exact *figures* for each month and (ii) by talking about the trend using some of the adverbs given in step 4.

6 Drawing graphs

Working in pairs, take it in turns to draw a graph and then describe it to your partner. Try to describe the curve you have drawn in two ways: (i) by using figures and (ii) by using adverbs.

7 Drill 1: Up and down . . .

When we are talking about the changes in the fortunes of a company, we use some of the following verbs:

go up and its opposite *go down*
increase and its opposite *decrease*
rise and its opposite *fall*

Now listen. Somebody is being corrected. She thinks that certain things happened to the company, but the person talking to her knows that the opposite is true.

Sales went up last year, didn't they?
As a matter of fact they didn't. They went down by 50%.

Total production fell last year, didn't it?
As a matter of fact, it didn't. It rose by 50%.

Now you go on in the same way.

Drill 2: Yes, that's right...

You are talking to a colleague about recent changes affecting the company. You confirm that he has the right information this time. Like this. Listen:

Prices of the ZB12 went up from £25 to £30 last year, didn't they?
Yes, that's right, they went up by £5.

But monthly sales fell from £12,000 to £10,000.
Yes, that's right, they fell by £2,000.

Each time, you have to say *by how much* things have changed. Now go on in the same way.

8 The present perfect tense

In the first part of the Unit we were discussing sales and export results for a period which is over. So we used the **simple past** tense:

Sales rose to £44,000 in September.
Exports fell slightly in November.

But if the period of time is not finished, we have to use the **present perfect** tense:

This year prices have risen by 10%.
This month we have sold £10,000 worth of goods.

In other words, prices could rise more before the year is finished and total sales for this month could be more than £10,000.

9 Last year and this year

Change these sentences from **simple past** to **present perfect**. Look at this example:

Last year sales rose by 10%. (This year: 20%)
This year sales have risen by 20%.

1 Last year prices rose by 15%. (This year: 12%)
2 Last year sales increased by 10%. (This year: 8%)
3 Last year exports to the USA fell by 10%. (This year: 5%)
4 Last year home sales improved by 12%. (This year: 9%)
5 Last year profits dropped by 6%. (This year: 4%)
6 Last year inflation went up by 5%. (This year: 1%)
7 Last year exports to the EEC went up by 7%. (This year: 9%)
8 Last year taxes rose by 8%. (This year: 12%)

10 Finding a market

Inflation rate

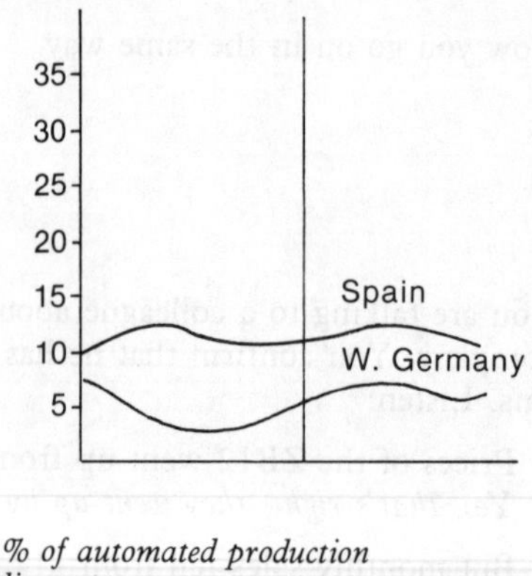

New factories opened

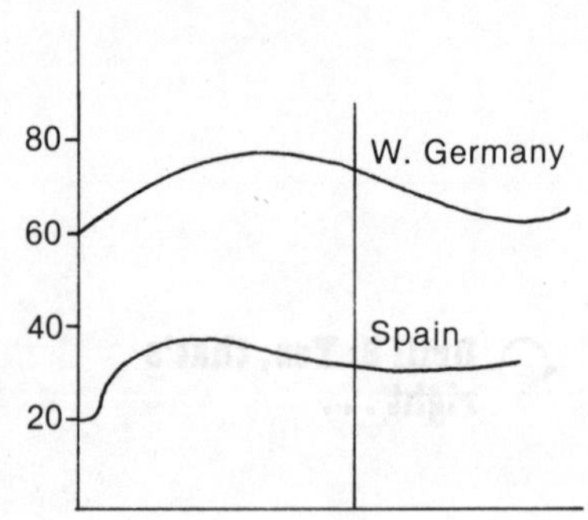

% of automated production lines

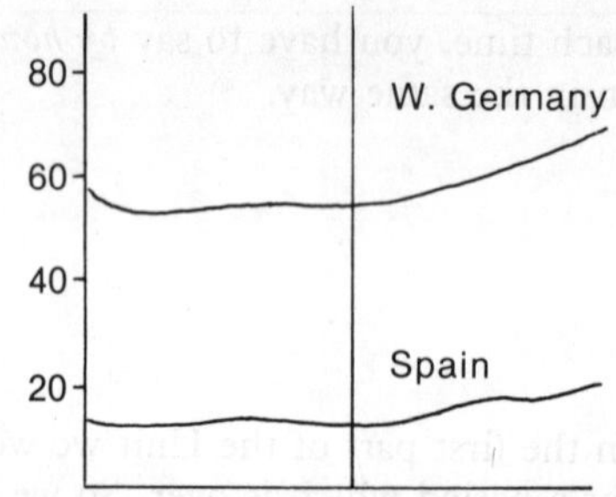

% of roller bearing systems imported

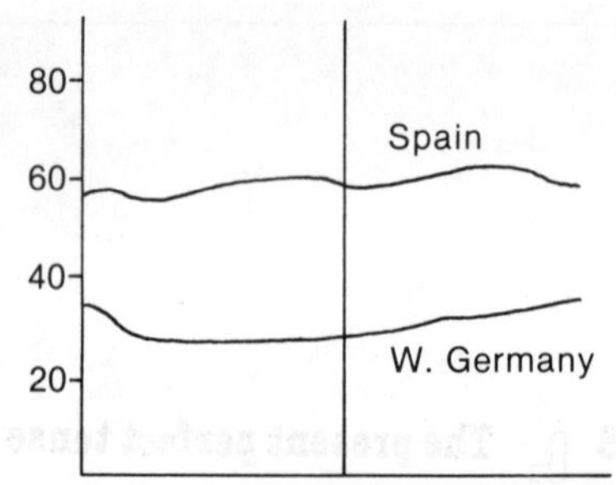

Read this text and transfer the information about Brazil onto the graphs above.

Economic Report
Profile of Brazil

Brazil is one of the fastest developing economies in Latin America and it's proving very popular with European exporters. Although the inflation rate is not as stable as it might be (last year it went up from 8% to 15% and this year has risen steadily to its current level of 27%), the economy shows no signs of slowing down. For example, the number of new factories opened each month has continued to rise. At the beginning of last year, just over 40 factories were being opened per month – there was a slight fall to the middle of the year (about 35 per month) but the final figure for the year was 38. This year has seen a steady advance, the current figure being 60 factory completions per month. Not all these factories are modern, however. Automated production lines are only slowly beginning to appear in Brazil. Throughout the whole of last year only 5% of factories were automated. This year, however, as a result of some joint ventures with Japan the figure has gradually risen – the current level is a healthy 16%.

A number of British companies are considering launching sales campaigns in Brazil. One of them is Ambermold Manchester. Mr Peter Dawes, Overseas Sales Manager, told us: 'Brazil is potentially a very interesting market for us. Nearly all their roller bearing systems are imported. Last year they imported about 80% of everything they needed and this year, despite setting up a roller bearing factory of their own, they are still importing 75%.'

So the outlook is quite good for British...

11 Allocating the marketing budget

You now have some information about Brazil, Spain and West Germany. Now imagine you are responsible for selling Ambermold's products – roller bearing systems used in automated production lines – and you have to decide how to spend a very limited marketing budget of £18,000.

Discuss in groups which market seems to be the most important for you and then allocate the budget accordingly; in other words, decide how you want to divide the marketing budget between the three countries. You can spend the whole budget on a campaign in one country if you like, or you can split the budget between two or three countries.

Be ready to explain your decision to the other group.

12 History of the company

You have been asked to write a short article about your company's activities for inclusion in a trade journal to be published shortly. Use the notes below as a basis and pay particular attention to your choice of past tenses.

1 Founding of company (1965)
2 Production of woollen goods and textiles (1960's and 1970's)
3 Diversification into retail shops (1974)
4 Extension of activities (since 1974)
5 Opening of first shop in US (May 1975)
6 Opening of subsidiary manufacturing company in France (September 1976)
7 Increase in turnover of £3½ million (June 1976 – now)
8 Inflation problems (1978 – 79)
9 Fall in inflation rate from 26% to 9% (1979 – now)
10 Slight fall in exports (this year)
11 Death of Chairman (January 1981)
12 Appointment of J Smithers as Chairman (last month)

Tapescript for step 1

Tape section 14

I'm sure you'd like a little more detail about those second-half figures from July to the end of the year. In July sales were at a fairly satisfactory level of £32,000. In August they went up by £2,000 to £34,000 and September brought a further increase of £10,000. Unfortunately we began to feel the effects of the recession at about this time when, for example, a big South American contract was suddenly cancelled and sales dropped to £35,000 in October. They fell another £5,000 in November but went up again in December to £32,000. And the figure for January was quite encouraging at £36,000. So as you can see, the period was rather unstable, but we did manage to end the year slightly ahead of the mid-year level. Now I don't know if there are any questions you want to put to me about any of the . . .

7 Here's how

There are 12 steps in Unit 7. You will:

- ask for and give directions
- look at regulations and instructions
- look at job descriptions

1 Giving directions

Look at the plan of the first floor of the Ambermold administration block. You are going to hear five short conversations. Each time, someone is asking the way to a different place.

Listen to the conversations and mark down where you think these places are.

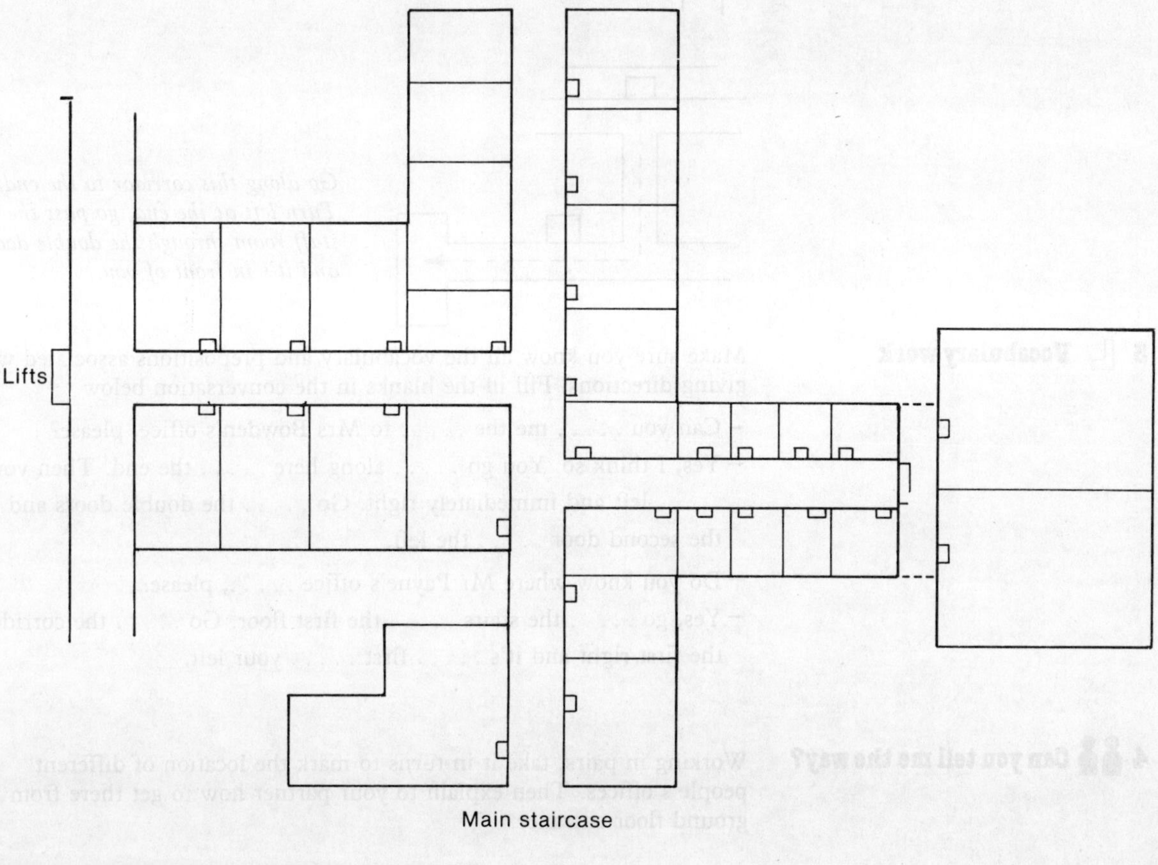

2 Asking for and giving directions

Here is how to ask the way:

Can you tell me where Mrs Bowden's office is, please?
Could you tell me the way to Mrs Bowden's office, please?
Do you know where Mrs Bowden's office is, please?

Giving directions is a little more complicated:

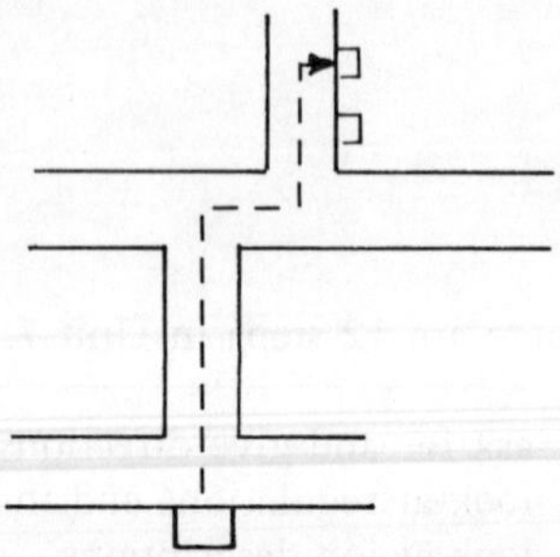

Go straight along the corridor to the end. Turn right and immediately left. It's the second door on the right.

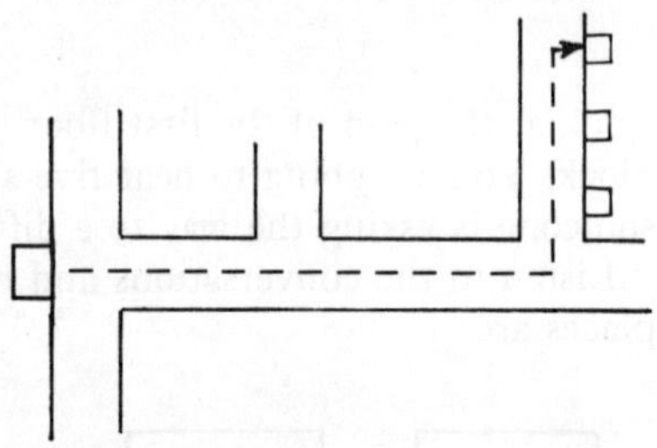

Walk down the corridor, take the second left and it's the last door on the right.

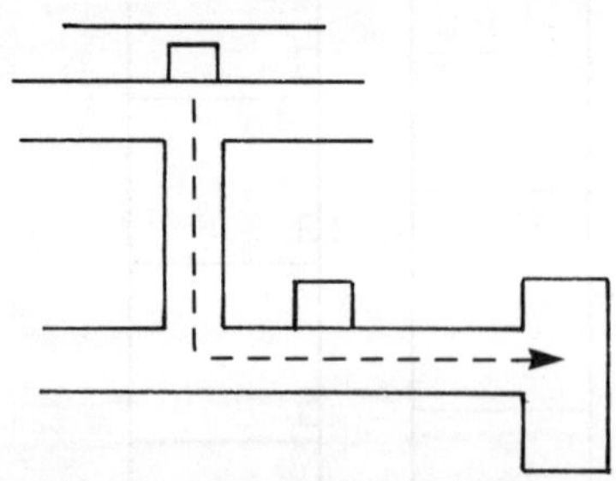

Go along this corridor to the end. Turn left at the end, go past the staff room through the double door and it's in front of you.

3 Vocabulary work

Make sure you know all the vocabulary and prepositions associated with giving directions. Fill in the blanks in the conversation below.

– Can you . . . . . me the . . . . . to Mrs Bowden's office, please?
– Yes, I think so. You go . . . . . along here . . . . . the end. Then you . . . . . left and immediately right. Go . . . . . the double doors and it's the second door . . . . . the left.
– Do you know where Mr Payne's office . . . . ., please?
– Yes, go . . . . . the stairs . . . . . the first floor. Go . . . . . the corridor, the first right and it's . . . . . first . . . . . your left.

4 Can you tell me the way?

Working in pairs, take it in turns to mark the location of different people's offices. Then explain to your partner how to get there from the ground floor entrance.

5 Exporting to Europe

Listen to this British businessman talking about the problem of exporting to EEC countries and to Eastern Europe. Note down in the table below whether the following things are necessary or not:

	EEC	Eastern Europe
Shipping documents		
Insurance policy		
Import licence		
Metric measurements		
Translations		
Notification to customs		
Notification to Board of Trade		

6 Rules and regulations

When discussing rules and regulations, we make a difference between what is necessary and what is not. If something is necessary, we say:

You have to inform the authorities.
You must inform the authorities.

To show that something is not required, we use a negative form:

You don't have to obtain a visa.
You don't need a visa.
A visa isn't required.

Asking about regulations is quite simple:

Do I have to get a visa?
Is it necessary to get a visa?
Is a visa required?
Must we apply for visas?

7 Necessary or not?

With the information you noted down in step 5, you can now make sentences like these:

For exports to the EEC and Eastern Europe you have to prepare shipping documents.
You don't have to use metric measurements for exports to Eastern Europe.

Make more sentences using *have to* and *don't have to* to indicate whether, for example, translations are necessary or not.

8 Exchanging information

Work with your partner to explain the rules and regulations which apply to the Britnat Credit Card and the Global Electric ZP11 Drilling Machine. Decide who will read which. Operating instructions for the ZP11 are at the end of the Unit.

Britnat Credit Card

Conditions of use

1 Minimum age of applicant: 18 years.
2 Credit limit: £200.00.
3 Interest charged at 1¾% per month. (True annual rate 29.56%.)
4 Minimum monthly repayment: 5% of outstanding balance OR £5.00, whichever is the higher.
5 Inform BRITNAT REGISTRATION CENTRE, P.O. Box 99, SOUTHAMPTON SO99 1XW immediately **IN WRITING** if card is lost or stolen.
6 BRITNAT credit card is non-transferable.
7 BRITNAT credit card is **NOT** restricted to customers of British National Bank Ltd. Customers of other banks are welcome to apply.

Some of the vocabulary in these two exercises is quite difficult. Read through the Britnat Credit Card Conditions of Use and the Global Electric ZP11 Drilling Machine Operating Instructions and try to find the words or phrases which mean the same as the following:

1 cannot be used by another person ....

2 yearly ....

3 money paid for the use of money ....

4 person making an official written request ....

5 national electricity provision system ....

6 rubbish ....

7 device for fixing bit in place ....

8 something that breaks an electric circuit ....

9 to stop working because it is stuck ....

12 Twenty questions

One member of the group thinks of a profession, the others must try to guess it, by asking questions beginning with:

Do you . . . . .?
Do you have to . . . . .?

For example:

Do you work inside or outside?
Do you have to wear protective clothing?

The person thinking of the profession can only answer 'Yes' or 'No'. Only twenty questions can be asked.

Tapescript for step 1

Tape section 16

a) —Can you tell me the way to Mr Thompson's office, please?
—Mr Thompson. Yes, just a moment. I think he's on the first floor. Oh yes, room 164. If you take the lift to the first floor and walk down the corridor to the end. . . Turn left and it's the last door on the right.
—Thanks very much.

b) —I've got an appointment with Mr James Turner. He said I should meet him in Mrs Bowden's office.
—That's on the first floor. It's probably quickest if you go up the stairs here. It's the second door on the right along the corridor in front of you.
—Thank you.

c) —Could you tell me where there's a gents' toilet, please?
—Yes, up the stairs, along the corridor, take the first right and it's the second door on the right.
—Thanks a lot.

d) —Can you tell me where Conference Room B is, please?
—Yes, if you get out of the lift at the first floor, go straight ahead along the corridor, turn right and immediately left. At the end there's a double door, go through that into a small lobby, and Conference Room B is on the right.
—Thank you.

e) —Do you know where the typing pool is, please?
—Yes. Take a lift to the first floor. Walk straight along the corridor in front of you, turn right at the end and it's the last door on the right before the stairs.
—Oh, thanks very much.

Tapescript for step 5

Tape section 17

The Government often talks about the need to increase exports to help our economy, but really with the number of rules and regulations there are, especially now we're in the EEC, it sometimes seems that they're actually trying to *stop* us sending our goods abroad! Of course it's not only our government that makes life difficult; it's often the government of the importing country who causes problems for the poor British exporter, especially in Eastern Europe where we have a lot of business.

The documents are probably the most complicated aspect. For all countries you have to prepare shipping documents, and you always need an insurance policy to cover the risks of transporting the goods. To export to Eastern Europe you have to apply for an import licence, but you don't need one for EEC countries. The weight of the goods must be given in metric measurements, in other words kilogrammes or metric tonnes, if you're sending something to an EEC country, but you can use British or metric measures for deliveries to Eastern Europe.

English is an official language of the EEC, so you don't have to translate documents intended for those countries. Unfortunately Eastern European countries require a translation into the local language.

Of course you have to inform the British customs authorities of *all* export shipments, but you only have to notify the Board of Trade in the case of consignments to Eastern Europe.

Information for step 8

GLOBAL ELECTRIC ZP11 DRILLING MACHINE
OPERATING INSTRUCTIONS

1 Make sure machine is connected to mains supply (240 V).
2 Clear all debris remaining from previous use of machine.
3 Check level of cooling fluid (min 75 ml, max 100 ml).
4 Fix protective guard in position at SLOT A.
5 Select and insert bit required (always tighten with chuck key).
6 Fix material to be worked on machine floor.
7 Turn machine on (green button)—no 'warming-up' time necessary.
8 Automatic cut-out system if drill jams—no need to use emergency switch.

NB Always wear protective clothing.

8 No sooner said than done!

There are 9 steps in Unit 8. You will:

- learn how to use the passive form of the verb
- find out how to describe processes
- discuss some business problems

1 Car production

Listen to an official from the EEC Import/Export Department giving information about car production in England and France. Note down details in the table below.

	France	England
Total number of cars produced last year		
Total number of cars to be produced this year (estimate)		
Location of factories		
Parts imported		
Percentage of cars exported last year		
Percentage of cars to be exported this year (estimate)		

2 The passive

We use the **passive** form of the verb when the focus of interest in the sentence is on the object of the verb. For example, we could say:

Workers produced 1,000,000 cars in Birmingham last year

but the important information in this sentence concerns the number of cars produced, not the workers. So we prefer to make this part of the sentence the subject:

1,000,000 cars were produced in Birmingham last year.

Forming the **passive** is quite simple. You take the verb *to be* in the appropriate tense and add the past participle.

Now make sentences about car production in England and France, using the information you have received from the EEC Import/Export Department.

3 Production statistics

Look at these block diagrams and make sentences using the passive form of the verb.

Now draw another block diagram showing details of production of sales figures of your company for the past few years as well as projections for the future.

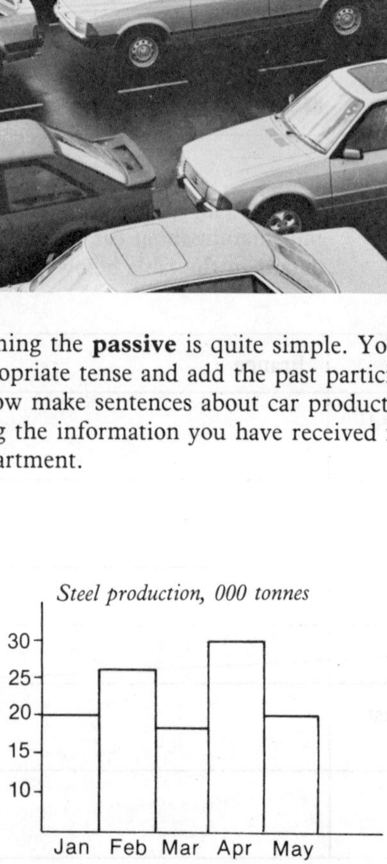

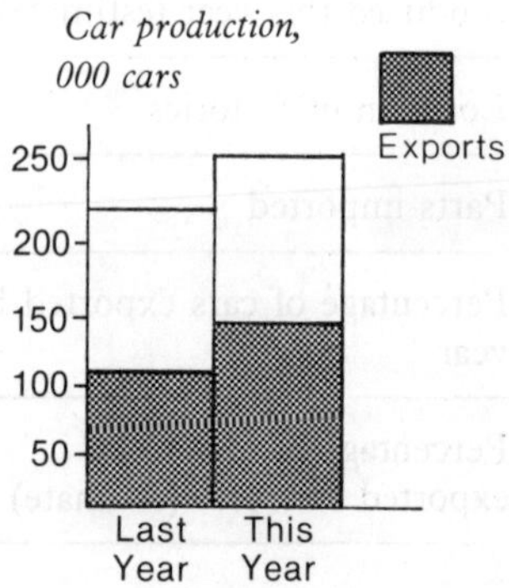

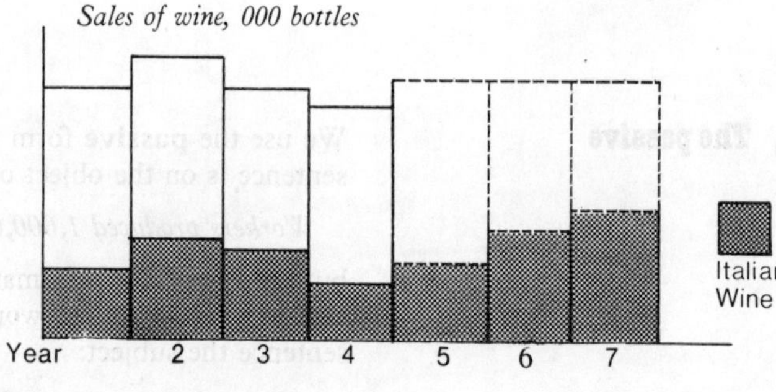

4 Processes

The passive form of the verb is often used when we are describing a process. For example, the different stages involved in building a house might be described like this:

> First the land is purchased. Then an architect is appointed to design the house. After that, planning permission is granted by local government. A builder is then asked to give an estimate of the cost of building the house. If this estimate is acceptable, a contract is signed and the house is built. Finally the house is offered for sale on the open market.

To show the connection between any two of these stages, we can make sentences using the **present perfect passive**.

> *After the land has been purchased, an architect is appointed to design the house.*

Now make similar sentences using *after* with the present perfect passive, like this:

> *After the architect has been appointed . . .*

5 Buying and selling goods

Below is a list of stages involved in purchasing goods from a company. First, put them in order and then write a paragraph linking the various parts of the process. Use the passive form wherever you think it is appropriate.

Dispatch	Confirmation	Order	Offer
Enquiry	Payment	Acknowledgement	Delivery
Invoice	Packing	Documents	

Some of these verbs may be useful:

> send deliver order prepare pay pack acknowledge make arrange dispatch place offer

6 Car manufacture

Look at the diagrams below, which show the stages of the manufacture of a car.

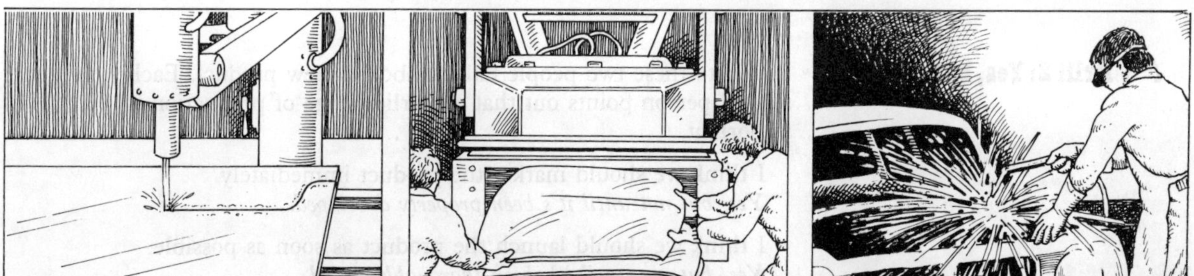

Listen to the tape and then write down the names of the various departments as well as details of what happens at each stage.

7 Drill 1: And what about . . .?

Listen to Alan Davies answering questions about car production at British Autocar's Birmingham plant.

Is the spraying done by the workers?
No, the cars are sprayed by robots.

And what about testing? Is that done in the main factory?
No, the cars are tested in the Quality Control Department.

Now you go on in the same way. The notes will help you. (Begin at number 3.)

1 by robots
2 in the Quality Control Department
3 here in Birmingham
4 manually
5 in that department over there
6 road transporter
7 in private showrooms
8 by all sorts of people

Drill 2: Yes, but . . .

Listen to these two people talking about a new product. Each time, the second person points out that an earlier stage of production is important.

I think we should market the product immediately.
Yes, but not until it's been properly developed.

I think we should launch the product as soon as possible.
Yes, but not until it's been thoroughly tested.

Now you go on in the same way. The notes will help you. (Begin at number 3.)

1 properly developed
2 thoroughly tested
3 tried out here in the UK
4 presented at the Trade Fair
5 accepted by the market in its present form
6 shown to important potential customers
7 sold in the south east
8 printed in English

8 Action taken

The Customer Service Department at Ambermold has to sort out customers' problems fast. Quick decision-making and accurate records are an essential part of the job. Look at this example:

TELEPHONE MESSAGE:

Breakdown of ABS 1200 system at Goodleigh Paper Mills – production line at standstill. Very important customer.

ACTION TAKEN:

Replacement ABS 1200 system sent by special delivery.
Ambermold service team sent to supervise installation.
Full report on breakdown requested.
Accounts Dept notified.

When making notes about action taken, the Customer Service Department does not write full sentences. In the above example they have used a reduced form of the **passive**.

Replacement ABS 1200 system sent by special delivery

is a short form for:

A replacement ABS 1200 system has been sent by special delivery.

Now look at these problems. Decide on the best way of dealing with them and then make a note of the action taken.

1 *Telephone message*

2 *Telex message*

3 *Telephone message*

4 *Telephone message*

5 *Message from Accounts Department*

1 ABS 700 system still hasn't arrived at Brinten's Ltd. Urgently needed for new production run. Delivery was promised two weeks ago.

2 FROM: J RABUTO, AMBERMOLD AGENT SOUTH EAST ASIA. URGENTLY NEED 200 COPIES CATALOGUE AND PRICE LIST. MR A BAIMAL OF INDONESIAN STEEL COMPANY VISITING EUROPE NEXT MONTH. CAN HE VISIT AMBERMOLD AND SEE ABS 1600 IN OPERATION? PLEASE CONFIRM SOONEST–

3 From Intermet Ltd: request for increased discount on orders (20%) from January next. Present discount rate 12½%. Possibility of placing business elsewhere if no increase is agreed.

4 From Booth and Wilson Ltd. Consignment of ABS 1500 received yesterday. 6 systems damaged in transit. Please advise.

5 Re: non-payment of account, J B Peters Ltd. Total amount outstanding £14,500. Company has cash-flow problem. Request six months extended credit. Please advise.

9 Memo writing

Here's a memo written by the Customer Service Department advising the management of action taken.

Now write similar memos giving details of action taken to solve some of the other problems.

```
Following a breakdown of an ABS 1200 at Goodleigh
Paper Mills, the following action has been taken:
A replacement system was sent by special delivery
this morning, together with a service team who
will supervise its installation.
A full report on the breakdown has been requested.
In the meantime the Accounts Dept has been notified.
```

Tapescript for step 1

Tape section 19

Hello. This is the EEC Import/Export Department. I'm ringing with some information you requested about the private car industry in Europe. Now I understand you want information about two particular countries, England and France, I think it was. Well, to take France first, the number of cars produced last year was 1,750,000 and this year the estimates are that just over 2,000,000 private cars will be produced. Most of the cars are made in and around Paris but there are also factories in Lyon. All the parts are made in France except the glass for the windows which is imported from Czechoslovakia and the tyres which are sent from West Germany. As far as exports are concerned, 35% of French-produced cars were exported last year and we think that just under that, 34% to be exact, will be exported this year.

The percentage of cars exported from England this year will probably be about 17%, which compares with 23.5% last year. The total number of cars produced in England last year was 1,225,000 and approximately 1,100,000 will, if our estimates are correct, be produced during this year. Factories producing cars are located in three areas: Birmingham, Oxford and London. No parts are imported apart from seats which come from Ireland.

Well, that's the latest information we have, but if you need to know anything else, just ring me – my name's Anderson – at my office here in London. The number's 01-557 4803 and ask for extension 340. Goodbye now.

Tapescript for step 6

Tape section 20

There are six main stages involved in car production. The basic material is strip metal and the first stage is cutting. Here the roll of strip metal is cut into lengths, after which it passes on to the pressing department, where the different parts of the chassis or body of the car, like the sides, wings and roof are pressed out. These pieces are then welded together in the welding department. Once the body has been built, the chassis passes on to the assembly line. Here the car itself is assembled. The engine is put in place, the electrical system installed, wheels and braking systems added, bumpers fixed, and so on. The next stage is spraying with a rust-retardant undercoat and a high-gloss coloured finish. The spraying department is usually separated from the rest of the manufacturing process to make sure that the vaporized paint doesn't get into the atmosphere. The final department is quality control where all the testing is done. All aspects of the car's performance are tested and special tests are run on individual components. Finally the cars are driven to the holding areas where they are kept until they are required for distribution.

9 Consolidation exercises

There are 8 steps in Unit 9, one for each of the Units you have completed so far. Each step consists of a reading (or interpretation) activity and a writing activity. These activities will help you revise what you have learned already.

1 The foam experts

Your company manufactures car seats and for some time now you have been looking for a new supplier of polystyrene foam. One day you pick up this brochure.

BAXCEL

The Foam Experts

Baxcel is fast building a reputation as one of the leading suppliers to the trade of all grades of polystyrene foam products; from luxury furniture to industrial floor coverings, from ladies' handbags to automated production lines, we can supply the right foam product for your specific purpose.

Just take a look at our record:

Baxcel Ltd (1) ..... in 1974 and since that time (2) ..... rapidly. Last December Peter Armstrong, Managing Director of Baxcel, (3) ..... profits for the year of £550,000 on an annual turnover of £1.6 million. Baxcel products (4) ..... all over Europe and the company (5) ..... by a network of agents world-wide. Baxcel (6) ..... public three years ago and (7) ..... by UMC, the Swiss Multinational, early last year.

So, what's special about Baxcel?

Firstly, the method of production. The liquid polystyrene (8) ..... very quickly and the air (9) ..... at high pressure at the beginning of the cooling process. The result: high quality, high-bulk foam. Secondly, the famous Baxcel service. We (10) ..... a wide range of foam products (120 different grades) and (11) ..... delivery to any U.K. address within ten days. Over the past year we (12) ..... our service further with the introduction of special discount schemes and credit arrangements. Please (13) ..... Sue Rayner at Baxcel Head Office for further details. We (14) ..... forward to hearing from you.

Exercise

Put the verbs in the list below into the correct tense: present, simple past or present perfect. Use the passive form where you think it is appropriate.

(1) found
(2) expand
(3) announce
(4) sell
(5) represent
(6) go
(7) take over
(8) cool
(9) inject
(10) offer
(11) guarantee
(12) improve
(13) contact
(14) look

2 Figures

You want more information about Baxcel before you decide to buy their products, so you ask your secretary to put together some statistics about Baxcel and your present suppliers, Petroplas Limited.

	Petroplas	Baxcel
Annual turnover last year	£3.5 million	£1.6 million
Profit before tax last year	£980,000	£550,000
Number of foam grades available	110	120
Total production last year (cubic metres)	4,000,000	2,500,000
Date established	1958	1974
Number of employees	1,250	1,100
Cost of standard product per cubic metre	£8.25	£7.95

Exercise

Write sentences comparing these seven aspects of the two companies. Don't forget to use intensifiers to show whether there is a large or small difference between them.

3 Telephone messages

You decide to telephone Baxcel's Sales Department to find out more information about their products and services. Here are your notes:

Do Baxcel produce foam suitable for car seats?
What's the foam made of?
Nearest Baxcel factory or warehouse to us?
Discount facilities available?
Average delivery period?
Guarantee on Baxcel products?
Is the foam resistant to fire?
Cost per cubic metre?

Exercise

Using polite forms (for example, 'Can you tell me . . .?') write out *in full* the questions you want to ask the Sales Department.

4 Details

Following your telephone conversation with the Sales Department at Baxcel, you receive details of foam products suitable for use in car seats.

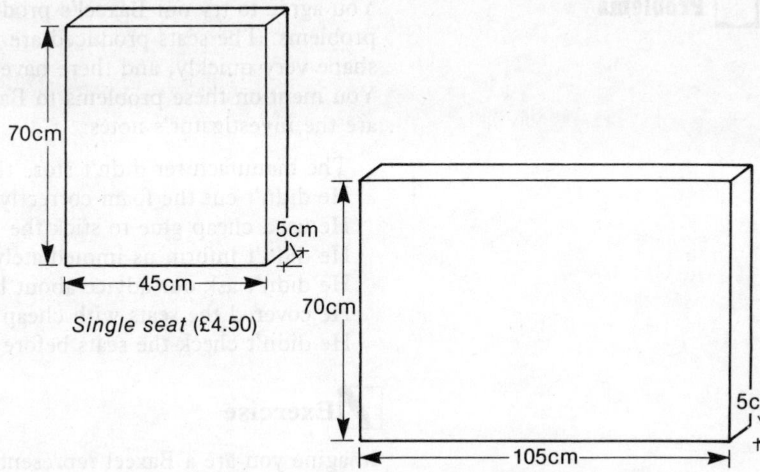

Single seat (£4.50)

Double seat (£8.25)

Exercise

Write a paragraph giving details of the dimensions of these two blocks of foam. Quote the price of each. Offer 10% discount on orders worth £100+. Promise prompt delivery.

5 Statistics

Baxcel also sent statistics to show that there is less danger from fire than there used to be.

Number of serious fires involving Baxcel foam products

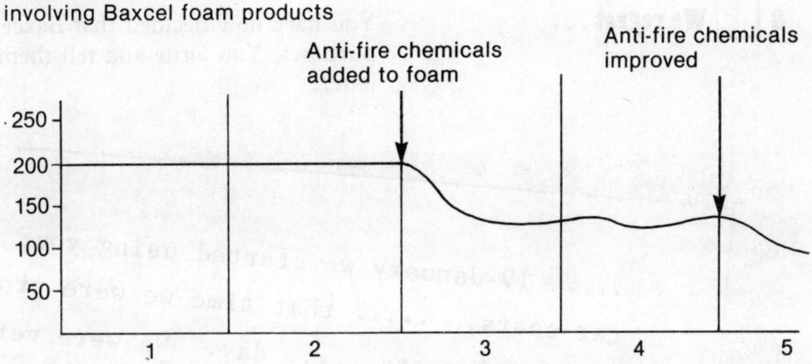

Exercise

Write a paragraph showing the improvement in safety of Baxcel products over the last five years. Explain why there has been such an improvement.

6 Getting there

You have decided to visit Baxcel to discuss your company's requirements fully. The Sales Manager's secretary sends you instructions about how to get there.

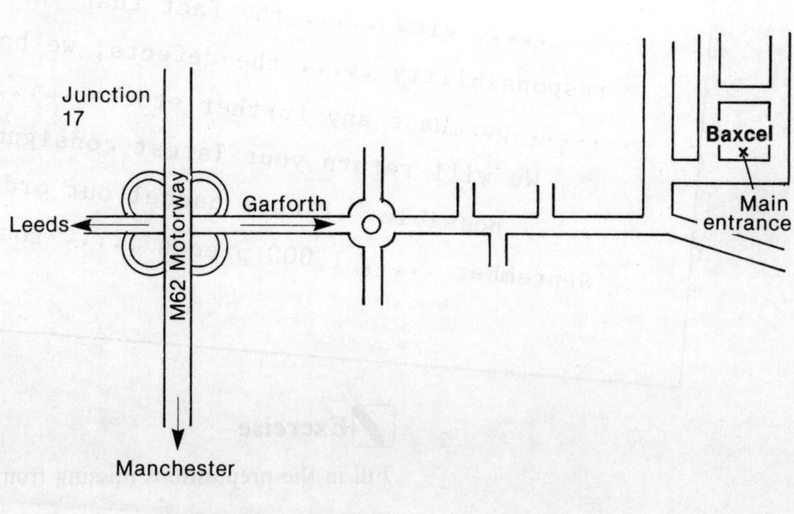

Exercise

Write instructions for someone travelling on the M62 motorway from Manchester to visit Baxcel.

7 Problems

You agree to try out Baxcel's products. Unfortunately, there are some problems. The seats produced are rather uncomfortable and lose their shape very quickly, and there have been complaints from customers. You mention these problems to Baxcel who investigate the matter. Here are the investigator's notes:

The manufacturer didn't store the foam according to instructions.
He didn't cut the foam correctly.
He used cheap glue to stick the foam to the seat.
He didn't inform us immediately of the problem.
He didn't ask our advice about how best to assemble the seats.
He covered the seats with cheap synthetic material.
He didn't check the seats before they left the factory.

Exercise

Imagine you are a Baxcel representative telephoning the customer to explain what he has done wrong and to explain why you cannot accept liability. Make sentences with *should have* and *shouldn't have*.

8 We regret . . .

You have now decided that Baxcel's products are not suitable for your purposes. You write and tell them of your decision. Here is part of the letter.

..... 19 January we started using your foam ..... our car seats. ..... that time we were producing ..... least 220 seats ..... day. We were very satisfied ..... the foam ..... first, but soon we started receiving complaints ..... our main customers, British Autocars Ltd.

..... view ..... the fact that you do not accept responsibility ..... the defects, we have decided not ..... purchase any further stocks ..... your company.

We will return your latest consignment ..... soon ..... possible. Please cancel our order ..... 14 September ..... 1,000 pieces ..... foam (size AB20).

Exercise

Fill in the prepositions missing from the above extract.

10 Plans, arrangements and decisions

There are 12 steps in Unit 10. You will read about:

- future plans and intentions
- facts about the future
- anticipating reactions to decisions
- ways of saving energy

1 Next week's programme

Listen to David Barker talking about his plans for the coming week. Write down details of his programme.

2 The present continuous tense

When we are talking about our personal plans for the future we often use the **present continuous** form of the verb.

I'm attending the conference next week.
I'm flying to Barcelona on Thursday.
We're having lunch in Vienna.

3 The simple future tense

However, if there is a condition attached to the plan we have, we use the **simple future** form and a clause with *if* or *unless* plus a verb in the **simple present** tense.

I'll probably fly to Vienna on Thursday, unless I get a phone call from London.
I'll stay at the Grand Hotel if there's no room at the Splendide.

Sometimes we have not finalized arrangements completely. If there are *two* possibilities but we are not sure which we shall actually do, we use the **simple future** with *either . . . or*.

We'll either go round the factory or just talk about the agency contract.
We'll eat either at Piero's or at that new Chinese restaurant, depending on how much time we've got.
Either I'll ring him tomorrow or Jim's secretary will send him a telex.

4 Discussing plans

From the notes you made about David Barker's plans, you should be able to practise these forms by making complete sentences like this:

On Monday he's meeting Hans Weber in Manchester.

Now go on to write about Mr Barker's plans for the rest of the week.

5 What about you?

Bob Grant and Nancy Harding have also been finalizing their plans for next week.

Working in pairs, take the parts of Bob and Nancy. Ask each other about your plans and note them down. The information about Nancy Harding is printed at the end of the Unit. Bob's plans are below.

Monday	Flight BA 246 to Barcelona 08.30. Lunch – Mr Santos. Afternoon – free.
Tuesday	Conference 10–5. Dinner with Mr Martinez.
Wednesday	Flight IB 403 to Madrid – 9.15. Meeting ROLA SA 11.00 (if confirmed).
Thursday	Free morning. Seminar at CEPESA 3.00.
Friday	either – Follow-up session at CEPESA or – marketing visit to local companies.
Saturday	Flight BA 310 to Manchester Ringway.

6 The new helicopter

Read this newspaper article about a new development in the aeronautical field.

New helicopter project will cost £1,000m

by our own correspondent

THE WL93 will be a large aircraft. It will be based on an American design made by Waverley under licence for use by the navy and air force, as well as for servicing oil and gas installations in the North Sea.

Its first employment will be as an anti-submarine military aircraft, packed with modern electronic systems designed to detect and follow enemy warships. In its civil form it will carry up to 40 passengers.

Of the total development costs of £1,000m, Waverley will contribute approximately £250m and the rest will be committed to the advanced electronics to be built into the project. These systems are being designed by British Cables Ltd.

Waverley is already recruiting technicians to work on the WL93 project, which, when it is in full assembly, may create up to 2,000 additional jobs. Many of the parts for the helicopter will be manufactured in France and Italy and then be transported to the UK for assembly, if present negotiations are successful.

Waverley expects to sell up to 750 WL93s, which at current prices would cost £5.5m each. The aircraft could be powered by engines made in Britain, France or the United States, depending on the technical specifications required.

7 True or false?

Read these statements about the new WL93 helicopter and decide if they are true or false.

1 The WL93 will be used against enemy submarines.
2 The helicopter will carry at least 40 passengers in its civil form.
3 Waverley will pay 25% of the development costs.
4 The cost of developing the necessary electronics will be £250m.
5 It is certain that 2,000 additional jobs will be created.
6 Some parts may be made in France and Italy and assembled in the UK.
7 British-made engines will power the helicopter.

8 Possibilities and probabilities

When we are discussing facts about the future or communicating decisions we often use the **simple future** tense.

Waverley will pay 25% of all development costs.
The navy will use the helicopter against enemy submarines.
The project will require substantial investment.

When these facts and decisions are public and impersonal, we often use the **simple future passive**.

25% of all development costs will be paid by Waverley.
The helicopter will be used by the navy against enemy submarines.
Substantial investment will be required.

However, we can never be completely certain about the future. To suggest that things could turn out differently, we use other modal verbs like *may, might, could*.

The helicopter could be powered by British engines.
Some parts may be made in France.
2,000 additional jobs might be created.

9 The simple future passive

Now make sentences from this information about Ambermold's policy decisions. Use the simple future passive form wherever possible.

		Certain	*Possible*
1	Set up new plant in South America:	☐	☑
2	Discuss annual wage rises before the end of next month:	☑	☐
3	Produce new version of ABS bearing system within five years:	☑	☐
4	Extend production area at Swinton Lane plant:	☐	☑
5	Negotiate new contract with Indonesian Government:	☑	☐
6	Use American motors to operate new production line:	☐	☑
7	Investigate potential of Scandinavian market:	☑	☐
8	Make 50 office workers redundant at Swinton Lane:	☐	☑

10 Drill 1: Tell me . . .

Look at Peter Milne's diary for the coming week.

Monday	2.30	Leave for Geneva
	5.00	Meet Herr Richard
Tuesday	10.00	Meet Managing Director of Metalco
	2.00	Attend Trade fair in Montreux
Wednesday	12.00	Play golf with David
	7.30	Have dinner with David
Thursday	9.15	Leave for London
	3.00	Report back to Ambermold Managers

Now listen to these examples:

When exactly are you leaving for Geneva, Peter?
Oh, I'm leaving for Geneva at 2.30 on Monday.

I see. And when exactly are you meeting Herr Richard?
Oh, I'm meeting Herr Richard at 5.00 on Monday.

Now imagine that you are Peter Milne. Answer your secretary's questions about your business trip.

Drill 2: And this year?

Listen to these two people talking about events in the company calendar.

Last year the company announced profits on 19 June, I think.
When will they be announced this year?

Oh, around the same date I suppose. And the annual conference, they held that in Blackpool last year.
Where will it be held this year?

Each time the second person asks a question using the passive form of the verb. Now you go on in the same way.

11 Save it!

The Government has for some time been encouraging companies all over the country to save energy, and a committee of managers at Ambermold has been asked to look into ways of reducing energy consumption at Swinton Lane. Here is their report:

PROPOSALS OF COMMITTE ON EFFECTIVE ENERGY USE

Chairman: B Anderson

The committee's brief was to suggest economies which would lead to a saving of £5,000 per annum on our energy budget.

We feel that the final decisions as to how this should be achieved are best left to an open meeting at which all departments are present.

However, we would report that any or all of the following alternatives are open to us.

(Note that all amounts refer to annual savings.)

Reduce lighting levels in production area:	
– by 10%	£1,250
– by 5%	£ 850
– by 2%	£ 310
Reduce central heating level in admin block:	
– to 20°C	£ 580
– to 18°C	£1,350
– to 16°C	£2,050
Turn off advertising sign at front of building:	
– in evenings	£ 650
– in evenings and at weekends	£ 900
Turn off boundary fence flood lighting:	
– at nights	£1,200
Close social club:	
– at 10.00pm	£ 600
– at 9.00pm	£ 900
– at 8.00pm	£1,200
Canteen to serve cold meals only:	
– in summer	£ 850
– all year	£1,750
– at lunch times	£ 400
Turn off extractor fan in factories:	
– during all working hours	£1,800

Department of Energy
SAVE IT

Discuss this problem in groups and decide how best to save the target amount of £5,000. Try to imagine the effect of your decisions.

Remember how we use *if* with the **simple present** followed by a clause in the **simple future** or with *could, may* or *might*:

If we reduce the heating, the office workers will/might/could/may complain.

Then discuss your decision with the other groups. Be prepared to defend your group's decision to the rest of the class.

12 Writing a memo

Write a memorandum to the board giving details of the decision of your group as to how you propose to reduce expenditure on energy. Use these notes to help you.

—Refer to the meeting.
—Give an outline of the choices available.
—Indicate which alternatives were selected, giving reasons.
—Assure the board that everything possible is being done to conserve energy.

Tapescript for step 1

Tape section 22

SECRETARY: Could you give me some details about your trip next week? Where are you going, exactly?

DAVID BARKER: Well, I'm not leaving until Tuesday now, because Hans Weber is over here in England so he's coming up to see me here in Manchester before I go. So I'm catching the Milan plane early on Tuesday morning, eight-thirty I think it takes off, and then I'm visiting the works outside Milan in the afternoon and catching the train on to Turin at about 6 o'clock. I'm staying at the Hotel Splendide near the station in Turin that night.

SECRETARY: I see, and what about the next morning?

DAVID BARKER: Well, on the Wednesday of course I'm attending the conference in Turin all day, and then I'll probably fly on to Vienna on the four-thirty plane unless I get a phone call from England. I'm not quite sure what's happening in Vienna. It depends on Herr Richard really. We're having lunch together on Thursday and then either he'll take me around the factory or we'll just talk about the agency contract and try and reach some agreement.

SECRETARY: And Friday?

DAVID BARKER: It's completely free at the moment. I'm planning to have a look at some of the museums and art galleries in the city during the day and then perhaps go to the opera or the theatre during the evening.

SECRETARY: And you're flying back to Manchester on Saturday.

DAVID BARKER: Yes, that's right. I'm catching the British Airways flight at 9 o'clock on Saturday morning. So I'll be back home by lunchtime. After quite an exhausting week.

SECRETARY: Yes, indeed.

Nancy Harding's plans for step 5

Monday	Final preparations for trip to Birmingham International Trade Fair. Train to Birmingham 7.00
Tuesday	TRADE FAIR Appointments Smith 10.15 Johnson 12.00 (lunch) Andrews 3.00
Wednesday	TRADE FAIR Seminar on roller bearings 11.00 Prepare press release (if time)
Thursday	TRADE FAIR Either Press Conference 11.00 OR Technical Seminar 11.15
Friday	Write report for Managing Director. See Managing Director 3.00 pm.
Saturday	FREE

11 Go West, young man!

There are 13 steps in Unit 11. You will learn how to:

- report questions
- report statements

1 Immigration procedures in the USA

Alan Haydock is going on a business trip to the USA on behalf of Ambermold. He is rather concerned about immigration procedures at American airports and so he asks a colleague, Bill Young, what happened when he went to Texas on business.

Listen to the conversation and note down the information which the immigration official wanted from Bill Young. There are six points in all. Begin like this:

1 Length of stay in US.

Listen again. This time write down the actual questions asked by the immigration officer. Begin like this:

1 How long are you staying in the United States?

2 Reporting questions

Here are the rules for changing a direct question into a reported question. Look at this example:

Where do you live?

To report this question, we need first of all an introductory verb:

He asked me . . .
He wanted to know . . .

Then we put the question into indirect speech. This means:

a) that the word order changes to that of a normal sentence;
b) the person and time change if necessary;
c) the tense of the verb changes:
simple present → simple past
simple past → past perfect (or **simple past)**

If there are two or more parts to the verb, the first part changes:

is/are → was/were   **can → could**
will → would   **may → might**
have → had

So the reported form of the question above is:

He asked me where I lived.

3 Press report

George Daniels was recently interviewed by a reporter from the *Sunday Chronicle* about his part in catching a bank robber. Imagine you are George. Write down the questions you were asked. Here are the reporter's questions:

1. What is your full name?
2. How old are you?
3. Where do you live?
4. Can you describe the events of the morning of 23 July?
5. What did you think when the robber pointed a gun straight at you?
6. How did you get the gun off him?
7. What happened when the police arrived?
8. Did you receive any reward from the bank?
9. What did your wife and family think about the whole episode?
10. Are you afraid of going into a bank now?

4 Arrangements for a trip

Alan Haydock receives a memorandum from his boss Peter Jackson. Read this memo and be ready to give the information in it to the US immigration officer.

Ambermold International

Memorandum

From: Peter Jackson
To: Alan Haydock

25 June 19--

This is just to let you know details of your ten-day trip to Denver, Colorado. A single room with bath has been reserved for you at the Holiday Inn, Denver, from 7 - 15 July inclusive.

I'm also enclosing your return air ticket (Heathrow-Denver-Heathrow), together with traveller's cheques to the value of $750. (The hotel bill will be settled by the company in advance.)

I hope you have a successful trip and I'm sure you'll be able to persuade US Motors that the ABS is exactly what they're looking for.

5 The immigration officer

Imagine you are Alan Haydock. Listen to the US Immigration Officer, who will ask you certain questions. Use the information in the memo to answer him.

6 Reporting back

Later, you telephone Bill Young to say that you've arrived safely. Tell him what questions you were asked at the airport. Listen to the immigration officer again if you need to be reminded about his questions.

7 Who's getting the contract?

Read this article from the *Denver Gleaner*. Can you re-enact the interviews that the reporter held with Burley H. Crawford, the 'unofficial source' and the representative of Stateside Bearings?

DENVER GLEANER

Huge USM contract for parts to go to England?

BURLEY H CRAWFORD, President of US Motors, today denied that the company was considering awarding a huge contract for parts to a British firm. Asked why representatives of a leading British manufacturer of bearings had traveled to Denver, Mr Crawford said it had been "an essentially exploratory and informational consultation session."

$100 million in 5 years

Unofficial sources yesterday disclosed that a contract in the region of $100 million was being discussed and that a definite decision would be made within the next few days. Other offers from companies in the US and Europe were being considered but the British had the best chance of landing the contract as things stood at the moment.

Protest by US manufacturers

A spokesman for Stateside Bearings, the largest manufacturer of ball bearings in the US, said today that he was shocked that the contract could be going abroad. He said that the US market needed large contracts very badly and that it didn't help at all if

please turn to page 4

8 Reporting statements

Remember that the only difference between reporting questions and reporting statements is the introductory verb used. These are the most commonly used for reporting statements:

He told me . . .
He said . . .

There are many other verbs, which also give information about *how* something was said.

He warned me . . .
He suggested . . .
He implied . . .
He promised . . .
He admitted . . .

9 Telephone messages

This morning you took two telephone messages for Alan Haydock. He is out on a job and is now phoning in to the office to find out if there is anything which needs urgent attention. Tell him about these two messages.

MEMORANDUM OF CALL

To: Alan Haydock

☒ You were called by— ☐ You were visited by—

Alexander Marshall

Of (Organization)

British Motors Ltd

☒ Please call

Phone No. Code/Ext. 021-635-9110

☐ Will call again

☐ Is waiting to see you

☐ Returned your call

☐ Wishes an appointment

Message

Mr Marshall has completed tests on ABS.1200 - several problems:
- overheating
- jamming at high speeds

Please call to arrange visit to factory

Received by JS

Date 26 Sept. Time 9.26

MEMORANDUM OF CALL

To: Alan Haydock

☒ You were called by— ☐ You were visited by—

Peter Masterton

Of (Organization)

UMC (London)

☒ Please call

Phone No. Code/Ext. 01-636-4098

☐ Will call again

☐ Is waiting to see you

☐ Returned your call

☐ Wishes an appointment

Message

Are target figures for next financial year ready yet? Please send to Masterton as soon as possible - copy to UMC Head Office (Financial Controller's Dept). Call if any problems

Received by JS

Date 26 Sept. Time 10.50

10 Drill 1: What did they ask?

You have just been interviewed for a job. In your book is part of the form you had to fill in:

1 Have you worked in a similar job before?
2 What relevant qualifications do you have?
3 Why are you looking for a new job?
4 What do you like most about your present job?
5 What do you like least about your present job?
6 How do you get on with your colleagues?
7 How did you hear about this job?
8 How much do you earn in your present job?

Tell a friend about the questions you had to answer:

So what did they ask you?
Well, they wanted to know if I had worked in a similar job before.

I see. And what about qualifications?
Well, they wanted to know what relevant qualifications I had.

Now you go on in the same way. (Look at the list of questions above, and begin at number 3.)

Drill 2: Yes, why . . .?

You are talking to your colleague after this interview. You are also interested to know the answer to the questions which the interviewer put to him. Listen to these examples:

He asked me why I was looking for a new job.
Yes, why are *you looking for a new job?*

And he wanted to know what qualifications I had.
Yes, what qualifications do *you have?*

Notice that the stress is on the first part of the verb. Repeat those questions again:

Yes, why are *you looking for a new job?*
Yes, what qualifications do *you have?*

Now you go on in the same way.

11 Two reports

You are now going to read two reports by Alan Haydock on his visit to Denver. Work in pairs, each of you reading one of the reports. The first report is printed on page 75; the second is at the end of the Unit.

Note down the information under the following headings.

1 Relations with Burley H Crawford.

2 BHC's opinion of the ABS 1200 system.

3 BHC's opinion of the trend towards smaller cars in the US.

4 ABS 1200 described in general or details?

5 Results of US Motors' enquiries to other companies.

6 Possible disadvantages of ABS 1200.

7 BHC's opinion of Ambermold prices and delivery dates.

8 Return visit by Haydock necessary? If so, why?

Imagine that the reports have been sent to you personally. Compare the version of events you have been given with the story Haydock told your colleague. Use phrases like:

Well, he told me . . .
He said to me
According to his report . . .

I had a most useful and illuminating talk with Burley H Crawford with whom I was immediately able to establish a friendly and cooperative working relationship.

He seemed interested in Ambermold's products, particularly the ABS 1200; one reason for this is that the ABS 1200 is suitable for use in smaller cars and there's a strong move here away from the large 'gas-guzzling' limousines often associated with the US. Petrol prices have risen considerably in the last two or three years and although they haven't yet reached European levels, the Americans are concerned to get the best possible return for expenditure on energy; building smaller cars is one way out of the problem.

I described the ABS 1200 in general terms and Mr Crawford was quite impressed. In fact he even suggested that I return to Denver at some future date in order to discuss the whole matter more fully.

US Motors have apparently made enquiries about similar components all over Europe and have not found anything at all suitable. Our prices are considered competitive and our delivery dates acceptable.

The conclusion must be that the contract could go to Ambermold. If we can arrange a follow-up visit soon, there should be no difficulty in winning the contract before the opposition can develop a viable alternative.

12 What really happened?

Now listen to Alan Haydock talking to Bill Young. Look back at your notes and write down what *really* happened in Denver, Colorado.

13 Discussion points

Look at these statements:

Personal advancement is more important than loyalty to the company.
Industrial espionage is inevitable in the modern world.

'Headhunting' (a secret approach to other companies' executives) is an acceptable way of filling top vacancies.
In business, small is beautiful.
Multinationals are outside the control of individual governments.

Choose one or two and write down three or four arguments for or against. Discuss your ideas with the rest of the group.

Tapescript for step 1 *Tape section 24*

ALAN HAYDOCK: Bill, I'm going to America in a couple of weeks and I'm a bit worried about the customs officers and what they ask you at the airport.
BILL YOUNG: You mean immigration?
ALAN HAYDOCK: Yes, that's right.
BILL YOUNG: Have you got your visa fixed up?
ALAN HAYDOCK: Yes, that came from the Embassy last week.
BILL YOUNG: Oh you'll be alright then. Just be prepared to answer lots of questions, that's all.
ALAN HAYDOCK: What sort of questions? What did they ask you?
BILL YOUNG: Well, the main thing they wanted to know was how long I was staying in the United States, and of course whether I was there on business or as a tourist.
ALAN HAYDOCK: I see. What else did they want to know?
BILL YOUNG: They asked me if I already had an address in the United States, and also where I lived in England. Oh yes, and they asked me how much money I had in travellers' cheques and cash.
ALAN HAYDOCK: That's OK then. I shouldn't have any problems there.
BILL YOUNG: I knew there was something else. Do you know, they actually asked me if I'd ever been to a psychiatrist.
ALAN HAYDOCK: Good Lord. I wonder why they wanted to know that. Well, thanks anyway for your help.
BILL YOUNG: That's alright. Have a good trip. And don't worry, they'll let you in.

Tapescript for step 5 *Tape section 25*

IMMIGRATION OFFICER: This way please sir. Your passport? Yes that's fine. Thank you very much. Now, I just have to ask you a few questions. First of all, how long are you planning to stay in the USA?
ALAN HAYDOCK: ....
IMMIGRATION OFFICER: I see. And do you have an address here?
ALAN HAYDOCK: ....
IMMIGRATION OFFICER: Fine. Colorado's a nice part of the country. Are you here on business or as a tourist?
ALAN HAYDOCK: ....
IMMIGRATION OFFICER: On business, OK. Could you tell me please, how much money do you have with you right now?
ALAN HAYDOCK: ....
IMMIGRATION OFFICER: Oh, that's plenty for ten days. The only other thing I have to know is the name of the company you work for back in the UK.
ALAN HAYDOCK: ....
IMMIGRATION OFFICER: Could you spell that, please?

ALAN HAYDOCK: ....

IMMIGRATION OFFICER: Thank you. Oh yes, one more question. Are you now or have you ever been a member of the Communist Party?

ALAN HAYDOCK: ....

Tapescript for step 12

Tape section 27

I got on extremely well with Burley Crawford right from the start. I described the ABS 1200 to him in detail but he said he thought it wouldn't be suitable for the kind of cars they manufacture. Although it's more or less the right size, now that smaller cars are being made in the US, he thought that the variation in temperature in the US might be a problem. In England we obviously don't have such extremes of temperature, and he thought we hadn't really taken these problems of design into account in this version of the ABS. Nevertheless, he was very impressed with the technology. They've tried everywhere in Europe to get a suitable component, but nowhere can supply exactly what they want, not even Germany. He thought our prices were reasonable, and our delivery dates quite acceptable, but felt that the ABS 1200 still wasn't quite right. And that decision is definite. Then we discussed the development of the ABS 1200 and I explained that I was very much involved right from the beginning. When he realized that I was responsible for most of the technology, he asked me if I'd ever thought of working in the States. And since I came back to Manchester, I've been thinking about it very seriously. In fact I'm hoping to go over to Denver for a formal interview and look around the factory very soon, if I can manage it.

Alan Haydock's second report for step 11

Burley H Crawford is by no means an easy person to get on with, although he clearly knows what he wants from suppliers: the right product at the right price!

He was not very impressed with my lengthy and detailed presentation of the ABS 1200 — I tried to emphasize the usefulness of the system for smaller cars, but he informed me that the trend was now back towards bigger cars, the worst of the oil crisis now being past.

He told me that several other companies were able to offer similar systems at a better price. A German company, for example, can supply US Motors with an excellent flexible system and deliver it much more quickly than we can.

It seemed to me that the only possibility would be to do a follow-up visit to Denver offering a modified version of the ABS 1200 tailored to US Motors' specific requirements. If we don't do this — and fast — we shall lose the contract to our German competitors.

12 What do you think?

There are 11 steps in Unit 12. You will be learning how to:

- ask about personal opinions
- give your own personal opinions
- generalize about other people's opinions
- agree and disagree at meetings
- put your point effectively
- interrupt at meetings

1 The public opinion survey

A national newspaper is carrying out a public opinion survey. Listen to an interview with a man in the street and tick the correct box on the questionnaire below. For example, if you think that the interviewee is very much against nuclear disarmament, put a tick in the box *Disagree strongly*.

	Agree strongly	*Agree*	*Disagree*	*Disagree strongly*	*Don't know*
1 Britain should give up all nuclear arms.	☐	☐	☐	☐	☐
2 Policemen should always carry arms.	☐	☐	☐	☐	☐
3 Tax on cigarettes should be doubled.	☐	☐	☐	☐	☐
4 Britain should drive on the right-hand side of the road.	☐	☐	☐	☐	☐
5 Workers should be represented on boards of directors.	☐	☐	☐	☐	☐
6 Britain should leave the EEC.	☐	☐	☐	☐	☐

2 Asking for opinions; giving opinions

There are various ways in which we can ask for somebody's opinion about a particular issue or problem. Here are some of them:

What do you think about . . .?
In your opinion, should . . . be done?
What are your views on . . .?
Do you think . . . should be done?
Do you agree or disagree with this statement?

Here are some ways of agreeing and disagreeing:

Yes, I think . . . should be done.	*I don't agree with that.*
I'm in favour of that.	*I'm not in favour of that.*
I would support that point of view.	*I'm absolutely against that.*

3 What about you?

Now find out your colleagues' opinions about the same issues and problems. Note down their opinions. Try to interview as many people as possible.

4 What they think

Here is part of the article which appeared later in the *Daily Herald* following the public opinion survey.

. . . which were put to randomly selected members of the public.

Strong feeling

Two issues which aroused particularly strong feelings were Britain's driving habits and tax on tobacco. There's a lot of support for a proposal to double the tax on cigarettes; nearly 72% of those interviewed thought this was a good idea and only 5% disagreed strongly.

Even stronger was the reaction to any suggestion of changing to driving on the right. 80% of those interviewed totally rejected the idea, with only 2% agreeing strongly.

No clear view on the EEC

People were less certain about Britain leaving the EEC. Here the percentage of 'don't knows' was relatively high — 18% — and the total number for was almost the same as the number against, 37% to 45%, so it's difficult to draw any definite conclusions. On the other hand there does seem to be a general feeling that policemen should not always be armed. A total of 64% agreed or agreed strongly with this statement.

Another point which emerged with some force from the survey was that

5 Making generalizations

When we are generalizing about people's opinions, some of these phrases are useful:

Most people tend to think that . . .
There's a lot of support for this viewpoint.
Ninety per cent of people are of the opinion that . . .
There seems to be a general feeling that . . .
There's no clear view about . . .

6 Survey results

Here are the results of the survey on two of the issues.

		Agree strongly	*Agree*	*Disagree*	*Disagree strongly*	*Don't know*
1	Britain should give up all nuclear arms.	10%	11%	34%	38%	7%
5	Workers should be represented on boards of directors.	17%	14%	20%	24%	25%

Write a paragraph about these two sets of figures, emphasizing the most important aspects. Use some of the phrases given in step 5 if you think they are appropriate. You should also be able to write a paragraph summarizing your colleagues' opinions on the same issues.

7 Next item on the agenda

Giving your opinion at a business meeting is rather different. Here is part of a meeting held recently to consider company policy on a particular matter. Listen to the discussion and note down information under these headings.

1 Agenda item: ....

2 Matter to be discussed: ....

3 Advantages of present system: ....

4 Result of vote: ....

8 Making your point at meetings

At a meeting it is essential to make your point clearly and logically. You also need more formal language to get your point across to your audience.

Imagine that you want to say that a particular project under discussion is too expensive, not well enough researched and requires expertise which is not available at the moment. You could say:

This project is too expensive. It isn't well enough researched and it requires expertise not available at the moment.

But it would be much better to say:

Well, the first thing I have to say is that this project is too expensive. It also seems to me that it hasn't been well enough researched. Perhaps the most important aspect, however, is that it requires expertise not available at the moment.

Each new idea is introduced with a short phrase to prepare the listener for another argument against the project. The result is that the speaker's arguments are more likely to convince his audience.

Other useful phrases in this context are:

I must emphasize that . . .
The point is . . .
The thing is . . .
Another point I'd like to make is . . .

It is also important to be able to break into a discussion and put your point of view without being rude. Here are some phrases which might be suitable for use at reasonably formal meetings.

Could I make a point there?
Could I come in here?
Perhaps I could just comment on that?
Sorry to interrupt, but . . .

(The last one is perhaps best used when you haven't understood something.)

After a speaker has been interrupted, he might start again, like this:

As I was saying . . .
What I was going to say was . . .
I was just about to point out that . . .

9 Putting forward your own ideas

Now practise putting forward your ideas to a group. Look at these situations, decide whether you are for or against the proposals and think of as many arguments as you can to support your point of view. Use the phrases you have learned in order to make your points as effectively as possible.

1. Your company is considering building a sports centre for the exclusive use of staff.
2. The company is proposing to extend the opening hours of the shopping centre until 9.00 pm Monday to Friday.
3. As a public relations exercise, the company intends to arrange public tours of the production area on two afternoons a week.
4. Mrs James, the tea lady, is to be replaced by hot-drink dispensers to be situated at suitable locations throughout the factory and offices.
5. Air conditioning is to be installed in the offices. All windows will be double-glazed and permanently sealed.

10 Drill 1: What do they think?

		Agree	Disagree	Don't know
1	Police should carry arms.	15%	75%	10%
2	Britain should leave the Common Market.	40%	55%	5%
3	The monarchy should be abolished.	10%	85%	5%
4	Workers should be represented on boards of directors.	32%	60%	8%
5	The UK should be a federal state.	57%	29%	14%
6	The metric system should be introduced in the UK.	61%	25%	14%
7	Britain should drive on the right.	12%	73%	15%
8	Health care should be free.	69%	24%	7%

Look at the questionnaire results and then answer the questions. Like this. Listen:

What do most people think about police carrying guns?
Most people think that the police shouldn't carry guns.

I see. And what do the majority think about Britain and the Common Market?
Most people think that Britain shouldn't leave the Common Market.

Now you go on in the same way.

Drill 2: Sorry to interrupt . . .

Listen to this person speaking. Occasionally he uses difficult words. When you do not understand a difficult word or phrase, interrupt and ask for an explanation. Like this. Listen:

And, of course, there's the problem of teething troubles.
Sorry to interrupt, but what do you mean by 'teething troubles'?

I mean the problems associated with introducing the interface technology.
Sorry to interrupt, but what do you mean by 'interface technology'?

Now you go on in the same way.

11 Two sides to the question

Ambermold has been spending more and more every year on central services. While only 3% of expenditure went on administration and management five years ago, this figure has risen alarmingly to nearly 5.5% in the last financial year. Something has to be done. The Managing Director is convinced that the Project Co-ordination Department (PCD) which employs one manager, four executives and three assistants, could be disbanded. The PCD was established to take over control of the development, production, marketing and sales of important products, particularly those which represent new technological developments.

Divide into two teams, Ambermold Management and PCD. Read the information given, and add any other ideas which you can think of to support your view. Then meet the other side to present your case and decide on the future of the PCD. Information for the PCD team is at the end of the Unit. Information for Ambermold management is printed below.

Ambermold Management

You are in favour of the immediate disbanding of the PCD for the following reasons:

1. All the functions carried out by the PCD at the moment could be fulfilled by the R & D Department, the Marketing Department, the sales team and the production engineers.
2. Sales of new products which are the responsibility of the PCD are much lower than sales of standard lines.
3. Unical Limited has disbanded PCD with no adverse effects.
4. Senior managers are threatening to leave because they feel that their authority is being undermined by the PCD.
5. PCD expenditure has risen every year since it was formed three years ago, with no visible result. We need to invest this money in more urgent projects, which will bring immediate returns.

Tapescript for step 1

Tape section 28

INTERVIEWER: Excuse me, would you mind answering a few questions?

MAN: Well, I don't know. I am in rather a hurry actually.

INTERVIEWER: It won't take a moment. We're doing a public opinion poll on some important political questions to try and find out if the Government really has support for its policies. The results are going to be published in a national newspaper.

MAN: Oh, all right then.

INTERVIEWER: Thanks, well, what I'll do is read out statements and you have to say whether you agree strongly, agree, disagree, disagree strongly or just don't know. OK?

MAN: Yes.

INTERVIEWER: Well, first of all what are your views on nuclear disarmament? 'Britain should give up all nuclear arms.' What do you think of that?

MAN: I absolutely agree. I think Britain should lead the way towards a European nuclear-free zone.

INTERVIEWER: Fine. Now, 'Policemen should always carry guns'. Do you agree with that?

MAN: No, not always. Not when they're just on normal duty. But if they're chasing a criminal who they know has got a gun, then they should be armed as well.

INTERVIEWER: There's a proposal by one of the parties to double the tax on cigarettes. Is that reasonable, in your opinion?

MAN: No, I don't think it is. I think the smoker pays enough tax already.

INTERVIEWER: Oh. 'Britain should drive on the right-hand side of the road.'

MAN: What rubbish! Why doesn't everybody else drive on the left!

INTERVIEWER: OK, next question: 'Workers should be represented on boards of directors'.

MAN: Mm, I don't know about that one. It depends. You'd have to be very careful to organize it properly. Erm . . ..

INTERVIEWER: All right. One more question: 'Britain should leave the EEC'.

MAN: That's a nasty question. I wasn't in favour of us joining but I think it would be difficult to leave now. I think we'll just have to stay in and make the best of it.

INTERVIEWER: OK. That's all, thanks very much.

Tapescript for step 7

Tape section 29

ALAN: Well, perhaps we could take the next point on the agenda? Roger?

ROGER: Thank you, Alan. Yes, well. 'Recommendations of Working Party on Computerization and Discussion.' Well, the first thing I have to say is that the working party hasn't yet completed its report, but we are hoping to do so by next week. The formal recommendations haven't been decided on yet, but there are one or two things we could profitably discuss now. Perhaps the most important matter to talk about at this point is whether we are in fact to computerize the payroll at the same time as the accounts and stock control system. The general feeling of the working party is to go for a fully computerized system, but I'd like to hear the views of this meeting.

THIRD SPEAKER: Well, I'd like to support Roger on this one. It seems to me sensible to computerize all the systems at one time. We're going to need an automated payroll eventually so I think we should go ahead now and make the extra investment.

FOURTH SPEAKER: Could I come in here? As the person with overall responsibility for the Wages and Salaries Department I must emphasize that the system at present works extremely efficiently. Mavis Ward has been with the company for thirty years now and does a first class job.

THIRD SPEAKER: No one's saying she doesn't, but you've got to move with the times, and a computerized system . . ..

FOURTH SPEAKER: If you'd just let me finish . . . She does a first class job which quite simply wouldn't be done as well by any computer, however sophisticated. The point is, Mavis and her team are able to take account of all sorts of little things that a computer just couldn't cope with. The human element, in fact.

FIFTH SPEAKER: Don't you think that's rather sentimental? After all, a computer only does what it's programmed to do. And anyway if

Mavis and her team were retrained as computer programmers, they'd be the ones in charge of the system.

ALAN: Peter, could I bring you in here? What are your feelings on the subject?

PETER: Well, I'm afraid I can't really agree with John on this. Apart from the initial teething troubles . . .

ALAN: Sorry to interrupt, but what do you mean by 'teething troubles'?

PETER: I mean the problems we're likely to meet when we're still setting up the system and finding out how best to use it. So, as I was saying, apart from those problems, I think that full computerization is the best thing to go for.

ALAN: Thank you. Well, perhaps we could move to a vote. All those in favour of a full computerization programme, to include wages and salaries . . .. Thank you. And those against . . .. Thank you. Well, that looks like the result the working party were hoping for . . .. Now, any other business?

PCD team information for step 11

You must defend the work done by your team over the last three years and argue for the continued existence of the department. Here are some arguments which will help you to put your case.

1. There is a need for a team which has overall control and knowledge of *all* aspects of a product.
2. R & D need advice about production *and* market opportunities when they are designing new products. The PCD can provide this advice.
3. The ABS 1750, the first product to be developed under the control of the PCD, is still selling very well.
4. Customers with problems need to have contact with just *one* department which can advise about technical, financial and delivery problems.
5. Because of technical and marketing skills available within the department, more effective market surveys can be carried out.
6. The PCD has helped with the training of the technical sales staff.

13 The customer is always right

There are 10 steps in Unit 13. You will be learning how to:

- make and deal with complaints
- explain and apologize
- promise and offer
- discuss a problem about noise

1 A dissatisfied customer

Ambermold receives a call from a dissatisfied customer. Listen to the conversation and note down the information below:

Customer Service Dept. Telephone Message

Date ______ Time ______

Customer's name & address ______

______

Details of order

Item: ______

Number ordered: ______

Date ordered: ______

Order no. ______

Details of delivery

Delivery date: ______

Invoice date: ______

Invoice no. ______

Details of complaint ______

______

Action taken ______

2 Tenses

Look at this extract from the conversation. Put the verbs into the correct tense, **present perfect** or **simple past**.

I'm ringing about a consignment of roller bearings you . . . . . (send) us about three weeks ago. We . . . . . (build) them into our Global 2000 model and we . . . . . (have) rather a high failure rate on our test run. We . . . . . (use) your bearing systems for ten years now and this . . . . . (never happen) before. And it's nothing to do with the way they were assembled. We . . . . . (already check) that. In fact we . . . . . (check) the whole production line last Tuesday.

3 Dealing with a complaint

Now look at this short dialogue. It shows all the basic elements of a complaint and how to deal with one.

CUSTOMER: The goods we ordered last week haven't arrived yet.
SALESMAN: Oh dear.
CUSTOMER: Can you tell me what the situation is?
SALESMAN: Just a moment . . . Hallo, I'm terribly sorry.
CUSTOMER: What's the problem?
SALESMAN: There's been a delay at our factory, you see.
CUSTOMER: Oh, I see.
SALESMAN: We'll send them to you as soon as possible.
CUSTOMER: Mmm.
SALESMAN: Shall I mark your order urgent?
CUSTOMER: Yes, please. If you would.
SALESMAN: OK. Goodbye.

Explaining the background:

We ordered the goods a week ago. They arrived yesterday. Some of them were quite badly damaged.

Request for action:

Do you think you could sort it out?
Can you tell me what's happened?

Apologizing:

I'm terribly sorry about this.
I'm so sorry this has happened.

Explaining and making excuses:

There was a strike at the factory, you see.
We couldn't get the raw materials.
I didn't know your phone number.

Promising:

Don't worry. We'll send a letter to the insurers.
We'll replace all the damaged goods.
I'll find out what's happened and phone you back.

Offering:

Shall I phone the carriers for you?
Would you like us to replace the goods?
Do you want me to inform the insurers?

Accepting an offer:

Yes please, if you would.
Yes, I'd be most grateful if you could.

Declining an offer:

No thanks. I'll do that.
No thank you. That won't be necessary.

4 Promises

As we saw in step 3, when we promise somebody to do something, we usually use the simple future tense.

Now work with your partner. Take it in turns to make promises in response to the following statements.

1 I want a corrected invoice by first post tomorrow.
2 Please inform the insurance company at once.
3 I certainly hope this won't happen again.
4 Please don't forget to send us a copy of your new price list when it's ready.
5 Please don't be late for the appointment on Thursday.
6 Next time I want the whole report translated into English.

5 Offers

The two phrases which are most useful when you want to offer your help to somebody are:

Shall I . . .?
Would you like me to . . .?

Now, with your partner, take it in turns to offer help in the following situations.

1 I've got an appointment on the other side of town at 3 o'clock and it's 2.30 already.
2 I'd like some more information about your company's products.
3 Oh dear, I haven't got any change for the phone.
4 I can't understand how this photocopier works.
5 Someone will have to take the minutes of the meeting.
6 I can't understand this letter – it's all in Italian.

6 Making a complaint

Look at the information on page 89. Working in pairs, build up dialogues for each of the situations described.

7 Drill 1: Don't worry

Somebody is ringing to complain about the service given by your company. Promise to do everything you can to help him. Like this. Listen:

I'm very concerned about the delay in sending the goods.
Don't worry. We'll send the goods as soon as possible.

And we've been waiting for ten days for you to forward the operating instructions.
Don't worry. We'll forward the operating instructions as soon as possible.

Now you go on in the same way.

	HOTEL	BANK	SUPPLIER
EXPLAIN BACKGROUND	Single room and bath reserved by phone 2 nights Jan 13 and 14. Confirmation letter received: single room (no bath) reserved 2 nights Jan 14 and 15.	Statement received. Items 12 and 18 are the same. £27 debited twice. Interest charged £1.85.	Goods ordered last week. Arrived damaged. Packing instructions ignored. Clearly stated: 'wooden crates' *not* cartons.
REQUEST FOR ACTION			
APOLOGY			
EXCUSE	Mistake— Confusion over name.	Computer error.	Special packing instructions on back of order overlooked.
PROMISE	Change dates of reservation. Reserve room with bath.	Credit £27. Reduce interest charges to 75p.	Send replacement goods. No charge for delivery.
OFFER	Confirm by letter?	Send corrected statement?	Collect damaged goods?
ACCEPT			

Drill 2: Can I help?

Your friend is having difficulty in carrying out certain tasks. You offer to help. Listen:

I've been trying to phone him for half an hour but I can't get through.
Would you like me to phone him for you?

And I've been trying to translate this report for two hours and I can't make head nor tail of it.
Would you like me to translate it for you?

Now you go on in the same way.

8 Too much noise! Read this letter and attached report which were sent to Ambermold Head Office in early September.

Town Hall

IN DEO FIDEMUS

Borough of Milton Keynes

Telephone: BLETCHLEY (0246) 29800
Telex: MILBORO 235879

The Managing Director
Ambermold International
Swinton Road
MANCHESTER

4 September 19--

Dear Sir,

I understand from the Directors of Rollerco (Milton Keynes) that their company is a wholly-owned subsidiary of Ambermold International, and I am accordingly writing to you to pass on complaints about noise levels at the Rollerco factory.

Over the last eighteen months, noise levels have been increasing gradually and the housing estate to the east of the site has been particularly badly affected. The most disturbing development, however, has been the introduction in early August of night-shift working at the plant between 10 pm and 4 am, and this has made life intolerable for many local residents.

The Council commissioned an independent investigation into the noise levels (copy report enclosed) and would point out that the factory appears to be exceeding the permitted limits, as laid down in Section 32b of the Noise Prevention Act (1972).

I should be pleased to receive your comments on the foregoing, together with any ideas you may have on how this situation may be remedied.

Yours faithfully,

George Hooper (Town Clerk)

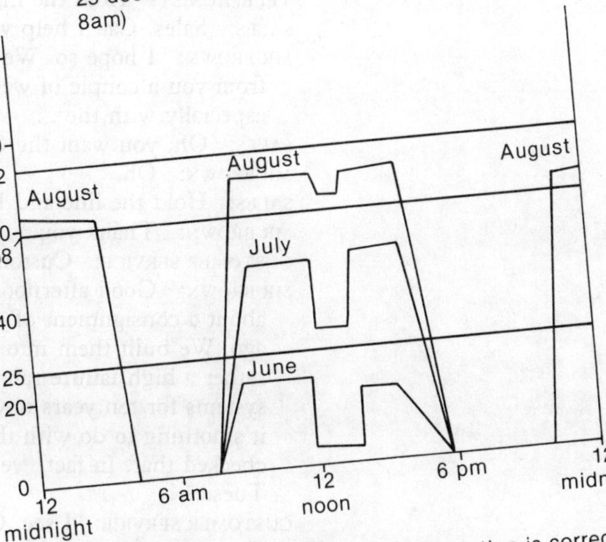

Report on Noise Levels in area surrounding Rollerco (Milton Keynes)

Measurements of noise levels were taken at regular intervals and in varying weather conditions from June to August. Average noise levels were calculated for each month to show trends more clearly.

Note that the maximum permitted noise levels under Section 32B of the Noise Prevention Act 1972 are:

72 decibels (for periods of up to five minutes per hour during working day)
58 decibels (for extended periods during working day)
25 decibels (for any period between 8pm and 8am)

We can confirm that the above information is correct to the best of our knowlege.

for Scientific Investigation Services Ltd.

A J Hobson.

A J HOBSON
Project Engineer

9 A conflict of interest

A meeting has been arranged to discuss the noise problem in Milton Keynes. It is to be held at the Rollerco factory and the aim is to reach a satisfactory compromise acceptable to all those involved. There are two main groups at the meeting: Ambermold/Rollerco Management, who want to keep full production going in order to meet important export delivery dates, and Milton Keynes Council/Local Residents Association, who are determined that the people of Milton Keynes should not have to suffer excessive noise.

Divide into groups and decide how best to present your argument. Then meet together to discuss the problem.

10 A conflict resolved

Following the meeting at Rollerco, Ambermold Management have to write a letter to Milton Keynes Council in which they formally agree to the compromise which has been reached. You write the letter. Some of the following phrases may be useful:

As agreed at the meeting on 13 September . . .
We confirm that . . .
We are sorry for any inconvenience caused.
Please contact us again if there are any further problems.

Tapescript for step 1

Tape section 31

MR BROWN: Good afternoon. I'd like to speak to someone about a consignment of roller bearings we received from you a few weeks ago.

TELEPHONIST: Hold the line and I'll put you through to Sales.

SALES: Sales. Can I help you?

MR BROWN: I hope so. We received a consignment of roller bearings from you a couple of weeks ago and we've had some problems, especially with the . . .

SALES: Oh, you want the Customer Service Department.

MR BROWN: Oh.

SALES: Hold the line and I'll get you transferred.

MR BROWN: Thank you.

CUSTOMER SERVICE: Customer Service. Can I help you?

MR BROWN: Good afternoon. This is Global Motors here. I'm ringing about a consignment of roller bearings you sent us about three weeks ago. We built them into our Global 2000 Model and we've had rather a high failure rate on our test run. We've used your bearing systems for ten years now and this has never happened before. And it's nothing to do with the way they were assembled. We've already checked that. In fact, we checked the whole production line last Tuesday.

CUSTOMER SERVICE: I see. Could you give me some more details of your order, please?

MR BROWN: Yes, they were ABS 120 bearing systems (seven hundred of them altogether) and they were ordered from you on 12 June, our order number PQ1046. They were delivered to us on 5 July and your invoice was dated 29 June. The number of that is A 294351.

CUSTOMER SERVICE: Just a moment and I'll see if I can find your original order in the sales records . . . Hallo. Yes, there seems to have been some mistake. Your order says quite clearly ABS 1200 which of course are completely unsuitable for use in private motor cars.

MR BROWN: Oh dear. Well look, we've only used about two hundred of them so far, so can I send the other five hundred back?

CUSTOMER SERVICE: Yes, of course. I'll issue a credit note for them. Let's see. That's five hundred at £25.00 each, which is £12,500 + VAT at 15% makes £14,375 altogether. Now do you want me to place an order for seven hundred of the ABS 120's?

MR BROWN: Yes, please, and can you confirm all this in writing to me; my name's Brown, at Global Motors, Global House, Barn Road, Birmingham 24.

CUSTOMER SERVICE: Fine, Mr Brown. I'll put through the credit note today and I'll send the order off immediately.

MR BROWN: Thank you very much. Goodbye.

CUSTOMER SERVICE: Goodbye.

14 A new appointment

There are 11 steps in Unit 14. You will practise:

- placing emphasis
- asking for clarification and further information
- writing a job advertisement
- interviewing techniques

1 The man for the job

Fittenwell Pharmaceuticals are planning to expand their laboratory equipment range and have decided to appoint a design engineer to strengthen their Research and Development team. Listen to the Personnel Manager and his assistant discussing the new post. The requirements for the job are determined by the duties to be performed. Note down what the duties will be and what attributes the candidates will need to carry out those duties.

	Requirements	*Duties*
Qualifications		
Experience		
Age range		
Personal qualities		
Languages		

2 Placing emphasis

We use the phrase *what . . . is/was* to emphasize part of a sentence and to persuade others of its importance. Look at these sentences:

We need someone who can speak French.
What we need is someone who can speak French.

The question of overtime payments is not yet resolved.
What is not yet resolved is the question of overtime payments.

3 Practice

Use the following adjectives to make sentences emphasizing the requirements for and duties of the job, like this:

What we're looking for is someone mature enough to lead a team.

1 mature
2 skilled
3 experienced
4 fluent in French
5 creative

Practise with your partner.

4 Asking for clarification

This is how we can ask for clarification:

Sorry, but what exactly do you mean by 'young middle age'?
I'm afraid I don't quite follow you.
Sorry, I didn't catch that.
How old did you say he should be?

An explanation will then be given:

By young middle age I mean 35 to 40.
What I'm trying to say is that the job will be a very demanding one.

When asking for an explanation of initials or abbreviations we ask:

What does XYZ stand for?

5 Abbreviations

Working in pairs, ask what the following abbreviations stand for, and write down the answers. The answers are at the end of the Unit.

1 UN
2 EEC
3 IMF
4 FAO
5 CIF
6 FOB
7 VAT
8 OPEC
9 eg
10 ie

6 Be more specific

If the information received is not precise enough, you can ask for more details. For example, look at these remarks made by candidates at an interview.

I've worked abroad with different companies for several years and have occasionally headed a negotiating team.
The general working atmosphere of a company is extremely important to me.

The interviewer might want to ask for specific facts and figures. The use of *just* and *exactly* emphasize the need for a precise answer.

Where exactly have you worked?

Which company/how many companies have you worked for?
How long did you work for United Cars?
Just how often have you headed a negotiating team?

Or he could ask more general questions:

Would you expand a little on that?
Could you be a bit more specific?

7 Tell me more

The following telex has just been received from an overseas customer. The points underlined need clarification. Working with a partner, make a telephone call to ask for the information needed. The customer's information is at the end of the Unit.

> ATTN. MR NY WRD
>
> NUMBER RECEIVED INSUFFICIENT. PLEASE SEND MORE DIRECT TO OUR OFFICES. HAVE HAD SERIOUS PROBLEMS WITH ONE OF YOUR COMPONENTS. PLEASE ADVISE.
>
> AM ARRIVING LONDON SOON. PLEASE ARRANGE TOP LEVEL MEETING.

8 The job advertisement

> Expanding Legal Consultancy requires from early next year mature, well-qualified bi-lingual (French/English) secretary to be responsible for most general office duties. Excellent pay and conditions. Send CV in confidence to:
> M A Personnel Services
> P O Box 198
> London SW1 5JN

Here is an advertisement for a secretarial position to appear in the classified advertisements page of a daily newspaper.

Note the order of adjectives. Although there is no fixed order when several adjectives are used together before a noun, certain rules generally apply.

1 Nearest the noun are adjectives which describe the purpose of something or its category.

an expanding legal consultancy
a busy sales office

2 Before these come adjectives describing what something is made of and its origin.

a plastic American credit card

3 Before those we put adjectives of colour, then shape, size, age and other adjectives.

a large, round, black, oak dining table
the sophisticated, new, computerized payroll

The adjective nearest to the noun is the most essential to the meaning, so the rules above may vary according to the situation.

Now write an advertisement for the job you heard discussed in step 1. Use the notes you made, but invent any other details you wish to include.

9 Letter of application

Here is a letter from an applicant for the secretarial post advertised in step 8.

Bluebell Cottage,
Bluebell Lane,
W. Muchington,
Nr Horsham, Sussex

M A Personnel Services,
P O Box 198,
London SWI 5JN

7 January 19--

Dear Sir,

I am interested in applying for the post of secretary in your company, which was advertised in the Daily Telegraph, 4 January 19--.

I am at present working for Watson & Clarke Ltd in Crawley, where I have been Personal Secretary to the Head of the Legal Department for the past 2 years. This position also includes responsibility for translating and occasional interpreting at meetings with overseas clients.

I enclose my curriculum vitae and will be happy to give you any further information, should you require it.

Yours faithfully,

JOAN SARGEANT

Write a similar letter in answer to the advertisement for the post of Design Engineer at Fittenwell, which you heard discussed in step 1.

10 Drill 1: Yes, but . . .

You are interviewing a candidate who does not appear to have the right qualifications for the job. Listen to these examples:

I speak fluent Russian and Japanese.
Yes, but what we need is someone who can speak French.

And I have three years' experience.
Yes, but what we need is someone with at least ten years' experience.

Now you go on in the same way. The notes show what sort of person you need for the job. (Begin at number 3.)

You need someone:

1 who can speak French
2 with at least ten years' experience
3 over thirty
4 with research experience
5 with an engineering degree
6 who can work in a team
7 who has worked overseas
8 who is willing to travel extensively

Drill 2: Sorry, but ...

During the interview you need to ask the meaning of certain abbreviations. Listen to these examples:

And as you see from my letter I have an MA in Business Administration.
Sorry, but what exactly does MA stand for?

Master of Arts. And after leaving university I worked for a year in Nigeria with the VSO.
Sorry, but what exactly does VSO stand for?

Now you go on in the same way.

11 The interview

In groups of six – three interviewers and three candidates – hold interviews for the post of Design Engineer in Fittenwell's Research and Development Department. Fittenwell's policy, when interviewing short-listed candidates, is that candidates should be seen separately by each member of the selection board, who then meet to discuss their impressions and reach a decision. Prior to the interview the board holds a brief co-ordination meeting to determine exactly what form the interviews should take, and what qualities they are to look for in the successful candidate. During this time the candidates should prepare a brief CV.

The interview record form provides a guide to areas which could be covered during the interviews.

Interview Record

Name ______ Age ______

Address ______ Tel. No. (Home) ______

Tel. No. (Business) ______

Present employer ______ Salary ______

Address ______

Position held ______ Reason for leaving ______

General knowledge ______ Adaptability ______ Reliability ______

Technical knowledge ______ Quality of work ______ Career outlook ______

Experience ______ Management potential ______ Team worker ______

Attitude to overtime ______ Initiative ______

Remarks ______

Tapescript for step 1

Tape section 33

ASSISTANT: So let's try and establish some sort of criteria. What sort of a candidate are we looking for?

MANAGER: Well, first of all qualifications – obviously he must have a degree in engineering, and what we really need is a design specialist, because of course he'll be working on our new product range.

ASSISTANT: Someone with a post graduate diploma in design engineering, you mean.

MANAGER: Yes, ideally. Of course we don't want a whizz kid straight out of college.

ASSISTANT: Sorry, I don't quite follow.

MANAGER: Well, what I mean is, he should've had a minimum of ten or twelve years' relevant experience – working on the design problems of precision equipment. He'll have to work largely on his own, you realize.

ASSISTANT: So what sort of age range are you thinking of?

MANAGER: Young middle age would be about right and I think . . .

ASSISTANT: Sorry, but what exactly do you mean by young middle age?

MANAGER: Thirty-five to forty, I suppose, mature enough to lead a team of junior engineers. Now the personal qualities. What we're after here is high motivation. He must be able to work without the boss breathing down his neck all the time, because he'll be totally in charge of his own section. Then creativity is most important, and an eye for detail. He must be able to initiate projects and supervise each step of the design phase. And, of course, he should be familiar with both COBOL and FORTRAN to be able to use our computers.

ASSISTANT: Sorry, I didn't catch that.

MANAGER: COBOL and FORTRAN?

ASSISTANT: Yes, what do they stand for?

MANAGER: 'Common business oriented language' and 'formula translation' – they are computer programming languages.

ASSISTANT: Oh, I see.

MANAGER: And of course what we really want is someone who can eventually take over responsibility for R and D at the new French plant.

ASSISTANT: So what we ought to do is advertise for someone fluent in English and French and possibly one other European language.

MANAGER: Yes, it sounds quite a tall order, doesn't it?

Abbreviations from step 5 written out in full

1 United Nations
2 European Economic Community
3 International Monetary Fund
4 Food and Agriculture Organization
5 Cost, Insurance and Freight
6 Free On Board
7 Value Added Tax
8 Organization of Petroleum Exporting Countries
9 for example (Latin: *exempli gratia*)
10 that is (Latin: *illud est*)

Customer's information for step 7

The telex is for the attention of Mr Hyman.
You have received one hundred stethoscopes and you ordered one hundred and fifty.
You want them sent to your main Sales Office.
You have had problems with the clamp fittings on the X15 microscope. Several have warped (possibly due to hot climate).
Your visit to London is next week.
You want to discuss a large new order with the Overseas Marketing Director.

15 What would you suggest?

There are 9 steps in Unit 15. You will:

- give and ask for advice and suggestions
- report advice and suggestions
- discuss investment possibilities

1 A neighbour's advice

Cedric Crawley, a forty-five year old clerk at Fittenwell, has just inherited £500,000. He's talking to his neighbour, Mrs Jamieson. She knows about money. Listen to their conversation and note the advice she gives. Try to decide how certain she is of her advice; is she very certain, quite certain or not very certain?

2 More advice

In addition to consulting Mrs Jamieson, Cedric has written for advice to his local newspaper and has asked some colleagues at Fittenwell for their suggestions.

Work with your partner. One of you is to read the letter Cedric received from the *Daily Chronicle* and note down the advice given. The other is to read and note down the suggestions of Cedric's colleagues (reproduced at the end of the Unit). As before, try to decide how certain of their advice these people are. You will be discussing this advice in step 4.

The Daily Chronicle

Dear Mr Crawley,

Thank you for your letter enquiring about investment possibilities for a sum of £500,000.

Since you state that you have little experience of financial affairs, we would not recommend your considering the stock market unless you put your affairs in the hands of a reputable stockbroker. Should you wish to do so you would be wise to consult your bank manager, who would certainly be able to recommend a reliable firm.

Unless you are certain that you will not be requiring to withdraw cash at short notice, we would advise against Local Authority Bonds, Government Stocks, and Gilt-Edged Securities - although with the present high minimum lending rate, interest rates on current issues are attractive.

Investment in either Building Societies or Unit Trusts might provide one solution. Unit Trusts are to be recommended as they spread the risks of Stock Market fluctuations, while at the same time, if well managed, taking advantage of upward trends in the market. Alternatively, you may wish to consider National Savings Certificates.

Without more details of your circumstances we are unable to be more specific but hope we have been of some assistance.

Do not hesitate to write again should you require further advice.

Yours sincerely,

Financial Section
The Daily Chronicle

3 Reporting advice and suggestions

In reported speech, advice and suggestions can be introduced by *advise* and the gerund.

He advised buying Krugerrands.

If you mention the person or people to whom the advice was given the verb *advise* is followed by the noun or pronoun and the infinitive.

He advised me to invest in diamonds.

Advice may be negative. Notice how this is done:

He advised against buying Krugerrands.
He advised me not to invest in diamonds.

Other verbs used to report advice and suggestions are: *suggest, recommend* and *advocate* (in more formal situations). These verbs are followed by the gerund if the person given the advice is not mentioned.

They suggested investing in shares.
We recommend selling your oil paintings.
The Board advocated raising additional capital.

If the person is mentioned, the introductory verb is followed by a *that* clause with *should* and the infinitive or the **present simple.**

They suggested that I should invest in shares.
The Board advocated that we raise additional capital.

When speaking, *that* is often omitted.

4 What did they advise Cedric to do?

Using the notes you made in step 2, report to your partner the advice given by the *Daily Chronicle* and Cedric's colleagues, like this:

A: What did Cedric's colleagues suggest?
B: *Well, one of them suggested investing all the money in Fittenwell shares, another advised him against . . .*

5 Giving advice; making suggestions

There are various ways of giving advice and making suggestions. The way we express advice depends on how familiar the person and the situation are, and how confident we are that our suggestions will be accepted.

Mrs Jamieson and Cedric's colleagues are generally very confident.

Straight into a building society with it!
What I'd do is buy property.
Why not buy a flat in this block?
You couldn't do better than buy Fittenwell shares.
You should buy as many as you can.
You must have a few Fittenwell shares.
I advocate buying shares.

The *Daily Chronicle*, answering an enquiry from an unknown reader, is less certain that the suggestions will be appropriate.

We would not recommend this unless you consult a stockbroker.
Should you wish to invest in the stock market, you should consult your bank manager.
Unit trusts might provide one solution.
You may wish to consider National Savings Certificates.
It might not be a bad idea to invest in gold.

The following expressions show that the suggestion may not be perfect but is one to which you cannot object.

You could always put the property in the hands of an estate agent.
If all else fails you could still sell at a good price.

Requests for advice also depend on the circumstances. In a formal situation you might ask:

I wonder if you could advise me on this?

But if you were with friends, you would say:

What would you advise?
Can you suggest anything?
Any ideas?

6 Can you suggest anything?

Here are some queries made by a foreign visitor to Britain. Work with your partner. Using the language forms above, take it in turns to ask for and give advice.

Query	*Suggestions*
What to do at the weekend:	play golf, go to a concert, go for a country walk
What to buy as presents for the family:	records, sweaters, English silver
Where to spend a week's vacation in Britain next summer with the family:	Scotland, the Lake District, Cornwall
How to get a job in Britain:	apply to an employment agency, advertise in the national newspapers, write directly to large companies
What to see and do in London:	a river trip to Greenwich, the National Gallery, the Tower of London, Harrods

Now imagine that a visitor to your country asks for similar advice. What would you suggest? What would you advise him not to do? Write ten sentences.

7 Yes or no?

Listen to the following conversation between Cedric and his bank manager. When you hear the bank manager's reactions, put a tick in the appropriate box in the checksheet below.

	Yes	*No*	*Get professional help*
Property	☐	☐	☐
Krugerrands	☐	☐	☐
Shares	☐	☐	☐
Building societies	☐	☐	☐
Unit trusts	☐	☐	☐

	Yes	No	Get Professional help
Art collection	☐	☐	☐
Own business	☐	☐	☐
Theatrical production	☐	☐	☐

8 Drill 1: What did he say?

You are Cedric. Using the notes you have made, answer your colleague's questions about your talk with the bank manager. Listen to these examples.

So you've been talking to the bank manager about your plans, Cedric. What did he have to say?
Well, he recommended investing in property.

Yes, anything else?
Well, he advised me not to invest in Krugerrands.

Mmm, and what about shares?
Well, he advised me not to invest in shares unless I got professional help.

Now you go on in the same way.

Drill 2: What would you advise?

You work for an advertising agency. A discussion with one of your clients is in progress. He is not impressed with your original ideas so you put forward a more conventional solution. Listen to these examples.

Now what would you advise for our new brand of cigarettes?
Well, I think you should hire a plane to write the brand name across the sky.
Oh no, that wouldn't reach a wide enough audience.
Well, you could always take out a large advertisement in a national paper.

Mmm, maybe, and what about our cigarette lighter campaign?
Well, I think you should scatter thousands of leaflets over London from helicopters.
I'm sure that's against the law.
Well, you could always try a direct mail shot.

Now you go on in the same way. (Use the notes below, beginning after the two examples.)

Original idea	*Alternative*
Hire a plane to write the brand name across the sky:	take out a large advertisement in a national newspaper
Scatter thousands of leaflets over London from helicopters:	try a direct mail shot
Recruit private car owners to advertise on their cars:	launch a poster campaign
Give a champagne reception for VIPs at next month's International Fair:	distribute free samples
Get the film star Mimi La Tour to advertise them on TV:	advertise on commercial radio
Sponsor a formula one racing car:	take your account to another agency

9 Cedric's dilemma

Despite all this conflicting advice – or perhaps because of it – Cedric is still unsure of what to do.

In small groups, discuss all the suggestions already made. Read the information on the right for more ideas. Discuss, and try to agree on, the best advice for Cedric.

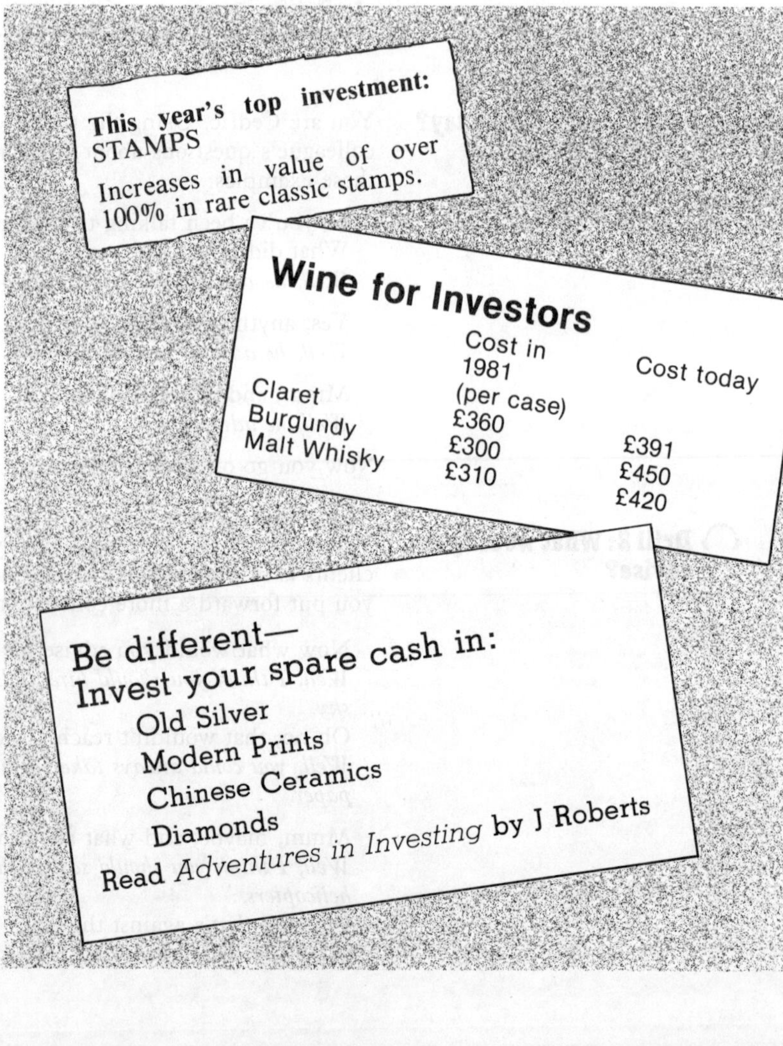

Tapescript for step 1

Tape section 35

CEDRIC: So you see I'm here with all this money – totally out of the blue. What would you do with it if you were in my shoes?

MRS JAMIESON: Well, dear, I must say I'm delighted for you. That's a really nice little nest egg for your old age. As for what to put it into, there's no doubt at all in my mind – straight into a building society with it for the time being. It'll be as safe as houses ha! ha! Excuse the pun! And you'll be getting 10% or so interest tax free. Then later on, what I'd do is buy property and let it out. You'd make a fortune – rents are going to go sky-high, you mark my words and house prices are always way above the inflation level. Why not buy another flat in this block? You could always put the management of the property in the hands of an estate agent, so you'd have no bother with the tenants. And have you thought of putting a bit aside for a rainy day – that's what I'd . . .

CEDRIC: Er, excuse me Mrs Jamieson – sorry to interrupt you, but time is really getting on. Thanks ever so much for your advice – I can see there is a good deal in what you say and I'll certainly think it over carefully.

Tapescript for step 7

Tape section 36

CEDRIC: Hello Mr White. I do hope you'll be able to help me make up my mind. So many people have given me advice and now I really feel totally confused. I'd like to know what you think of all the suggestions I've had.

BANK MANAGER: Well, I'll certainly help if I can.

CEDRIC: Well, several people have suggested buying property – what do you think?

BANK MANAGER: Yes, property is generally a safe investment.

CEDRIC: Then others advise investing in shares – what do you think about that?

BANK MANAGER: Well, shares are always a risk – they're worth considering but you'll need to take professional advice.

CEDRIC: I see . . . and what about gold? Some of my colleagues recommended buying Krugerrands.

BANK MANAGER: Now there I would say no. The price of gold is just too high at the moment for it to be worth considering.

CEDRIC: Mmm . . . well then, there are unit trust funds and building societies. A lot of people seem to think the money would be safest there . . .

BANK MANAGER: Yes, I'd certainly agree as far as building societies are concerned, but unit trust funds can vary enormously in their performance and I would definitely say you should take professional advice before deciding . . .

CEDRIC: Yes, that's what I thought . . . Then another idea was starting some sort of collection – rare stamps or paintings . . .

BANK MANAGER: Ah, now do you have any specialist knowledge about stamps or art?

CEDRIC: Well, no, not really.

BANK MANAGER: Then in that case I'd definitely advise against it – it's so easy to make very costly mistakes.

CEDRIC: Yes, I was afraid you might say that. Now what about starting a business of my own? Do you think that's a good idea?

BANK MANAGER: Well, it's a possibility, but you should definitely think it all through very carefully and get expert help before you take such a step.

CEDRIC: There's just one other thing – I hardly like to mention this, but I've often wondered about helping to finance a theatrical production. I've always been fascinated by the stage . . .

BANK MANAGER: My dear Mr Crawley, what an idea! Don't even consider it! More money has been lost by inexperienced amateurs backing ill-advised theatrical ventures than . . ..

Information for step 2

Cedric Crawley's immediate superior at Fittenwell Pharmaceuticals is Daniel Kidd, the General Services Manager. He has strong views on the subject of investment. Rose Marwell, from Clinical Research, and John Kennedy, from Research and Development, also have views on the matter.

KIDD: Well, what I think is, he couldn't do better than buy a few Fittenwell shares. With the new plant opening shortly – and we all know it's going to be a tremendous success – the price of shares will rocket. Get in while you can, that's my advice. He should buy up just as many as he can.

KENNEDY: I really don't think he ought to put all his eggs in one basket like that. But I do advocate buying just a few shares, they'd be just the thing for Cedric. It'd give him an interest in life to have a portfolio to manage. And certainly he must have a few Fittenwell shares too.

MARWELL: Well, personally I feel it might not be a bad idea to invest in a few Krugerrands. As my father always said, nothing beats gold as an investment. With the way things seem to be going on the economic front, inflation is going to eat into any other form of savings. Then if all else fails, he could still sell at a good price. Gold is the best possible hedge against inflation.

16 Weighing it up

There are 12 steps in Unit 16. You will practise:

- comparing and contrasting
- expressing preferences
- summing up and evaluating alternatives

1 A flat in London

Your company is thinking of purchasing or renting a flat in London. Read the advertisements and note down the following information on each:

—location and distance from the office in Piccadilly
—size and price (or rent)
—facilities and conditions (length of lease, ground rent and service charge)

1. **REGENTS PARK:** 1st floor apartment available in exclusive block in very select area. Porter. Lift. Video entry-phone. 2 bedrooms. Lounge. 2 Bathrooms. Luxury kitchen. Imposing entrance hall. 29-year lease. **£120,000** — Ground rent/service charge £1,500.

2. **MAIDA VALE:** Service studio flats. Luxury bathroom. Kitchen. Fully equipped and furnished. £500 per month. Public telephone in entrance hall. Restaurant. No children or animals.

3. **HAMPSTEAD:** Pleasant ground floor flat in solid Victorian house. 3 bedrooms. Lounge. Dining Room. Kitchen. 2 bathrooms. Use of garden. Needs some modernisation, hence realistic price. 85-year lease. **£95,000.**

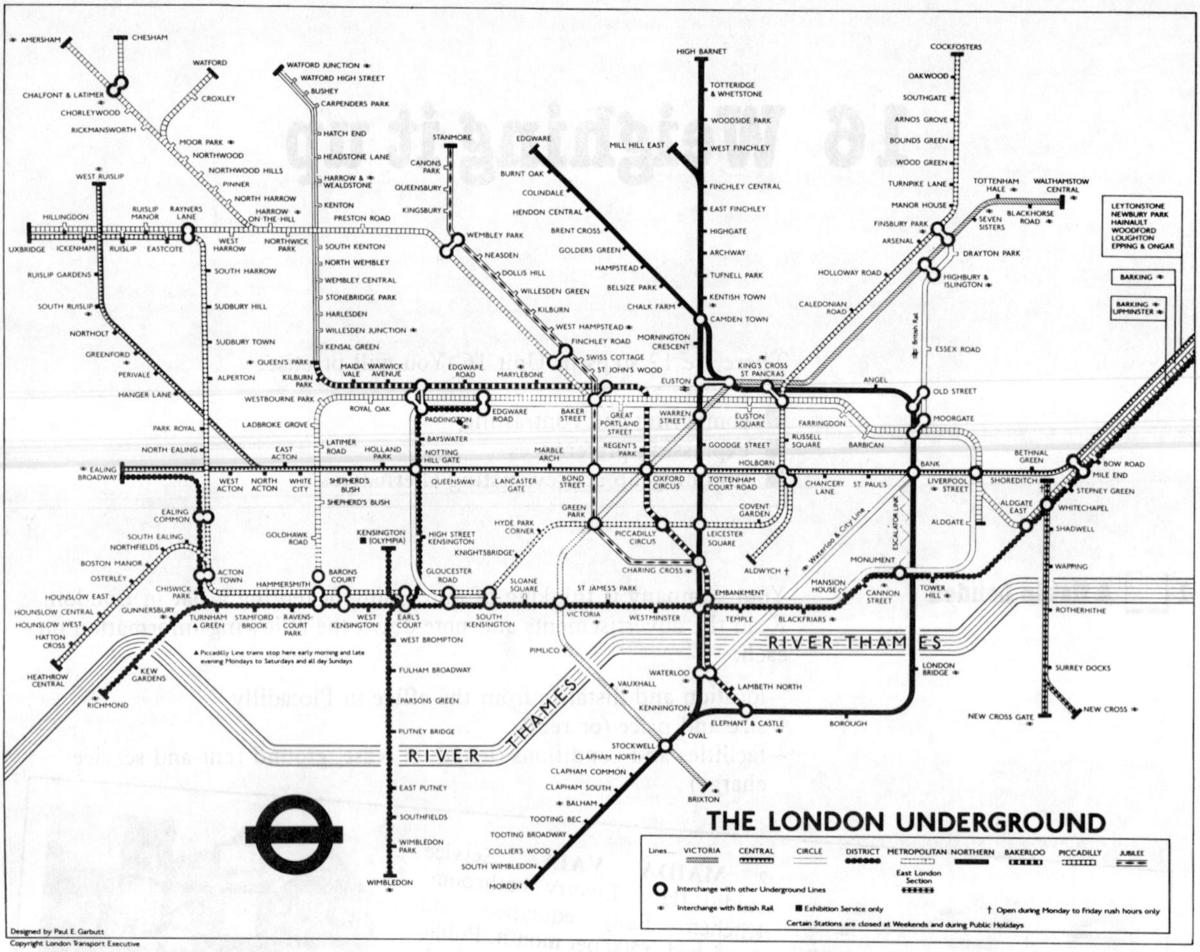

2 Differences and similarities

You practised comparing and contrasting in Unit 3. Here are some more expressions to compare similar things:

There's no difference between the two.
There's very little to choose between them.
In size, A is the same as B.

to compare differences in general terms:

There's no comparison between the two.

to compare specific differences:

The studio flat is the cheapest of all.
This area is the most exclusive in London.
While/Whereas a flat is more convenient, it's less spacious than a house.

3 Intensifiers

These show how big the difference between two things is:

a lot . . . *much . . .* *a good deal . . .* *a little . . .* *a bit . . .*	*cheaper* *more expensive*

Other intensifiers can be used in the same way:

in positive comparisons:	in negative comparisons:
incomparably . . .	*nearly . . .*
far . . .	*anything like . . .*
comparatively . . .	
relatively . . .	
somewhat . . .	

The flat in Regents Park is far nearer Piccadilly.
The price is relatively low.
He isn't nearly as hardworking as his boss.
Paris isn't anything like as big as Tokyo.

When you want to show how big the similarity between two things is, you can use these intensifiers:

almost . . .	*exactly . . .*
pretty well . . .	*just . . .*
roughly . . .	*just about . . .*

In size, A is exactly as big as B.
B was built at roughly the same date as A.

4 The quotation

Quotations have been received from these roller bearing manufacturers for bearing systems ordered by Global Motors.

Company	*Product range*	*Home market share*	*Export markets*	*Steel quality*	*Delivery*	*Unit price (single row)*
British Bearings	1 row bearings	10%	EEC	C	6 weeks	£46.50
Aluco	1, 2, 4 row, thrust bearings	23%	EEC North Africa	A	20 days	£48.50
Ambermold	1, 2, 4 row bearings	25%	EEC Spain North Africa North America	A1	21 days	£48.99

Now complete this report on the quotations using each of these expressions once only.

roughly	*not nearly*	*somewhat*	*incomparably*
slightly	*far more*	*almost*	*more or less*
a good deal	*great*	*definitely*	

While British Bearings' quotation for supplying the parts required for CX135 is . . . lower than Aluco's, the quality of the steel is . . . inferior. Similarly their delivery dates are . . . so satisfactory. Aluco seem to be a . . . efficient company altogether. Furthermore, Aluco has an . . . wider range, and their UK market share was . . . the same as Ambermold's last year, although they are . . . less well-known abroad. There appears to be no . . . difference between the offers of Aluco and Ambermold. The prices quoted are . . . the same, and their delivery dates too are . . . identical. I think we can definitely exclude British Bearings but should give . . . more thought to both Ambermold and Aluco.

5 Regents Park, Hampstead or Maida Vale?

Using the expressions from step 4, compare the three flats you read about in step 1. Talk about size, cost, distance from Piccadilly, facilities and conditions. Practise with your partner. In real life, which would be most suitable for your company? Begin your sentences with:

From the point of view (of size, etc) . . .

6 Decision making

With the cost of hotel accommodation constantly increasing, Fittenwell are considering whether it would be cheaper to invest in private accommodation in the cities visited by their executives. Listen to three Fittenwell managers discussing Algiers, Dubai and London. For each city note down:

the number of visits per year
the average length of stay
average monthly rent for a flat
average price of a two-bedroom flat
their recommendation (to buy, to rent or to continue with hotels)

7 Preferences

When talking about what *you* would rather do in the future, say:

I would prefer to stay in a flat rather than a hotel.
I would sooner/rather stay in a hotel.
I'd go for buying a flat. (informal)

When talking about what you would prefer *someone else* to do:

We'd prefer you to make out a written report.
I'd rather/sooner we came to a decision today.

When the preference expressed is more impersonal:

It would be preferable/better to keep to the present arrangements.

If you do not think that one course of action is preferable to the others:

I've no real preference.
I (really) don't mind.
It doesn't make any difference.
It doesn't matter either way.
It's all the same to me. (informal)

The examples below illustrate common expressions used to sum up and evaluate opinions.

So all in all you support the idea.
On balance I feel we should go ahead with the purchase.
On the whole the present arrangement is the best.
It wouldn't be worth investing any more money in the project.
It's worth trying.
We'd better wait for the working party's report.
In general the smaller the hotel the better the service is.

8 On the whole I'd rather . . .

Write one sentence in answer to each of these questions, using the expressions in step 7.

Would you prefer:

— to get a higher salary or to pay less tax?
— to take a month's holiday in August or two weeks in June and two in September?
— a company car or a generous petrol allowance?
— flexi-time or fixed working hours?
— open-plan or traditional office design?
— a continuous working day or a lengthy lunch break?

Would you prefer your son or daughter:

— to become an engineer or an actor?
— to marry early or late?
— to have a large or small family?
— to go to a school with fairly strict discipline or to a more progressive one?

9 Telex

After their discussion on the relative merits of buying or renting a flat and hotel accommodation, the following telex was sent from Fittenwell head office to their managing director in Dubai.

```
ATTN. J SIMPSON

CONSIDERING RENTING APARTMENT DUBAI FOR USE OF
VISITING COMPANY EMPLOYEES. KINDLY MAKE INITIAL
ENQUIRIES RE FORMALITIES, PRICE RANGE, AVAILABILITY.
THOMPSON, OVERSEAS PERSONNEL, TO VISIT AND INSPECT
APARTMENTS EARLY FEBRUARY.
BEST REGARDS
H KESSLER
```

Now write a similar telex to the director of Fittenwell's UK subsidiary. Inform him of the decision taken at the meeting and that Herman Kaufmann will be arriving in London on 22 March to make the final selection.

10 Drill 1: You or me?

Your secretary is checking the jobs to be done while you are away from the office. Some of them you would rather do yourself. Listen to these examples:

Now you wanted to make an appointment with Mr Smith. Do you want to make that yourself?
No, actually I'd rather you made it.

And what about the telex from the London office. Shall I reply to it?
No, actually I'd rather reply to it myself.

Now you go on in the same way. Your secretary is always wrong about who should do the jobs!

Drill 2: Yes, but . . .

After a discussion on changes to be made in the office you have this conversation with your secretary. Listen to these examples:

You realize that most of these changes will mean a great deal more expense?
Yes, but on balance I think it's worth doing to improve efficiency.

For example, you want to change the invoicing system. We'll need at least three more office staff.
Yes, but on balance I think it's worth doing to simplify our records.

Now you go on in the same way. Give reasons for your decisions. The notes will help you. (Begin at number 3.)

1 Changes will improve efficiency.
2 New invoicing system will simplify our records.
3 Purchasing another photocopier will save time.
4 Having an in-house magazine will improve internal communication.
5 Holding weekly departmental meetings will encourage more team spirit.
6 Setting up a Customer Service Department will create goodwill.
7 Installing word processors will speed up order processing.
8 Appointing Mr Jeffries as Head of Advertising will counteract the inexperience of the rest of the team.

11 Siting a factory

A large US car manufacturer has decided to set up a 150,000-cars-per-year plant in Britain. They have drawn up a list of six sites to be inspected during their feasibility study.

Divide into groups to represent the site owners and the car manufacturer. In each group, two or three students represent the owners of two or three of the sites on the shortlist; they should stress the advantages of their sites (good communications and transport, low cost area, government assistance, and so on). Their information is at the end of the Unit. The other two or three students in each group should decide on the best site for their factory by asking about:

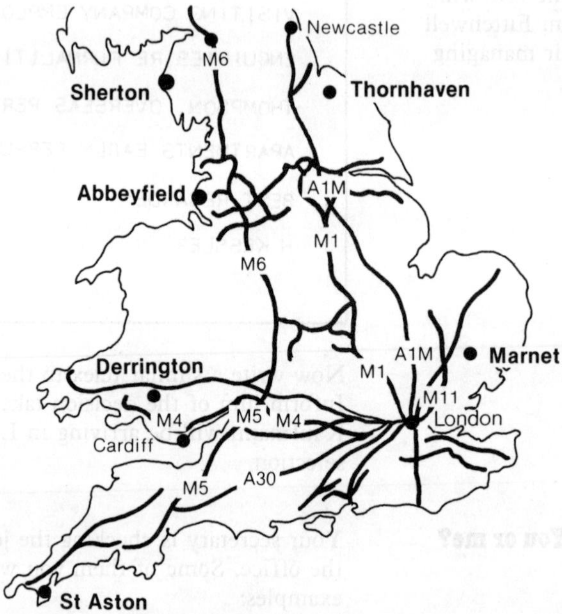

the area of land available (you need 2,000 hectares)
cost and availability of land
transport and freight facilities
availability of skilled labour
state of labour relations
availability of government grants for investment
proximity of components suppliers

12 A report

Write a brief report on the decision you came to regarding the choice of site for the car company. Use the report in step 4 for guidance. Include these points:

1 A comparison of the two short-listed sites
2 The advantages and disadvantages of the site chosen
3 The justification for your choice

Tapescript for step 6

Tape section 38

BOB: I suggest we take the three centres in alphabetical order – first Algiers. The figures we have for last year show eighteen trips altogether, each lasting an average of ten days, though some have necessitated stays as long as three weeks. Business is very encouraging in that area and those figures are likely to be considerably increased. We may even have to consider opening some sort of permanent office there in fact. John, you're an old hand at North Africa, let's hear from you.

JOHN: Yes, well you know there's no question of buying an apartment in Algiers – that's out for foreigners, and rents are getting higher each year. It's the most expensive country in the area. Personally I'd rather stay in an hotel. There are a number of pretty good ones – they're used to businessmen and while they may not be quite as efficient – or as clean – as one might wish, they're better than many I've stayed in. On the whole I'd sooner be in a centrally located hotel, where you're within easy reach of government offices, than staying out in the suburbs way out of town.

BOB: And you don't think it would be worth buying a flat to economize on expenses?

JOHN: Bob, I've just told you we can't buy a flat there and rent for a decent place would be around £400 a month – plus maintenance and domestic help.

BOB: So on balance perhaps we'd better leave things as they are for the time being and look at it again next year. Right. Now Dubai. We seem to have had someone there almost continuously this last year. Twenty separate trips, each lasting considerably longer than the Algiers visits – eighteen days on average. And the cost of each trip has been positively alarming. David, you're our Gulf representative. What do you think?

DAVID: Yes, well the hotels in that part of the world are quite luxurious. And correspondingly highly expensive. But property prices are also definitely the highest in that part of the world and rents too – £1,000 a month is a fairly average rent. Buying property is out of the question – the regulations are more or less the same as in Algiers, nationals only – but food and the general cost of living is relatively low.

JOHN: So all in all, it's probably worth thinking about renting something – even at those prices – considering the number of visits we make. The more people we have to send, the more economical it would be.

DAVID: You're probably right. Personally it wouldn't make much difference to me, and I know a number of our people would definitely prefer to stay in a flat – particularly on the longer trips.

BOB: Right, then London – here again it's been a year of constant coming and going. Twenty-five trips – roughly one week each, though

Site owners' information for step 11

Site	*Area and location*	*Price range*	*Transport: road, rail, sea*	*Unemployment rate*	*Government grants for building and equipment*	*Other information*
1 Thornhaven	2,000 hectares NE 30 miles inland	low	all excellent	17%	50% (top rate)	Four separate land owners.
2 Sherton	2,500 hectares NW Coast	middle	poor road links	15%	50%	Housing land. Would have to be redesignated for industrial use.
3 Abbeyfield	2,500 hectares NW Coast	middle	good	10%	35%	600 hectares available immediately. 1,400 obtainable from two private owners.
4 Derrington	2,050 hectares South Wales 30 miles inland	low	very good	12%	40%	Seven private owners. History of poor labour relations.
5 Marnet	3,000 hectares 60 miles NE of London	middle	poor road and rail links	6%	25%	2,500 hectares owned by British nationalized industry.
6 St Aston	2,200 hectares SW Coast	middle	poor road and rail links	9%	30%	Two private owners. New section of motorway opening next year to north of site.

some much shorter. I know London flat prices are high, but hotel accommodation must be about the highest in Europe.

JOHN: Yes, I don't really feel it would be worth renting a flat. There would be no great saving if we had to pay out three or four hundred a month. There are no restrictions on purchasing property and it would be one of the safest investments we could make. We could get something reasonable for around £100,000 . . ..

BOB: Fine, so those are the recommendations. We'll put them to the Board. Peter, if you could draft a brief report to that effect. I'd sooner it was all settled as quickly as possible.

17 Better than ever

There are 12 steps in Unit 17. You will practise:

- making a presentation
- raising objections
- querying information
- dealing with objections and queries
- referring to visual aids

1 Presenting the product

Mr Cassell of Fittenwell's European Marketing team is presenting a modified version of one of their analgesic drugs, a painkiller for children, to a group of pharmacists visiting Fittenwell's head office.

Listen to this part of his talk and answer the following questions:

1 What has been changed?

....

....

....

....

2 What is the purpose of the changes?

....

....

....

....

3 What has not been changed?

....

....

....

2 Presentation techniques

The presentation of a product or service to potential customers has one aim – to persuade them to buy. To achieve this it is important to present factual information so that the advantages of the product or service are emphasized. Each item should be introduced clearly and linked to the preceding and following ones.

May I begin by welcoming you all here today.
Perhaps I could start by telling you something of the company's history.
I'd like to move on now to the question of packaging.
And now we come to the most important point – safety.
Finally, I would just like to thank you all for coming here today.

You may wish to make comparisons and contrasts:

Soluble analgesics act far faster than non-soluble ones.
No other manufacturer conducts more stringent tests.

Changing the usual order of words in a sentence focuses the attention of listeners:

We feel that under no circumstances must children be put at risk.
Never, I can confidently assert, has a manufacturer carried out more stringent tests.

You can use *what . . . is* to draw attention to a clause or verb and *it is* to draw attention to a noun:

It is the safety factor which has always been our main concern.
What we were trying to do was eliminate the usual side-effects.

The passive form emphasizes the subject:

Every aspect of the problem has been carefully studied.

The auxiliaries *do, does* and *did* emphasize the verb in affirmative sentences:

We do appreciate that cost is an important factor.

3 Welcome to the company

Here are the notes for part of a talk given by the Managing Director to trainees on their first day with the company. Rearrange them into a logical order and introduce each item with one of the linking expressions from step 2.

- hand you over to our personnel manager for a tour of the building
- explain to you the management structure
- What we expect from our employees
- give an outline of the company's history
- welcome you to Fittenwell

4 We can help

An employment agency wants to put the following information in their brochure explaining their services. Change the sentences to focus attention on the words in italics. Begin your sentences with the words in brackets.

1 The most time-consuming task for a personnel department is *shortlisting candidates for interview.* (Shortlisting . . .)
2 *You need a reliable agency* to relieve the pressure of routine recruitment. (What . . .)
3 Our agency can solve *all your recruitment problems.* (All . . .)
4 We *only* pass on to you for interview *the most suitable applicants.* (Only . . .)
5 *We have never failed to* satisfy our customers' requirements. (Never . . .)
6 *We understand* your needs. (We do . . .)

5 Any questions?

After Mr Cassell's speech, the pharmacists are invited to ask questions. Listen to this part of the recording and note down whether the following statements are true or false.

	True	*False*
The containers have only been tested on children.	☐	☐
They are now guaranteed child-proof.	☐	☐
The drug will be far more expensive than other similar brands.	☐	☐
Clinical trials show side-effects in 0.02% of cases.	☐	☐
19% of children found the taste of the dissolved aspirin pleasant.	☐	☐
There is a warning to parents on the label to get a doctor's advice after twenty-four hours if symptoms persist.	☐	☐

6 A good question

In step 5 you heard a number of phrases which are often used to ask and answer questions after a speech or presentation.

Referring back to what the speaker said

Questions following a speech or presentation are often introduced by a phrase which situates it in the context of the speech.

You mentioned the cost of the new drug being rather high.
On the subject of taste, you said that 84% disliked the undissolved tablets.
I'd like to go back to your statement about clinical trials.

Making a point

The purpose of raising a point during a question/answer session may be to obtain information:

You mentioned the cost of the new drug being rather high. Could you tell us exactly how high it will be?

to discredit the speaker:

You said, earlier in your speech, that 9% of children under five were able to open the containers. Later you quoted a figure of only 6%. Can you explain this discrepancy?

to put forward your own ideas:

Could I go back to your statement about clinical trials? I have always thought the law regarding these is out of date.

to throw doubt on the speaker's assumptions:

On the subject of taste, you said that 84% of children tested disliked the undissolved tablets. Do you really consider that sufficient evidence of their safety?

Dealing with questions raised

When questions have been asked, you must deal with them effectively. If you know the answer, say something like this:

Yes, I have the figures here – two hundred and fifty thousand.

Should be, likely to, approximately, on average, probably are used when you do not have exact facts or figures:

The new version should be in production next year.
We have a work force of approximately 18,000.

If the point made by a questioner is incorrect, or your remarks have been misunderstood, say something like this:

You seem to have misunderstood me, I said 6% of adults were unable to open the containers, not 6% of children.
I'm afraid your information is out of date; the law regarding clinical trials has changed.
Perhaps I didn't explain that clearly enough . . .
If I could put it another way . . .

If you did not give all the facts:

Yes, I'm sorry, I should have said that this applies to EEC countries only.

If your facts are wrong, or you are justly criticized:

Yes, you're right, it is 6% not 16%.
You may be right, I'll check those figures again.
Yes, I accept that, the results are not good.
Yes, I take your point, there is room for improvement.

If you don't know the answer, give yourself time to think:

Yes, as a matter of fact, that's a very interesting question . . .

– change the subject:

I'm glad you brought up/raised the question of cost, I wanted to say a few words about our pricing policy in general.

– ask the questioner or others present for their opinion:

A very good point. What are your own views on the matter?

– admit it:

I'm afraid I just don't know.
I'm sorry, I don't have that information to hand.

7 Make your point

During the discussion following a lecture on the future of public transport, you wish to raise certain points. Make sentences for each of the following, referring to the speaker's statement and making your point.

	Speaker's statement	*Your point*
1	We must make a distinction between urban and rural areas.	Why?
2	(a) Public transport is as essential as water and electricity supplies. (b) Most families today own cars.	If (b) is true, why (a)?
3	Government must subsidize public transport.	Would tax payers agree?
4	Private cars should be banned from inner cities.	First public transport must be made more efficient.
5	Public transport cannot be a profit-making operation.	Not true. Many private rail and bus companies exist.

If you were the speaker, how would you deal with these points?

8 Fittenwell on the spot

Mr Cassell went on to make the following remarks about Fittenwell's achievements this year.

1 Turnover up by 12%
2 Five new products in the pharmaceutical division.
3 Excellent reputation for product reliability.
4 Considerable expansion over last few years. Further expansion planned for next year.
5 No labour problems.
6 Large increase this year in Fittenwell's share of the Japanese market.

Working in pairs, one partner raises the following points.

1 You want to know the exact turnover figures for this year and last year.
2 You know that a rival company claims two of the new products are the result of their research and are threatening legal action.
3 You've heard that sales of one of Fittenwell's antibiotics was banned in the USA.
4 Fittenwell have closed sales offices in several parts of North and Central America. You want details of their expansion programme.
5 Fittenwell had two major strikes in the UK last year.
6 Their share of the Japanese market is still only .05%.

The other, representing Fittenwell, should answer these points using the notes at the end of the Unit.

9 Visual aids

Most presentations will involve the use of charts, graphs, diagrams, slides, overhead transparencies.

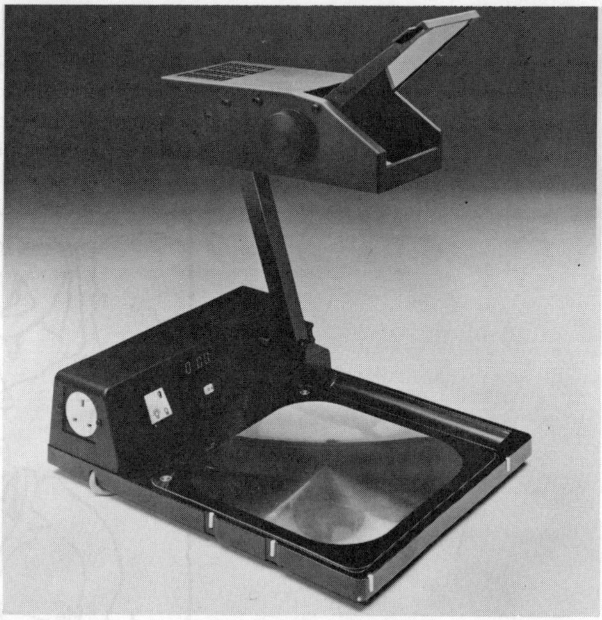

Here are examples of how you introduce information using visual aids:

This slide shows the cell structure in detail.
As you can see from this chart, the process has three main stages.
This diagram illustrates what I was saying about our laboratory facilities.

10 A new approach to order processing

These are notes for part of a talk on improved efficiency in order processing. Write the paragraph out in full, including references to visual aids.

1. Present system consists of six separate stages (flow chart).
2. Proposed new system, only three (flow chart).
3. Advantages: speed, efficiency, reduction in manpower.
4. Possible objections: increased workload in order processing department, possibility of errors.
5. Proposals to overcome objections:
   (i) salary review for staff concerned (diagram)
   (ii) appointment of "order processing controller"
6. The new system works (graph showing increase in orders in rival company using similar system).

11 Drill 1: You mentioned . . .

There are discrepancies between the salesman's claims and the information in the catalogue. Listen to these examples.

Now are there any questions about operating the machine?
Yes, you mentioned ease of operation, but I see here that there are forty pages of operating instructions.

Yes, but I think you'll find it is really quite simple. Now any queries about the material?
Yes, you mentioned lightweight material, but I see here that it weighs thirty kilos.

Now you go on in the same way. The notes show the speaker's claims about the machine and the information from the sales catalogue. (Note that they are not in the order in which you will hear them.)

Speaker's claims	*Catalogue information*
lightweight material	it weighs 30 kilos
low price	it costs £25,000
prompt delivery	the delivery period is six months
ease of operation	there are 40 pages of operating instructions
trouble free maintenance	it needs servicing every four weeks
inexpensive servicing contract	it costs £500 a year
above average durability	it is guaranteed for 18 months

Drill 2: Yes, but . . .

The manager of one of Fittenwell's divisions has been presenting last year's figures. He accepts the directors' criticism of his division's poor results last year. Fortunately he can show that the situation is much better this year.

These figures are appalling. Your overseas sales were the lowest in the group last year.
Yes, I take your point, but this graph shows how high overseas sales are this year.

And you must reduce costs. Your production costs were far too high last year.

Yes, I take your point, but this graph shows how low production costs are this year.

Now you go on in the same way. Remember to stress the important words: *low* or *high* and *this year.*

12 Take the floor

Prepare a brief speech on a topic of your choice, including references to visual aids. While you are listening to other students' speeches note down one or two points you wish to raise. Conduct a question and answer session after each speech to deal with the points raised.

Tapescript for step 1

Tape section 40

. . . is familiar to you all.

Perhaps I should start by reassuring you that the basic properties of Vitas, our aspirin for children, remain unchanged. This diagram shows that the active ingredients are the same. So, too, is the speed with which it acts – far faster, as I'm sure you realize, than non-soluble aspirin.

But what is new, unique in fact, is the great improvement in safety precautions. We are extremely disturbed by reports of the increasing numbers of children poisoned by swallowing drugs and other household substances. Under no circumstances, we feel, must children be put at risk. A new ingredient, therefore, which clinical trials have proved to be totally safe, has been incorporated in the tablets. This gives the tablets an unpleasant, bitter taste if taken without water, and will discourage children from thinking of them as sweets. In our tests 84% of children disliked them intensely. Dissolved in water, of course, they have the same pleasant orange flavour as before.

Another improvement is in the design of the container. Our former containers could be, and I'm afraid, were often opened by any lively three year old, but now, after extensive testing – and no other manufacturer conducts more stringent tests – we can safely say that the new container is child-resistant. Only 9% of children under five were able to open it, while just 6% of adults were unable to do so. This, I think you'll agree, strikes the right balance.

Finally could I just point out the new layout of the instructions and labelling on the container. Some mothers, apparently, found the old instructions confusing. As you can see from this enlarged photograph, the new design is a model of clarity.

One drawback is that the additional research costs have necessitated an increase in the price. We do appreciate that cost is an important factor, but for us, and I'm sure for you, it is safety which is our main concern.

Tapescript for step 5

Tape section 41

FIRST QUESTIONER: You said at the beginning of your speech that 9% of children under five were able to open the container. Later you quoted a figure of only 6% – can you explain this discrepancy?

MR CASSELL: No, actually, you seem to have misunderstood me. I said 6% of adults were unable to open the containers.

FIRST QUESTIONER: Oh, I see. Thank you.

SECOND QUESTIONER: On the subject of taste, you said that 84% of children tested disliked the undissolved tablets. Do you really consider that sufficient evidence of their safety?

MR CASSELL: Well, we are not claiming that they are childproof. What we are saying is that they are child-resistant, and that we have made a really positive contribution to safety.

THIRD QUESTIONER: Won't this bitter taste discourage parents from buying Vitas?

MR CASSELL: Perhaps I didn't explain myself clearly enough – 90% of children positively liked the taste of the tablets dissolved in water – and that is how they should be given of course – and may I remind you of the very low incidence of side-effects, in our clinical trials, .02%.

FOURTH QUESTIONER: You emphasized the clarity of the instructions and labelling. What exactly are the instructions?

MR CASSELL: Yes, I'm sorry I should've said that there are instructions on the dose related to the age of the child, and we warn parents to consult a doctor if symptoms continue after twenty-four hours.

FIFTH QUESTIONER: You mentioned the cost being high. Could you tell us exactly how high it will be?

MR CASSELL: Yes, I'm glad you raised that question. I admit it is substantially more than other similar brands, and I'd like to say a few words about our pricing policy . . ..

Fittenwell representative's information for step 8

1 Annual turnover this year: 250,000,000 Swiss Francs; last year: 225,000,000 Swiss Francs. 10% increase.
2 Not true. All Fittenwell's research is entirely original.
3 True – but only because USA has exceptionally strict regulations. Sales of the same drug have increased in Europe and the rest of the world.
4 Two or three sales offices closed – one in Toronto, one in Detroit, and one somewhere in Mexico. This year one assembly plant to open in Peterborough UK and one sales office in Abu Nafat.
5 Fittenwell UK had one strike lasting three days and one partial strike at their sales office (drivers and warehousemen only).
6 Exact figure not known. But Fittenwell's market share has definitely increased.

18 Consolidation exercises

There are seven steps in Unit 9, which will help you revise the work you have already done.

1 Appointments

You are a member of the Project Coordination Department of your company. Here is your diary for next week.

Monday	Meeting with Directors of Metalco 10.30 Lunch in Executive Dining Room 13.00 Discussion with Metalco Directors about manufacturing ZB11 under licence 14.30
Tuesday	Mr Jacques arrives 11.00 Show him round factory 11.30 – 13.00 Negotiate terms of agency agreement 14.00
Wednesday	10.00 Report to Board on current projects Afternoon – visit Leeds factory
Thursday	Morning – prepare production statistics for accounts department 2.15 – meeting to discuss development of new range to replace ZB

Exercise

Write a paragraph describing your appointments for next week. Use the present continuous tense.

2 Redesign

The PCD has been asked for its comments on proposals put forward by the Research and Development team to redesign completely the ZB range of products. Here is part of the R & D report together with some notes you have made.

Report	*Notes*
Stop production of the ZB range next year:	Customers certain to complain
Close Leeds factory temporarily:	Unions certain to take industrial action
Spend £150,000 on designing replacement:	Other projects likely to suffer
Tell the press of our plans:	Shares likely to fall
Ask the bank to finance the project:	Bank certain to charge extremely high rates of interest
Submit the plan to the Board before all the details are finalized:	Board certain to reject it
Buy cheaper components:	Quality and reliability likely to be a problem

Exercise

Now make sentences with *if*, showing the result of implementing these recommendations. Use *will* if the result is certain, use *might* or *could* if it is likely. Look at this example:

If we stop production of the ZB range next year, our customers will complain.

3 Minutes

You have a meeting with the R & D people to discuss their ideas about replacing the ZB range with a completely new product. You have been asked to write the minutes of this meeting. Here is an extract from your notes.

meeting R&D + PCD
24 Sept 2·30 pm.

Peter Elton (R&D Head)
- ZB range is out of date. Sales have been falling steadily. Customers are turning to competitors, eg. Corbridge Electronics. Is it worth spending money marketing an unsuccessful product?

D. Young (PCD)
- asked PE: Do you have statistics to support these statements? Which customers are we losing?

PE
- total sales of ZB range have fallen by 17% during last six months. Birtley's are dissatisfied with the ZB.

Miss E Winter
- wouldn't it be better to develop the new project range before we stop production of ZB?

PE
- we have large stocks – enough for 9 months. In that time we can develop prototype of replacement.

Exercise

Now write a paragraph using indirect speech giving details of what was said at the meeting. Use introductory verbs like the following:

He said . . .

He stated . . .

He pointed out . . .

He asked . . .

Don't forget to change the verb in the sentence which follows.

4 Complaints

Peter Elton mentioned that Birtley's were not satisfied with the ZB range. Here is part of their letter.

We . . . . . to inform you that we are not . . . . . with the ZB in its present form. More of our customers are reporting breakdowns of machines in which the ZB is a . . . . . . As you will . . . . ., we cannot allow our . . . . . for reliability to be threatened in this way.

Accordingly, we have approached other . . . . . who are able to . . . . . similar parts which make use of the latest microchip . . . . . . Unless you are able to offer us similar high-quality, low-cost products, we shall have no . . . . . but to take our business elsewhere.

Exercise

These are the words missing from the letter. Can you put them in the right place?

1	reputation	4	alternative	7	component
2	technology	5	supply	8	regret
3	satisfied	6	appreciate	9	manufacturers

5 Clarification

Birtley's complaint about the ZB range is not very specific. You decide to ring up and ask for more details about the problems they have been having. Here are the notes you made after reading their letter.

1 Some of Birtley's customers have complained.
2 Birtley's have used the ZB range for a long time.
3 The ZB is no longer suitable for Birtley's products.
4 Some of our competitors can supply a better component.
5 Birtley's are founder-members of FIDM.
6 They sent another letter of complaint a few months ago.
7 Someone in their Purchasing Department is responsible for their final decision.

Exercise

Write sentences asking Birtley's for more specific information about the phrases underlined. Use the following expressions.

When exactly . . .?
Exactly how long . . .?
Exactly how many . . .?
What exactly do you mean by . . .?
What does . . . stand for?
Just who . . .?

6 Suggestions

The R & D team have convinced you, the Project Coordination Department, that the ZB range must be redesigned. But you have some suggestions as to how this can be done without threatening the stability of the company. Here are your suggestions to the Board.

1 Don't stop production of the ZB for the moment.
2 Inform unions of the plans and assure them that jobs are not at risk.

3 Tell customers that the ZB range is being modernized – ask for comments.
4 Carry out a small-scale feasibility study first.
5 Approach the bank *now* for help with finance next year.
6 Send production engineers on training course immediately.
7 Don't change the name of the product.

Exercise

Write a memorandum to the Board setting out the PCD's proposals. Some of these phrases might be useful:

We would suggest that . . .

We would suggest . . . – ing . . .

We would advise you to . . .

We would advise against . . . – ing . . .

We think it would be a good idea to . . .

7 Prototype

The replacement for the ZB is called the ZB Micro and has been tested in prototype form by five companies. They were asked to give marks out of ten for the ZB Micro in various categories.

ZB MICRO

	Britton Ltd	F P Taylor Ltd	Intercal	Global Motors	BTF Ltd
Flexibility	7	6	7	8	6
Reliability	5	7	6	7	7
Price	2	3	5	2	4
Workmanship	6	6	5	7	7
Economy	8	8	9	7	9
Speed	9	9	10	8	9
Accuracy	9	9	9	8	8
Ease of handling	6	7	7	4	6

Exercise

Write a report to the head of the PCD summarizing these results and drawing general conclusions.

19 Expanding overseas

There are 11 steps in Unit 19. It contains:

- practice and revision of the past tenses
- passive forms of the verb
- graphs and statistics
- a discussion of new markets

1 Abu Nafat – an expert's view

The Fittenwell group is considering expanding its network of sales companies and agents. The state of Abu Nafat has been selected as a possible springboard for a deeper penetration of the market in the area.

You have been asked to submit a brief report at a meeting of the department. It so happens that there is, this morning, an interview on the radio which has a direct bearing on the subject. Listen to the interview and note down information under the following headings.

Topic	*Information*
Geographical situation	
Religion	
History early 1800–1918 1918–1946 1946–1965 1965–now	
Politics 1965–today Political alignment Political stability Future plans	
The economy today oil other industry financial standing	

2 Past tenses

There are examples in the interview of the **simple past, past continuous, present perfect, past perfect** tenses. The use of the correct tense is very important in indicating the order in which things happened, the relative importance of these things, their effect on the present and the time when they occurred.

The **simple past** indicates that *time* is important. The time is usually stated. We use this tense when relating a sequence of events.

In 1946 Jamil Sultan became the country's first president.
Immediately after this he nationalized the oil companies.
The steel plant was opened five years ago.

The **past continuous** is used when something was in progress at a certain time in the past. It is not used to indicate a completed action.

Oil, by this time, was proving to be the country's most valuable asset.
When he came to power many people were feeling very discontented.

Notice the difference between the last sentence above, which shows that the feeling of discontent began before he came to power, and the following.

When he came to power, many people felt discontented.

This indicates a sequence of events – *first* he came to power, *then* people felt discontented.

The **present perfect** is used when *either* the event itself continues up until now *or* the present effect or result of the event is more important than the time when it occurred. The time of the event is not stated, unless the period of time has not finished – this week, today, this year. If the event is still in progress, or the length of time taken is important the **continuous present perfect** can be used.

He has been ruling the country for ten years.
They have never held a general election.
The economic situation has improved this year.
I have already seen that film.

The **past perfect** is used when reporting a **past simple** or **present perfect** tense.

He said he had never met John Brown.
He mentioned that he had started working there in 1975.

The **past perfect** is also used when the event referred to occurred before another event in the past. The two events must be linked closely by an expression of time such as *as soon as, when, after,* or introduced by *previously* or *prior to this.*

He got the job in 1972. Previously he had worked for an oil company.
When he had finished speaking, he left the room.

3 Which tense?

Here is a report on archaeology in Abu Nafat. Write out, in the correct tense, all the verbs in brackets.

For over eighty years archaeologists (1 *be*) very interested in Abu Nafat. The present team of French archaeologists (2 *work*) there since 1980, and (3 *discover*) a number of pre-Islamic statues. While they (4 *work*) on a site in the north they (5 *find*) ancient tombs, some of which date back to 4000 BC.

When they (6 *arrive*) the French team were surprised to learn that, several years previously, a British team (7 *explore*) the same site but (8 *have*) to abandon their project through lack of funds.

Most of the French archaeologists' finds (9 *classify*) immediately and (10 *take*) to the National Museum, although the President just (11 *give*) permission for a number of items to be exhibited in Paris next year.

The President officially (12 *open*) the museum three years ago and, since then, the permanent collection (13 *increase*) rapidly. It is now an important centre for archaeological research.

Strangely enough, while they (14 *dig*) the foundations of the museum, workers (15 *unearth*) the remains of a Greek temple, and the authorities (16 *decide*) to move the museum to another site.

4 The passive

There is frequent use of the passive in the radio interview you heard in step 1. We use the **passive** form of the verb when the subject of a verb is less important than the object or the action itself.

It is often unnecessary to mention who performs the action, particularly when it is 'the Government' or 'the authorities'.

British advisers were requested to leave.
The people felt they were being exploited.
Foreign military bases have been closed.
Plans have been put forward for a new constitution.

But sometimes the passive form is used to emphasize the most important element of the sentence.

Abu Nafat was ruled by a Turkish governor.
Sheikh Abdullah was overthrown by a group of officers.

'Abu Nafat' and 'Sheikh Abdullah' are more important than 'the Turkish governor' and the 'group of officers'.

With certain verbs – *think, believe, report* and *say* – the impersonal *it* is used in the passive, to avoid beginning with a *that* clause.

It is said that the President works sixteen hours a day.
It is reported that elections will take place next year.

After **modals** – *must, have to, may, might, can, could, ought to, should* – it is the infinitive which takes the passive form.

The work must be done.
No policy decisions could be made without the consent of British advisers.

5 Achievements and projects

From these notes, make sentences about the Government's achievements in the past, work being done now, and future projects.

1969:	opened new steel plant
1969 – today:	priority given to investment in industry
ten years ago:	held first international Trade Fair in Abu Nafat
last five years:	built two hospitals and fifteen new schools
now:	investing 10% of the GNP in new industries
now:	constructing a six-lane motorway
next year:	completion of second phase of agricultural reform
in three years' time:	opening of new university buildings

6 North African projects

The following article was written by a foreign correspondent of an American newspaper. A local journalist, writing for North African readers, would place more emphasis on the projects themselves. Rewrite the article from the local journalist's viewpoint. This will involve changing sentences from the active to the passive form and vice versa, and possibly omitting or adding the agent. Look at this example:

Foreign journalist:
The World Bank has arranged a loan of £100m.
Local journalist:
A loan of £100m has been arranged by the World Bank.

International Cooperation

UN economists are discussing the financing of a number of projects in North Africa. International credit markets have already financed an important part of the gas pipeline network, and it is reported that the loans will be guaranteed by the central banks of the countries concerned. The World Bank has arranged a long-term loan for the construction of a dam in the north east, and World Bank experts are at present surveying the site.

The Food and Agriculture Organization may be asked to advise on pest control in some countries. If experts were needed, the FAO would probably send one team to each affected area.

UNESCO is also planning a symposium on the return of African works of art to national museums. This is a contentious issue which

7 Expressions of time relating to past events

A number of such expressions occur in the radio interview.

Abu Nafat was inhabited as far back as the year 4000 BC.
Prior to the Turkish occupation, Abu Nafat had been ruled by the Al-Watani family.
Over the last ten years considerable progress has been made.
Shortly after taking power they set up the national oil company.

Write down the following expressions, numbering them to show where they should occur in the passage below to make the sequence of events clear.

in recent years	*not until*	*meanwhile*
shortly before	*by the time*	*during*
immediately after	*prior to*	*as far back as*

(1) . . . . . 1918 it was known that the country had considerable deposits of oil, but it was (2) . . . . . 1935 that drilling operations began on a large scale. (3) . . . . . this, the country's only exports had been agricultural produce – fruit and some meat. (4) . . . . . the war, large natural gas reserves were also discovered but (5) . . . . . the war years, no gas was extracted. (6) . . . . . the war, expansion of industry world wide created a growing demand for fuel, and (7) . . . . . the massive increase in oil prices was decided, the annual production had quadrupled. (8) . . . . . the oil industry had been nationalized and the country's economy was booming. It is now realized that, eventually, the oil will run out and so, (9) . . . . ., a lot of investment and research has gone into diversifying the country's industrial base.

8 Drill 1: Yes, we did . . .

Your company had an excellent record in the seventies but has not been doing so well recently. Listen to these examples:

In the seventies your company sold a lot of goods abroad.
Yes, we did, but latterly we've been having difficulty in selling goods abroad.

And you also paid very high salaries.
Yes, we did, but latterly we've been having difficulty in paying high salaries.

Now you go on in the same way.

Drill 2: Right . . .

You are making notes on messages to be passed on to your boss when he returns from his holiday. Listen to these examples:

Now don't forget to tell him that the plumber came and has mended the radiator.
Right, the radiator has been mended.

And the new typist – you know the one who can't spell – well, she is typing the sales report now.
Right, the sales report is being typed now.

Now you go on in the same way.

9 Strictly between you and me

Listen to this telephone conversation between Mr Morley of Fittenwell's Export Marketing team, and a friend of his who has recently returned from Abu Nafat. The opinions expressed are very frank. Note down whether his comments about the following are positive (✓) or negative (x):

	Positive/Negative
1 climate	
2 social life	
3 financial returns	
4 paperwork	
5 the president	
6 political stability	
7 scenery	

10 A more acceptable turn of phrase

Some of the expressions in the conversation are very colloquial and would only be used between people who know each other well. Which expressions in the dialogue could be replaced, in a more formal situation, by the following?

he's very strong-willed ....
the climate is unpleasant ....
do not particularly like him ....
to follow bureaucratic procedures ....
strongly support ....
I would go even further ....

11 Decision time

You now have a considerable amount of information about Abu Nafat. Divide into two groups to discuss these aspects:

Group 1:
political situation
marketing opportunities
(You will find extra information from the Abu Nafat Embassy at the end of the Unit.)

Group 2:
geographical and cultural problems
economic factors
(Extra information from the Abu Nafat Embassy is printed below.)

Then compare your conclusions and decide whether you would advise Fittenwell Management to consider Abu Nafat as a suitable potential market for their pharmaceutical products and hospital equipment.

Abu Nafat: key figures of the economy

1 *Consumer prices*

It will be noted from this how the Government's policy of investments in local industries, reducing foreign imports, and subsidizing basic foods has stabilized the cost of living.

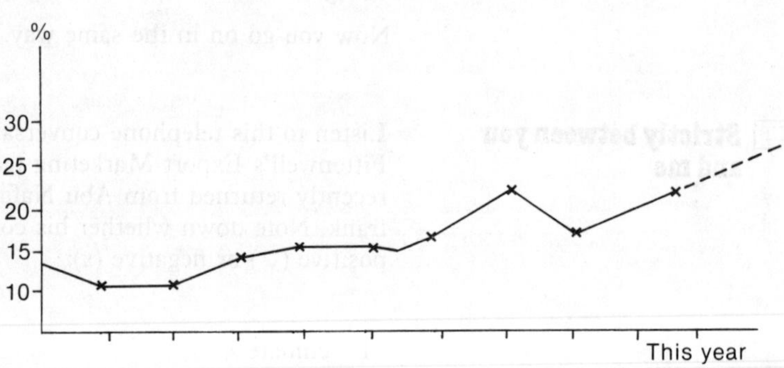

2 *Balance of trade*

A healthy economic position which we intend to maintain and improve.

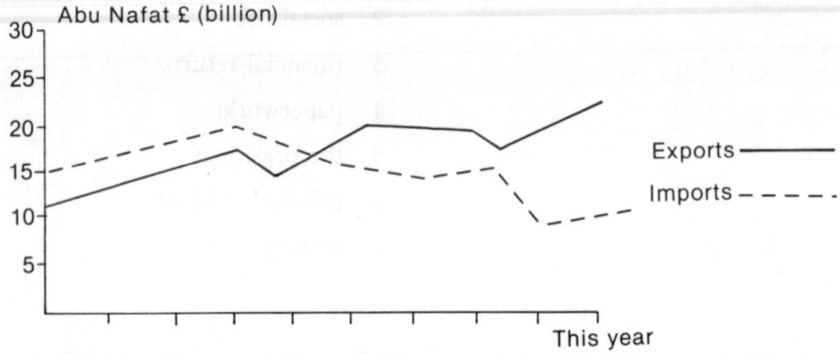

3 *Currency reserves ($ billion)*

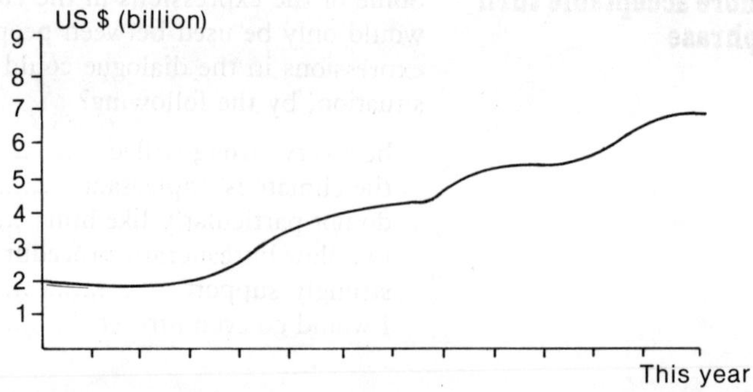

Tapescript for step 1

Tape section 43

INTERVIEWER: . . . and I asked Nicholas Murray of the Central School of International Studies, if he could tell me a little about the state of Abu Nafat.

MURRAY: Yes, well, it's true, Abu Nafat is not exactly a household name, but it does in fact have a long and interesting history. As far as archaeologists have been able to determine, Abu Nafat was inhabited as far back as the year 4000 BC. Its geographical position – as you know it's a large peninsula on the Arabian Red Sea Coast – and its excellent natural harbour, made it a regular port of call for merchants and sailors from earliest times. Early in the seventh century the inhabitants of Abu Nafat were converted to Islam and this is still, of course, the state religion.

INTERVIEWER: Abu Nafat was part of the Ottoman empire for many years I believe?

MURRAY: Yes indeed, for over a century – right up to the First World War in fact – Abu Nafat was ruled by Constantinople, with a Turkish governor and administration, who did little for the people.

INTERVIEWER: And what about this century?

MURRAY: Well, prior to the Turkish occupation, Abu Nafat had been ruled by members of the Al-Watani family for generations, and almost immediately after the First World War the British supported the family's claim to the throne. So from 1918 to 1946 Abu Nafat was ruled by Sheikh Abdullah – but in reality, under the terms of a special treaty arrangement, no policy decisions, defence agreements etc., could be made without the approval of British advisers. This caused considerable resentment among the growing numbers of educated young people and in 1946 the inevitable happened – Sheikh Abdullah was overthrown by a group of young British-trained officers, in a bloodless coup, and the British advisers were requested to leave, the treaty abrogated and Jamil Sultan, the leader of the group, became the country's first president.

INTERVIEWER: What was the new government's attitude to the West?

MURRAY: Well, of course, they were still very dependent economically on the West. American and European oil companies had the monopoly of the oil production – which by this time was already proving vastly superior in both quantity and quality than experts had originally supposed.

INTERVIEWER: I suppose this too was a cause of resentment among the population?

MURRAY: Yes, certainly – and in fact the downfall of Jamil Sultan's regime in 1965 – brought about by another army coup – was probably mainly due to the fact that he did not take a strong enough line with the oil companies. The people felt very strongly that their resources were being exploited and they themselves were not benefiting.

INTERVIEWER: So the new government was basically anti-Western in attitude?

MURRAY: Well, I wouldn't go so far as to say that. They did indeed take a much firmer line with the oil companies. Shortly after taking power they renegotiated contracts and agreements and set up the Abu Nafat National Oil Company which controls 51% of the oil industry in Abu Nafat. Foreign military bases have been closed – previously both the Americans and the British had forces stationed there – and the present government's aim is to preserve its status as a founder member of the group of non-aligned nations.

INTERVIEWER: How stable do you consider the present government?

MURRAY: Well, there's no organized opposition to the Government and during the last few months plans have been put forward for a new constitution and the election of a National Assembly – so I would say the Government must be feeling fairly confident.

INTERVIEWER: And the economic situation – has that improved since 1965?

MURRAY: Yes, indeed, I think it's fair to say that there have been remarkable successes. The policy has been to diversify away from an entirely oil-based economy and there has been considerable investment in petrochemical plants, steel, and agriculture. Over the last ten years Abu Nafat has had no difficulty in raising loans on the international credit markets – which is proof I think that financiers have confidence in the present economic policy of Abu Nafat.

INTERVIEWER: Yes, indeed. Well, thank you, Nicholas Murray. Next week our special guest will be . . .

Tapescript for step 9

Tape section 45

MORLEY: Extension 62, please.

BRONWELL: Hello, Export Sales Department. Bronwell speaking.

MORLEY: John, hello, Morley here, from Fittenwell. Listen, we're thinking of going into the market in Abu Nafat. I was wondering . . .

BRONWELL: Oh, that place!

MORLEY: You don't exactly sound enthusiastic!

BRONWELL: That's putting it mildly! The climate is foul – hell in the summer and grey and miserable in winter. And there's nothing to do – no cinemas, no theatres, nothing.

MORLEY: Well, why did you stay so long?

BRONWELL: I can tell you that in one word – money!

MORLEY: Ah, so you'd say it's a good place to do business?

BRONWELL: Well . . . yes and no. We got a couple of good contracts while I was there, but you wouldn't believe the time it takes to get through all the red tape. They accepted our tender in March last year but it was December before we could really get started.

MORLEY: And what about the political situation – how popular is the President?

BRONWELL: Most people can take him or leave him, as far as I could make out.

MORLEY: Really!

BRONWELL: Yes, but he's a bit of an autocrat. Never listens to anyone apparently. Still, I reckon he's there to stay. The army is right behind him and that's what counts. Listen, if you're free this evening, why don't you come over to my place. I'll show you some slides I took there. I must say there's some pretty spectacular scenery.

MORLEY: OK.

BRONWELL: See you later, then.

Group 1's information for step 11

The Embassy of Abu Nafat was happy to send information on the economy and investment prospects in Abu Nafat.

Embassy of Abu Nafat

Commercial Section

Investment Opportunities in Abu Nafat

Over the last ten years, Abu Nafat has encouraged the inflow of direct foreign investments, provided that the type of product and scale of operation has been consistent with the Government's development plans. The current 5-year plan lays emphasis on developing the sectors of health, education and agriculture, and companies working in these areas are welcomed.

Legislation: generally freedom for investments of up to 50%

Abu Nafat offers:

- a significant and growing market
- a high degree of political stability
- foreign trade 45% of GDP
- $6 billion reserves.

For further information contact:
Ministry of Trade and Development
DHOMS
ABU NAFAT

20 Business abroad

There are 9 steps in Unit 20. You will:

- practise making and responding to requests and offers
  on the telephone
  in negotiations
  in letter writing

1 Phoning the travel agent

Before leaving for Abu Nafat, Jonathan Morley has a number of matters to see to and arrangements to make. His secretary, Janice Freeman, phones a travel agency to enquire about flights to Abu Nafat.

Listen to the dialogue and write down the information requested and given.

2 Making and responding to offers

As you have heard in the dialogue, there are a number of ways of making offers. Some (direct) are more suitable in an informal situation; others (tentative) are more formal.

Tentative *We could alter the design, should you wish it.*
Would you like me to check that for you?
I could always change it, if you don't like it.
I'll show you the way, if you like.
Shall I retype the whole thing?
Direct *Can I get you anything?*

There are also a variety of ways in which you can respond to an offer.

Positive
↓
Thank you, that would be most helpful.
Thank you, I'd be very grateful.
That's very kind of you.
Yes, could you?
Would you?
Yes, please.
If you like.
Thank you, but it's not really necessary.
I can manage, thank you.
No, you needn't bother, thank you.
Negative *No, thank you.*

3 Making and responding to requests

Here are various ways of making requests. How would you classify them according to their degree of formality? Number them 1 – 9 (1 for the least formal, 9 for the most formal).

- Will you type this letter for me, please? ☐
- I'd be grateful if you could send me the following information. ☐
- Let's have a look! ☐
- Would you be so kind as to open the window? ☐
- Could you reserve two seats on flight 315? ☐
- I wonder if you could phone back later? ☐
- Would you mind starting an hour later? ☐
- I'd like some information. ☐
- Do you think you could possibly lend me £50? ☐

Which of the following responses shows the most enthusiasm? Which the least? Number them 1 – 9 (1 for the least enthusiastic, 9 for the most enthusiastic).

- I'll see what can be done. ☐
- We'll do our best. ☐
- I'm afraid that's just not possible. ☐
- Certainly. ☐
- It's out of the question. ☐
- Well, that may be a little difficult. ☐
- Of course. ☐
- No, I'm afraid not. ☐
- Yes, by all means. ☐

4 Problems

Look at this dialogue.

> A: John, I'm overdrawn at the bank and I'm going to London this weekend. Do you think you could possibly lend me £50?
> B: I'm afraid not, Bill. I'm a bit short myself, but I could let you have £10.
> A: No thanks. That wouldn't be enough. I guess I'll just have to stay at home.

Make up similar dialogues using the following expressions.

Requests	Responses
Could you . . .	*Well, that may be a little difficult . . .*
I wonder if you could possibly . . .	*Yes, by all means . . .*
Would you mind . . .	*We'll do our best, but . . .*
Offers	**Responses**
We could . . . if you wish. *I'll . . .* *Would you like me to . . .?*	*That's very kind of you . . .* *Yes, could you?* *Thank you, that would be most helpful.*

1 *Employee and employer:*

A: Excuse me, Mr Morley. My sister's getting married next week. . . . . .?

B: . . . . .

A: . . . . .

2 *Potential customer and salesman:*

A: We're interested in replacing some of our office equipment. . . . . .?

B: . . . .?

A: . . . . .

3 *Purchasing manager and supplier:*

A: We need those spare parts urgently. . . . . .?

B: . . . . ., but . . . . .

A: . . . . .

5 Making a phone call

Go back to the notes you made while listening to Janice Freeman and the travel agent, and in pairs re-enact their conversation.

6 Special requests

Work in pairs playing the parts of the travel agent and Janice Freeman from Fittenwell. The travel agent's information is printed on page 00 at the end of the Unit.

Fittenwell

You eventually decide to take the direct flight on Wednesday but have one or two special requests to make:

— Morley is a vegetarian and therefore cannot eat normal airline food.
— You want to take various samples of drugs and your latest laboratory microscope. These are fragile and you are worried about them being put in the hold with the other luggage. Also some of the drugs should be stored in a refrigerator.
— You are not sure whether a hotel room has been booked and would like the agency to check on this.

Phone the travel agency and make the appropriate requests.

7 Drill 1: I could if you like . . .

The Marketing Manager is busy, so you offer to help him. Listen to these examples:

I need this letter typed.
I could type it if you like.

Someone ought to reply to this enquiry.
I could reply to it if you like.

Now you go on in the same way.

Drill 2: Do you think you could . . .?

You are using your Manchester colleague's office. You need some work done, but you don't know how busy his secretary is, so you ask her politely. Listen to these examples:

I wonder if she would bring me the Sales Director's report.
Er . . . Miss Haylock, do you think you could possibly bring me the Sales Director's report?

I wonder if she would type this letter for me?
Er . . . Miss Haylock, do you think you could possibly type this letter for me?

Now you go on in the same way.

8 Negotiations in Abu Nafat

First read the following passage and underline the expressions in the text which mean:

total obedience
drinking no alcohol
were caused by
principally
in contrast to this

On arrival in Abu Nafat, Jonathan Morley and his secretary were met by officials of the Ministry of Trade and taken to the hotel. They were pleasantly surprised at how comfortable, even luxurious, it was, although strict adherence to Islamic prohibitions on alcohol meant that they spent a teetotal evening.

The following morning Jonathan Morley went along to the Ministry where he had an appointment with the Head of the Foreign Trade Department. He was surprised to find that there was little official enthusiasm for their setting up a sales company in Abu Nafat. The Ministry's objections stemmed mainly from the fact that a sales company would employ few local employees and would contribute little to the development of the Health Service in Abu Nafat.

On the other hand they positively encouraged the establishment of a manufacturing company to produce a wide range of Fittenwell products. A further meeting was arranged for that afternoon when a senior representative of the Ministry of Health would also be present.

In small groups divide into two teams – Fittenwell representatives and Abu Nafat government officials – and prepare your arguments. Using the notes provided, put forward your requests, listen and respond to those of the other side. Make any offers you feel appropriate. On some points you may feel you cannot give a definite answer as yet. Ask for more time to consider the question. Make notes on the responses of the other side.

Notes for the Fittenwell representatives are printed at the end of the Unit.

Abu Nafat government officials

You require:
- complete technical and clinical data on products
- workforce to be 75% local
- training of local employees
- participation in Dhoms University medical research programme
- preference to be given to the local market
- expatriate staff to comply with local customs regarding alcohol, dress and so on
- advice to Ministry of Health on Family Planning programme

You offer:
- assistance in local recruitment
- advice on local conditions, climate, laws and so on
- one year tax holiday
- repatriation of 60% of profits at advantageous exchange rates
- access to Red Sea Free Trade Area

9 Letter writing

When making a request in writing (for information, for advice, for a brochure, for a catalogue) the letter includes, apart from the greeting and ending:

i) an explanation of why you are making the request
ii) the request

When writing to offer your goods or services you would mention:

i) why you feel your offer would be of interest
ii) the offer

The more formal expressions for requesting and offering are generally suitable for business letters.

> **GLOBAL MEDICARE**
>
> INSTANT, EFFICIENT, DAY OR NIGHT INTERNATIONAL SERVICE. GLOBAL MEDICARE repatriates company personnel promptly and efficiently in well-equipped air ambulances from all parts of the world.
>
> IF THE WELFARE OF YOUR OVERSEAS PERSONNEL IS A PRIORITY FOR YOUR COMPANY, WRITE AT ONCE FOR DETAILS OF OUR INTERNATIONAL COMPANIES PLAN.
>
> Director of Services GLOBAL MEDICARE FREEPOST LONDON SW6 2BQ

1 This advertisement caught the eye of the Fittenwell Personnel Manager, who felt that a scheme of this nature would be of value to the company, operating as it does in parts of the world where health care is not always of the highest standard. Write his letter requesting further information.

2 In response to the letter from the Fittenwell Personnel Manager, write offering to send one of your representatives to the company to explain the Global Medicare scheme in detail.

Tapescript for step 1

Tape section 46

TRAVEL AGENT: Atlantic Travel, can I help you?

JANICE: Good morning. This is Miss Freeman from Fittenwell. I'd like some information on flights to Dhoms, Abu Nafat.

TRAVEL AGENT: Dhoms?

JANICE: Yes, D-H-O-M-S on the Red Sea. Could you please give me details of frequency of flights, fares and departure and arrival times?

TRAVEL AGENT: Dhoms . . . Dhoms . . . Ah yes, here we are . . . Oh, well, I'm afraid there seems to be only one direct flight a week. That's on Wednesday, leaving Heathrow at 7.30, arriving Dhoms at 17.30 local time.

JANICE: Only one a week . . .mmm. I wonder if you could check on flights from other European capitals – Paris, Brussels, for example.

TRAVEL AGENT: Yes, if you'll just hold on a moment I'll look for you. Ah . . . there's a flight from Paris on Thursdays and from Frankfurt every Saturday and Monday. Would you like me to work out connecting flights?

JANICE: Yes, would you, please.

TRAVEL AGENT: Actually, I'd better just check up on this. Do you think you could possibly ring back in say, half an hour? We don't get many enquiries for Abu Nafat and I may have overlooked something . . . or I could put the information in the post if you wish.

JANICE: Yes, I'd prefer that, if you would, and will you also enclose details of fares, flying times and return flights? If you could let us have it as soon as possible, I'd be grateful.

TRAVEL AGENT: Certainly, I'll send it off today.

Information for the travel agent for step 6

Atlantic Travel Agency receives a phone call from Fittenwell. Two passengers to Abu Nafat have a number of queries about their flights. The following extract from the airline's regulations will help you formulate your response to their requests.

Regulations

Passengers requiring special diet

..... passengers requiring special menus on religious or medical grounds should make their requirements known not later than seven days prior to departure date .....

Fragile Goods

..... the transportation of fragile items in the cabin of the aircraft is permitted at the discretion of the cabin crew. Passengers transporting such items should inform the airline representative not later than two hours before take-off.

A refrigerator is available on board the aircraft for small items such as a baby's feeding bottle .....

Notes for the Fittenwell representatives for step 8

You request:

- information on available sites
- permission to purchase land
- ministry assistance in recruiting local employees
- information on facilities for importing raw materials
- free repatriation of capital and profits
- access to Red Sea Free Trade Area
- drug trials facilities at local hospital

You offer:

- some government participation
- up to 60% local work force
- training scheme; seminars for local medical staff and so on
- research on particular local needs

21 That's what must have happened

There are 11 steps in Unit 21. You will practise:

- talking about ability and achievements
- expressing certainty and uncertainty about events in the past

1 An encouraging start

Listen to Robert Cave, a sales representative, reporting on his visit to a large pharmaceutical chain store.

Was he able to:

		Yes	*No*
1	see the Purchasing Manager?	☐	☐
2	explain Fittenwell's full range of products?	☐	☐
3	interest Mr Avon in the service provided by Fittenwell?	☐	☐
4	find out about their present purchasing arrangements?	☐	☐
5	make another appointment?	☐	☐
6	obtain a firm order?	☐	☐

2 Dialogue

Now listen again and write down the words missed out below:

SALES MANAGER: So you say you . . . . to see their purchasing manager?

ROBERT CAVE: Oh yes, I . . . . in the end, although his secretary did her best to prevent me, saying he was in conference, had an urgent appointment and so on. But I stood my ground and we . . . . . talk for about five minutes. Of course I . . . . ., in that short time, give him anything but the sketchiest outline of our product range, but I think I . . . . . catching his interest. He told his secretary to make an appointment for next week – Tuesday morning in fact. I . . . . . really . . . . . to go into details with him then, and with any luck come away with a firm order – and a large one, I hope! One thing I did . . . . . doing, though, was find out about their present purchasing arrangements. Of course I . . . . . ask him about them outright, but I . . . . . to get the information indirectly from his secretary.

3 Ability and achievement

In affirmative statements about the past,

could refers to an ability to do something
was or *were able to* refers both to this ability and what was actually achieved
managed to refers to something which was achieved with difficulty
succeeded in refers to the goal achieved

I finally managed to see Mr Avon.
He could only give me fifteen minutes.
We were able to arrange an appointment for next week.
However, I succeeded in obtaining an order.

In negative statements about the past, *could not (couldn't)* and *was/were not able to* are used for both ability and using an ability to achieve something.

I couldn't/I wasn't able to show him all our literature.

In statements about the future, *can* and *cannot (can't)* express the speaker's certainty about future ability.

We can't deliver before the end of the month.

Will be able to expresses a less definite attitude about the future. *May* or *might be able to* are used if the future ability is uncertain.

I'm sure we'll be able to reach agreement.
Their supplier may not be able to meet our deadline.

4 Ups and downs

United Construction Ltd had mixed fortunes last year. Make one sentence about each of last year's achievements and failures, beginning *we were able to* and *we couldn't* or *we weren't able to.*

Achievements	*Failures*
increase in domestic market share expansion of sales force	no increase in overseas sales failed in our bid to take over the ACM group
£2.5 million profit opening of new plant in Yorkshire repayment of bank loan	no major overseas contract no investment in new machinery sales of new product below target

5 A brighter future

Last year was disastrous for Global Motors. Sales slumped, there were frequent industrial disputes, 600 of the workforce were laid off when one of the smaller plants had to close through lack of orders. There was no money for investment in badly needed new machinery and repairs to existing buildings, and the shareholders received a dividend lower than in any previous year.

However, the company has just been awarded two extremely lucrative contracts – one in the Middle East and the other in South East Asia.

Make a list of things the company can now plan to do, for example

repair the roof at headquarters
take back all the men made redundant
pay off part of the bank loan

Decide how definite these plans are. Introduce those which are most definite with *Now we can . . .*, those less definite with *we'll be able to . . .*, and the more remote or improbable ideas with *we may be able to . . . .*

6 What can have happened?

When Robert Cave, Fittenwell's sales representative, called on Mr Avon the following week as arranged, he was informed that Mr Avon was in London on business. Cave found this hard to believe.

Listen to his conversation with his Sales Manager on his return to the office.

Are their ideas and hypotheses about the missed appointment, in his pinion, (a) certainly true, (b) possibly true, or (c) impossible?

Hypotheses	*Certain*	*Possible*	*Impossible*
Robert mistook the date.	☐	☐	☐
Robert mistook the time.	☐	☐	☐
Mr Avon forgot the appointment.	☐	☐	☐
Mr Avon was in the office but didn't want to see Robert.	☐	☐	☐
The receptionist made a mistake.	☐	☐	☐
Mr Avon was called away on an emergency.	☐	☐	☐

7 Did he . . . ?

Must have + past participle expresses certainty about a past event which we did not actually witness. The certainty is based on evidence or logical reasoning.

Mr Avon must have forgotten the appointment.

Can't or *couldn't have* express certainty that a past event did not take place (*couldn't* is a little less definite than *can't*).

I can't have mistaken the date, I wrote it in my diary.

May have or *might have* express the possibility of a past event having taken place.

I might have written down the wrong date.
He may have forgotten to telephone.

8 Who's who?

Three men went to three different cities for different reasons and stayed for different lengths of time. From the clues below you can work out the purpose, time and place of each man's visit.

As you work out the answer, fill in the information on this table, using ✗ or ✓, and complete the gaps in the sentences using *must have, couldn't have* or *might have* + past participle.

	London	Paris	New York	One month	Five days	Two days	Trade Fair	Sales visit	Language course
Mr Brown									
Mr White									
Mr Green									
Trade Fair									
Sales visit									
Language course									
One month									
Five days									
Two days									

1 The longest trip was to Paris. The sales visit lasted two days.

The sales visit . . . . . in Paris.
The Trade Fair . . . . . in Paris.

2 Mr White didn't go on the shortest trip and he didn't go to London.

So Mr White . . . . . on the sales visit but he . . . . . on a language course or to the Trade Fair.

3 Mr Green's trip was longer than Mr White's.

So Mr Green . . . . . to Paris, Mr Brown . . . . . to London, and Mr White . . . . . to New York.

4 Mr Brown's trip was the shortest. He . . . . . on the sales visit to London.

Mr White didn't go on the language course. He . . . . . to the Trade Fair in New York. So Mr Green . . . . .

9 Drill 1: When I was sixteen . . .

At a job interview a candidate is questioned about her previous experience. Listen to these examples:

I hear you had a great variety of holiday jobs while you were still at school. It's unusual for a girl to get a job as lifeguard at a swimming pool, isn't it?
Yes, I was able to get that job because I could swim very well when I was sixteen.

And another one was at a horse riding school.
Yes, I was able to get that job because I could ride very well when I was sixteen.

Now you go on in the same way. The notes will help you:

swim	cook
type	sing
dance	sew
ride	speak French and German

Drill 2: What do you think?

The boss has just sent a message to say that he wishes to speak to you about a very serious matter. With a colleague you try to work out what the reason might be. Listen to these examples:

Do you think he's found out about the customers' complaints?
Yes, he might have found out about that, I suppose.

Or could he have discovered that error in last month's accounts?
No, he can't have found out about that. I corrected it immediately.

Now you go on in the same way. The notes will help you. (Begin after the two examples.)

the customers' complaints	possible
error in the accounts	impossible; I corrected it immediately
arriving late	possible
borrowing from the petty cash	impossible; I paid it back last week
losing the files	impossible; I found them yesterday
breaking the office window	possible
leaving early in the evening	impossible; he always leaves before me
personal phone calls	possible

10 Could this have been prevented?

Jack Foster, a senior engineer, collapsed while working on a Fittenwell project in Central Africa. He was supervising the erection of the State Pharmaceutical Company plant – a joint venture with the National Department of Industry. He is now in intensive care in a London hospital and still in a critical condition. Emergency treatment at the local hospital was slow and inadequate. Arrangements for his repatriation to the UK were badly organized and the journey involved two changes of plane and considerable hardship. His family have made strong representation to the company, criticizing the repatriation procedure and threatening court action. A meeting has been called to discuss company procedure in the light of this case.

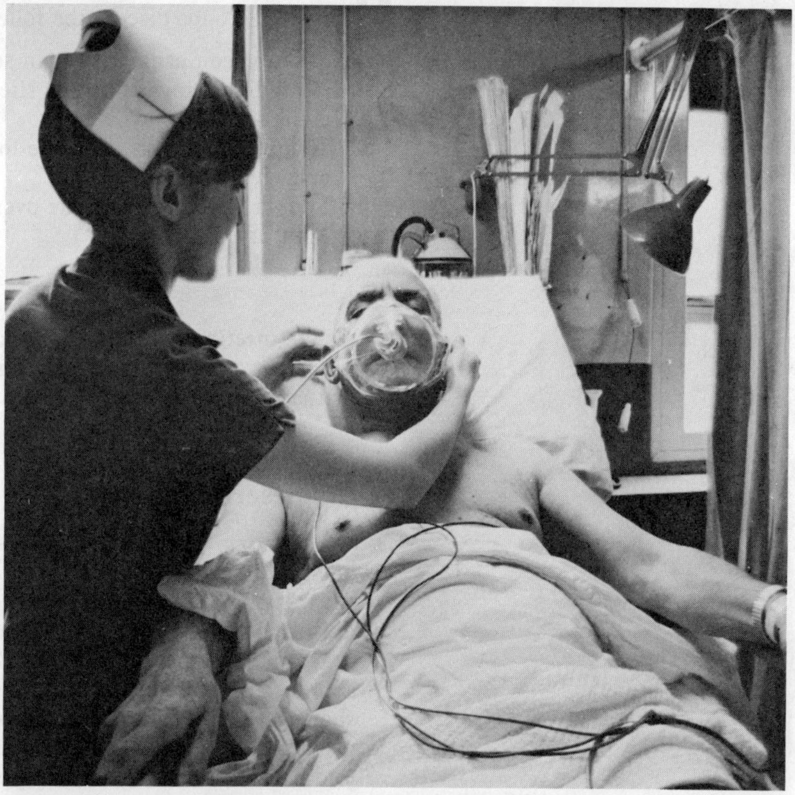

Read these extracts from reports submitted by the personnel department, the manager in charge of the African project, and the Foster family's solicitor.

Project manager

... in view of his age (60) it was suggested to Mr Foster that his assistant should go to Africa in his place. However, Mr Foster was most insistant that, since he had worked on the project from its inception, he should see it through to completion. He was passed as fit for overseas assignment three months prior to his departure...

Family solicitor

.... worked harder than anyone - 16-hour day was not uncommon. He showed no more than normal fatigue and seemed able to cope with the climate better, in fact, than many of the younger men. His collapse came as a great shock to us all. We had no doctor on the site so some delay in obtaining medical attention was inevitable. The nearest hospital was 100 kms from the site. Though small and poorly equipped they were able to give him adequate care, and he was repatriated by the first available flight to Europe. Waiting for a direct flight would have necessitated a further 5-day delay.

Personnel

.... maintain that the company must have been aware that Mr Foster was unfit to work in such extreme conditions. Medical and repatriation arrangements could definitely have been better organized. We should appreciate...

In small groups discuss the following questions.

1 Was the company at fault in sending Mr Foster to Africa?
2 Why didn't anyone on the site realize that he was unfit before he collapsed?
3 Who, if anyone, is to blame for the poor repatriation arrangements?
4 Should Fittenwell alter its overseas recruitment procedure in the light of this case?

11 Letter

After the meeting, write to the solicitor representing Mr Foster and summarize your conclusions, suggesting a meeting with him to explain the situation in full.

Tapescript for step 1

Tape section 48

SALES MANAGER: So you say you weren't able to see their purchasing manager?

ROBERT CAVE: Oh yes, I managed to in the end, although his secretary did her best to prevent me, saying he was in conference, had an urgent appointment and so on. But I stood my ground and we were able to talk for about five minutes. Of course, I couldn't, in that short time, give him anything but the sketchiest outline of our product range, but I think I succeeded in catching his interest. He told his secretary to make an appointment for next week – Tuesday morning in fact. I'll really be able to go into details with him then, and with any luck come away with a firm order – and a large one, I hope! One thing I did succeed in doing, though, was find out about their present purchasing arrangements. Of course I couldn't ask him about them outright, but I managed to get the information indirectly from his secretary. Apparently . . . .

Tapescript for step 6

Tape section 49

ROBERT CAVE: Yes, I arrived right on time – the appointment was for 10.30 – only to be told by the receptionist that Mr Avon was out of the office and not expected back that day. I just couldn't believe it.

SALES MANAGER: Well, Robert you must've got the wrong date – check in your diary.

ROBERT CAVE: No, I'm absolutely sure I'm right. I wrote it down immediately we'd made the appointment. Here it is, see – 10.30, on Tuesday 22 March. And I phoned him later in the week to confirm it. I can't possibly have made a mistake there.

SALES MANAGER: Well, maybe Mr Avon forgot to write down the appointment. Did you ask his secretary to check his diary?

ROBERT CAVE: No, I didn't. I suppose he might have forgotten, but I doubt it . . .. After all, I did confirm it with him personally.

SALES MANAGER: Do you think the receptionist might have made a mistake? Perhaps she thought he was out but he was really there waiting for you – or in another part of the building.

ROBERT CAVE: No, she can't've made that mistake – she even phoned his secretary to check.

SALES MANAGER: It's just possible Avon was in his office all the time but didn't want to see you for some reason.

ROBERT CAVE: Well, I didn't go up to his office to check, so I suppose he might've been there, but I think it's hardly likely. No, what must have happened is that there was an emergency at their London branch – the receptionist said that that was where he'd gone. He must've had to leave very suddenly and had no time to contact me. There just can't be any other explanation . . ..

22 The new production plant

There are 9 steps in Unit 22. You will:

- deal with rumours
- practise talking about future plans, arrangements, and decisions
- use different forms to show how certain a future event is
- make notes on a meeting
- discuss a public relations film

1 The information meeting

The Fittenwell Managing Director is to address a meeting to familiarize his managers with his plans for a new production plant. The managers have already received the following memo.

Now listen to the Managing Director and note down what he says on each of these points. Also, decide how certain he is of his plans. For each point, note down whether his plans are (a) definite, (b) probable, (c) possible or (d) vague.

MEMORANDUM
To: All Heads of Department 28 October 19--

NEW PRODUCTION PLANT

An information meeting will be held tomorrow at 10am in my office.

1 Date for taking possession
2 Date for commencing production
3 Recruitment of senior management
4 Recruitment of shop floor workers
5 Plans for Marketing Department
6 Transfer of staff
7 Recreation facilities
8 Housing
9 Production target - first 6 months
10 Insurance
11 AOB

2 Decisions, plans, intentions

During the information meeting the Managing Director is talking about plans, intentions and decisions that have been made. Here are some of the ways of doing this.

Definite decisions, statements of fact, spontaneous decisions:

The Production Manager will be appointed by Head Office.
I myself will be Managing Director.
The F134 will be our main product.
I'll just ask my secretary to bring some coffee.

Definite arrangements:

They are sending a team of Risk Management consultants.

What will occur as a matter of course; what will be happening at a particular time in the future:

We'll be taking possession of the factory on 1st April.
They'll be looking into the problem.
I'll be attending a meeting in Geneva this time next week.

Definite intentions and plans:

We do not intend to involve any but a handful of our present staff.
We mean to keep the centre open.
We are planning to carry out a certain number of alterations.

Less definite intentions and plans:

We hope to begin production two months later.
If all goes well, further appointments may be envisaged.

Less definite statements about the future:

They may recommend certain changes.
We would have to modify our plans.
We should have a fairly good idea of how things are going by then.
Should any of your department be interested, we would consider them of course.

Plans and arrangements for the future that did not materialize:

We were going to introduce flexible working hours, but the majority of the staff were against it.
The report was to have been published today, but it has been delayed because of the printers' strike.

3 Have you heard the latest?

Rumours are rife at Fittenwell UK. Internal communications are not of the best and, although plans for the opening of the new manufacturing subsidiary are by now fairly well in hand, little factual information has been passed on to any but the most senior management staff.

Below, in note form, are some of the rumours that have been circulating. After listening to the tape (step 1), confirm or deny the rumours and add any further information or corrections from the information you possess.

Remember that rumours are often introduced by expressions such as the following.

Have you heard . . .
Apparently . . .
Did you know . . .?
It seems that . . .

Here are the rumours:

1 Difficulty choosing a site; going to cancel the whole project.
2 Have to rebuild factory completely; no production for at least a year.
3 Managing Director thinking of resigning; totally opposed to Head Office policy.
4 Offices here to be closed down; all administrative staff to move to new plant.
5 Sales targets for first year unrealistically high; no plans to increase sales force.
6 New building a fire hazard, no insurance company will accept the risk.
7 Company having difficulty raising the capital they need.
8 Most of the top jobs in the new plant already promised to friends and relations of the Managing Director.

4 Probability

The way we express the future depends on how definite and factual the future event is. When we assess the probability of something happening in the future we use expressions like the following.

I am sure it will go well. ↑
I am confident it will go well. 90%
We expect the work to be completed by next month.
There is a good chance of promotion.
Housing is likely to be something of a problem.
There is some hope of sales rising. 50%
There is some danger of sales falling.
Many of the present staff are unlikely to want to move. 10%
There is very little chance of a 10% rise in salary this year. ↓

When the future event depends on another event, we use the conditional forms.

(i) When the condition is likely to be fulfilled, we use the **present simple** tense after *if* or *unless* and the **future** with *will* or *may*.

If sales improve, we'll be able to expand.
We won't meet the delivery date unless the components arrive tomorrow.

(ii) When it is unlikely or impossible that the condition will be fulfilled, we use the **simple past** tense after *if* or *unless* and the **conditional** form with *could, would* or *might*.

If we didn't have such fierce competition from abroad, our sales would rise dramatically.
Absenteeism would be reduced if we changed to flexi-time.

In more formal spoken and written English, *should* + **infinitive** can be used in place of *if* + **simple past**.

Should any of your department be interested in the new posts, we would consider them.

5 A gloomy outlook

Below are some notes made by a member of the financial team after listening to a lecture on 'Present Economic Trends'.

Use the expressions of probability and the conditional forms above to make complete sentences to summarize the points made in the lecture.

	Degree of probability	*Prediction*	*Condition*
1	above average	increase in number of unemployed	if world economic recession continues
2	average	continuing increase in inflation	unless stricter monetary control by governments
3	very high	rise in interest rates	–
4	average	stabilization of gold prices	if no major world crisis
5	low	reduction in the gulf separating North and South	unless considerable change in world economic order
6	very low	an alternative to nuclear power	if the present low priority given to research continues

6 What do you think?

In small groups, discuss the probability of the following events, and then compare the conclusions you reached.

1 The price of gold moving 10% up or down in the next six months.
2 A nuclear attack in any part of the world.
3 Finding a cure for cancer this century.
4 A major oil tanker disaster this year.
5 Discovering life on another planet.
6 A military coup in Britain within the next ten years.
7 One or more non-member countries joining the EEC this year.
8 Any member of the class becoming rich and famous.

7 The minister's plans

Listen to the Minister of the Environment talking about his department's projects for the next ten years. Note down how definite each one is. Then write a brief press release from the ministry for the national press, using the following expressions.

We mean to . . .	*If the committee agrees we will . . .*
. . . will be ________ed . . .	*We are thinking of ________ing . . .*
We will be ________ing . . .	*There is a chance that we may . . .*

The plans are:

1 to begin construction of the Channel tunnel
2 to reduce the Government's grant to local councils
3 to introduce measures to protect the countryside
4 to charge motorists a fee for using motorways
5 to set up a public enquiry into oil pollution on the Scottish coastline.
6 to appoint a troubleshooter to investigate complaints from the public.

8 Drill 1: There may be some delay . . .

You are talking to a visitor about plans for the new factory at Peterborough. She wants to know when they will be starting. Look at your cuesheet and listen to these examples.

So you've decided to redecorate the offices. When will work on that be starting?
Well, it should be starting next Monday, but there may be some delay.

And work on the new social centre – when will that be starting?
Well, it should be starting in June but there may be some delay.

Now you go on in the same way. The cuesheet will give the dates you need. (Note that the cues are not printed in the order in which you will hear them.)

Cuesheet

check electrical system	10 April
transfer of staff	1 April
overhaul fire precautions	15 April
redecoration of office area	next Monday
production	June
social centre	June
interviews	next Wednesday
advertising campaign	beginning of May

Drill 2: If they weren't so expensive . . .

Some of the office staff are complaining about working conditions and would like to see some changes made. You, however, are worried about costs. Listen to these examples:

The office typewriters are getting very unreliable. You should replace some of them.
Well, we would replace them if they weren't so expensive.

And the lighting is so poor. Why can't you install new lighting?
Well, we would install it if it weren't so expensive.

Now you go on in the same way.

9 Filming Fittenwell

To mark the fiftieth anniversary of the company, the Board of Directors has approved the production of a thirty-minute documentary film to illustrate the varied activities of the Fittenwell group in all parts of the world. It will be shown to:

—school and college students, during the company's annual recruiting campaigns
—the press
—investors and bankers
—customers and suppliers

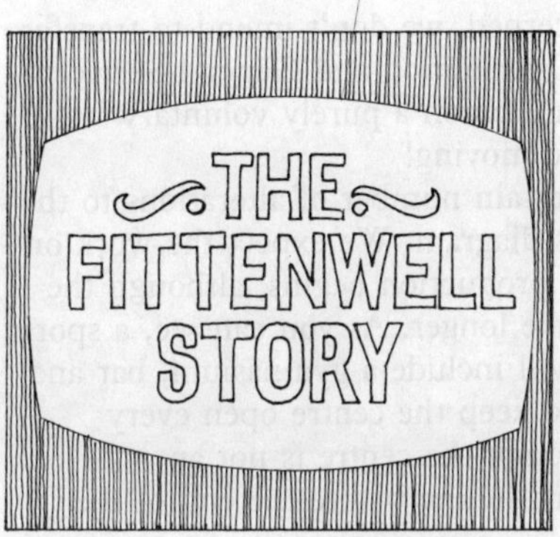

With this audience in mind, you have been asked to:

1 decide which sectors of the group's activities to include as being most likely to create a favourable image of the organization
2 plan a synopsis of the film
3 work out the best order in which to film the different sectors.

Total filming time will be two months. The budget is not overgenerous.

Tapescript for step 1

Tape section 51

MANAGING DIRECTOR: Good morning, Gentlemen. I know how busy you all are so I'll be as brief as possible. As you know I've been in Geneva for the past week, and I want to put you all in the picture as to our plans for the new plant at Peterborough.

First, dates. The lease has been signed and we'll be taking possession of the factory on 1st April. Provisionally we hope to begin production two months later. So by the end of the year we'll have completed six months on full production and we should have a fairly good idea of how things are going.

Now the question of recruitment. It has been estimated that we'll require several senior management staff. One of these, the Production Manager, will be Swiss – he has already been appointed by Head Office. Three other posts will be advertised in the national press. Should any of your department be interested in applying, John, we would consider them of course. In fact, I feel it might well be advantageous to fill at least one of the posts by internal appointment. It seems likely that one or two other posts will be filled by Head Office staff on temporary loan. I myself will be sharing my time between our company here and the new plant, as Managing Director of both – at any rate initially. If all goes well, as I'm confident it will, then further appointments may be envisaged next year. The Marketing Department will, for the time being, remain here, but of course our present marketing team will have to be considerably increased.

We don't anticipate any problems in the recruiting of local shop floor workers. United Optics in Peterborough is due to close down at the end of this month and approaches are being made to their workforce – many of whom already have the sort of skills we'll be needing.

As far as staff from here are concerned, we don't intend to transfer any but a handful – mainly in the Distribution and General Service departments. And any transfer would be on a purely voluntary basis – no one will be pressured into moving!

We are planning to carry out a certain number of alterations to the premises – details are shown on this diagram. We expect the work on the interior to be completed before production begins, although the major structural work could well take longer. As you can see, a sports and social centre is planned – and will include a gymnasium, bar and indoor swimming pool. We mean to keep the centre open every evening and at weekends – and although the centre is not an immediate priority, it should be functioning before the end of the year.

Housing is likely to be something of a problem. There is a serious shortage in Peterborough, as elsewhere, but we do hope to recruit a large proportion of our staff locally, and they, presumably, will already live in the area. We are sending a team to Peterborough shortly and they will be looking into the question then.

Now a brief mention of our target figures for the first six months. As you know the F134 microscope will be our main product, and it's hoped that we will achieve an average five hundred a month by then, rising to seven hundred and fifty in the second six months.

QUESTIONER: What about insurance? I see you have that down on the memo . . ..

MANAGING DIRECTOR: Insurance, yes, well, there appear to be one or two problem areas. Apparently there is some danger of the company being unwilling to insure the plant as it stands. They are sending some of their people to visit the factory in about two weeks' time. They may recommend certain changes and, should they do so, we could have to modify our alteration and expansion plans slightly. Anyway I'll keep you informed of developments there. Now are there any other points you'd like to raise . . .? No, well then I'll just ask Cynthia to bring in coffee.

Tapescript for step 7

Tape section 52

MINISTER: As you are all no doubt aware, public spending in all departments will have to be considerably curtailed over the next few years and this department is no exception. We have therefore, with regret, to announce that from the beginning of the next financial year the Government's grant to local councils will be reduced by two per cent. And in a further effort to improve and maintain our road network, we are considering the possibility of charging motorists a fee for using our motorways. Further details will be announced later, should we decide to go ahead.

Now on a more cheerful note – discussions with our French counterparts on the Channel Tunnel issue have resumed and while no announcement can be made yet, the prospect of beginning construction work in the foreseeable future should not be discounted.

We will also, during the next session of Parliament, be introducing measures designed to protect the countryside – areas of outstanding natural beauty – from building and industrial development. Following the recent controversy we also intend to set up a public enquiry into oil pollution along the Scottish coastline.

Finally, the appointment of a trouble shooter to deal with complaints from the public is still under discussion, but, subject to the committee's agreement, an appointment will be made early next year.

Thank you for your time, Gentlemen. You will, of course, be informed in due course of any further developments.

23 Could I have your views?

There are 10 steps in Unit 23. You will practise how to:

- chair a meeting
- ask opinions
- express agreement and disagreement
- talk about suitability

1 The meeting (1)

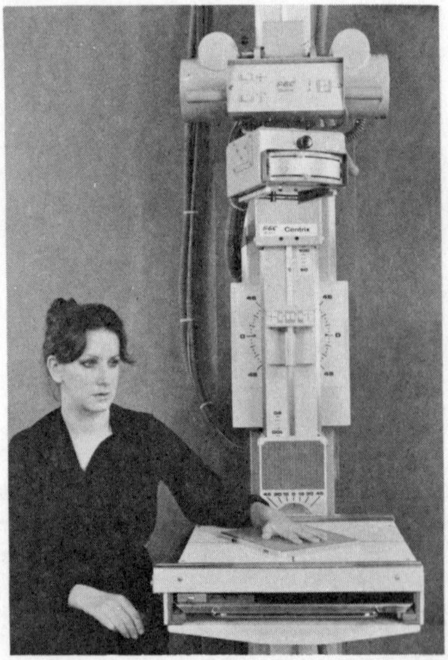

Managing Directors of the principal Fittenwell manufacturing subsidiaries have arrived in Geneva for a meeting to discuss a new design for X-ray equipment. The main features of the new design are (a) the use of a new, light-weight and extremely durable material, (b) mobility and ease of operation and (c) improved safety devices.

The meeting has been called to decide:

(i) whether it should be added to the standard range of Fittenwell hospital and laboratory equipment.
(ii) which of the manufacturing subsidiaries should produce it.
(iii) whether the time is right for setting up a manufacturing subsidiary in the UK.

The meeting is opened by the Chairman, Hans Kessler, member of the Board of Directors, Head of Production and Technology. Listen to the first part of the meeting and note down the opinions expressed for and against starting production of the new equipment.

2 Giving opinions

Some of the opinions expressed in step 1 are strong and confident.

I am in no doubt whatever that the new product will be a success.
I am confident that we will overcome the initial problems.
There's no doubt in my mind that R & D have developed a really worthwhile product.

When we feel that our opinion may not be shared by others we use expressions like the following.

Well, from our point of view, it will fulfill a need.
Personally, I don't think we should delay.

To encourage discussion, the Chairman invites others to give their opinion.

Does anyone have any strong views on the subject?
Would anyone like to comment on that?

It is easy to express agreement.

I agree totally (entirely/absolutely).
That's quite correct (true/right).
Just what I was thinking.

But often we want to express reservations or to disagree. In most business situations it is important to do this tactfully. It is usually better to avoid curt statements such as 'You are wrong' or 'I don't agree'. Here are some ways of disagreeing diplomatically.

I'd go along with that, though I'm not entirely convinced about the timing.
Well, I accept that, but aren't there going to be administrative problems?
That may be true, but it doesn't mean we have to reject the whole idea.
Yes, but on the other hand we must consider the cost.
I'm afraid I can't agree.

3 The meeting (2)

The meeting continues with a discussion of the second point – which of the manufacturing subsidiaries should produce the new equipment.

In small groups, take the parts of Hans Kessler and the Managing Directors of Italy, Spain, France, Germany and the UK. Use the expressions and the notes given below to continue the discussion in your own words.

MD ITALY: *Well, I accept that, but aren't there going to be . . .?*
Technical problems of starting production at other plants.
New equipment developed solely in Switzerland.
Need for consultations with R & D team.

KESSLER: (Agrees – asks for comments.)

MD SPAIN: *I'm afraid I can't agree . . .*
Production of C219 stopped.
Considerable spare capacity.
If Spanish subsidiary doesn't start producing new equipment there will be redundancies and labour unrest.

MD UK: *That may be true but . . .*
Doubts about size of market in Spain.
Why not limit production to two areas only?

MD FRANCE: *Yes, but on the other hand . . .*
Great interest shown in new product.

MD GERMANY: *I'd go along with that, though I'm not entirely convinced . . .*
Perhaps not all manufacturing subsidiaries to be involved at first.

MD ITALY: *Just what I was thinking. It's my view that . . .*
Begin production in Switzerland and extend to other subsidiaries (France, Germany, Spain?) if successful.

Now listen to the tape. How does it compare with your version?

4 Is it right for the job?

To support an opinion on whether something is suitable or right for a particular situation we use *enough, too, such, so*+adjective. Note the position of the adjective in these negative sentences.

Our plant is not large enough for production on a large scale.
Production costs in Europe are too high to compete on the world market.

Here is a positive sentence.

Demand for our product is high enough to warrant large scale production.

Note that if *enough* or *too* are followed by a verb, the verb takes the infinite form with *to.* If followed by a noun, *for* is used.

So and *such* can be used to support negative or positive opinion.

Competition is so intense that we may have to reduce our profit margin.
There is such high unemployment in the area that recruitment will be easy.

Note that *so* is followed by an adjective; *such* by adjective+noun.

5 Just what we need . . . or is it?

Using the forms in step 4, make sentences to support your opinion about how this pressing machine meets or fails to meet the customer's requirements.

Machine specifications	*Customer's requirements*
1 dimensions: 2 m×6 m×3 m.	floor space available: 2 sq m
2 price: £20,000	budget allowed: £10,000–£15,000
3 average output: 480 units per hour	performance requirements: minimum 400 units per hour
4 weight: one tonne	workshop on 1st floor, maximum weight: 500 kg
5 suitable large scale production on automated line	machine to be used once per month for small production runs of two to three thousand
6 simple to operate: one operator required	only one skilled operator available

6 The chairman's role

The Chairman of any meeting has to:
—open and close the meeting
—ensure that all points on the agenda are covered and decisions taken
—assign responsibility for carrying out the decisions of the meeting
—make sure those present keep to the point
—give everyone a fair hearing
—organize a vote, if necessary

Here are some useful expressions for keeping the di /ussion moving and to the point:

Perhaps we could move on now to the next point.
I'm afraid we must keep to the agenda.
That's settled then, we'll limit production to our Swiss plant.

For assigning responsibility:

Perhaps you would see to the distribution of this report, Bob?
Your department will work out the arrangements for the visit, Roger.
Could I ask you to explain the new timetable to the men, Bill?

For including everyone in the discussion:

Thank you for your views, John. Bob, I think you wanted to come in here.
As Head of Quality Control, Bill, what are your views?
Could I bring you in on this, Fred?

For organizing a vote:

I think we'd better take a vote on this.
Those in favour?
Those against?
Any abstentions?
Thank you. That's carried unanimously.
The motion is defeated by six votes to two.

7 The meeting (3)

Now continue with the discussion of the third point. Is the time right for setting up a manufacturing subsidiary in the UK? Below are some points you might want to make. The Chairman should ensure that everyone has a chance to give an opinion and that the discussion ends with a decision.

For	*Against*
skilled labour available	poor labour relations
government incentives for industry	inefficient management
good communications	powerful Trade Unions
relatively low wages	frequent strikes
tax holiday (up to five years)	high taxation
easy access to City capital market	sterling unstable
export opportunities (USA, Commonwealth)	inflation
oil	high interest rates

8 Drill 1: True, but . . .

You disagree with your colleague's view that your products would be successful in Japan. Listen to these examples.

Compared with the rest of Europe our prices are very competitive.
That may be true, but they're not competitive enough for the Japanese market.

And there's no doubt our methods are considered extremely efficient.
That may be true, but they're not efficient enough for the Japanese market.

Now you go on in the same way.

Drill 2: I'm afraid . . .

At a meeting of your department, colleagues find it difficult to keep to the point. You are the Chairman and you have to interrupt the speakers. Listen to these examples.

So he asked me what I thought of the new policy manual and I said . . .
I'm afraid we must keep to the agenda. We're discussing the training budget, not the policy manual.

And I've heard that there is to be a new Head of Personnel. Apparently he . . .
I'm afraid we must keep to the agenda. We're discussing staffing levels, not the Head of Personnel.

Now you go on in the same way. Look at the agenda. (Begin with item 3.)

1 the training budget
2 staffing levels
3 overtime payments
4 absenteeism
5 the sales report
6 staff suggestions
7 the Middle East contract
8 the trade fair

9 Innovation for industry

Every year the *Observer* newspaper organizes a competition to encourage and support new ideas. Divide into small groups, choose a chairman and discuss the relative merits of each of the ideas below. The following points should be considered when evaluating the entries:

1 originality of the idea
2 potential market
3 capital investment required
4 labour and production costs
5 development potential
6 feasibility of mass production

Here are some of the ideas entered for the competition:

1 A door phone with hidden camera and video screen. Visitors can be seen and identified before opening door. Visitors can also be filmed and recorded on tape.

2 Computer which responds to speech defects. Invaluable for teaching the deaf and handicapped to speak normally.

3 Plastic pipe lines. Unaffected by extremes of temperature, bacteria, corrosion. Can be adapted to carry water, oil, gas, cables, under or over the ground.

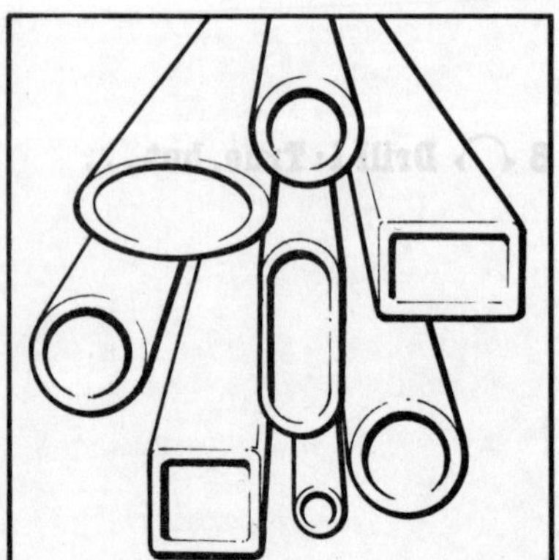

4 Burglar alarm small enough to fit on personal items – handbags, suitcases, radios, for example.

5 Vibrating pads which can be fitted to seats of office workers, long distance drivers, and so on, to prevent stiffness and muscular pain.

6 Miniature satellite dish to receive TV transmissions from all over the world. Small enough to fit on the top of standard TV set.

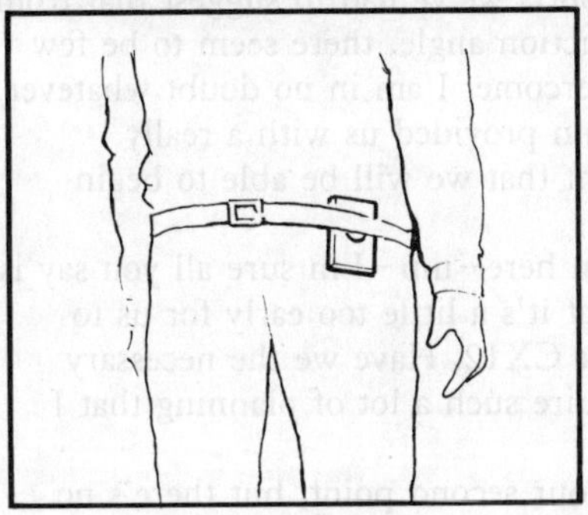

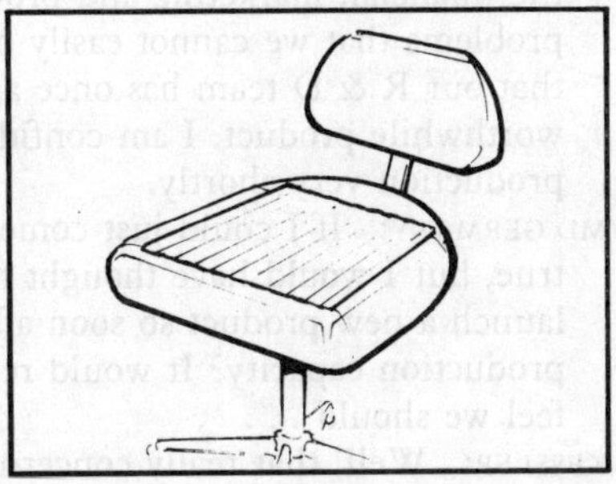

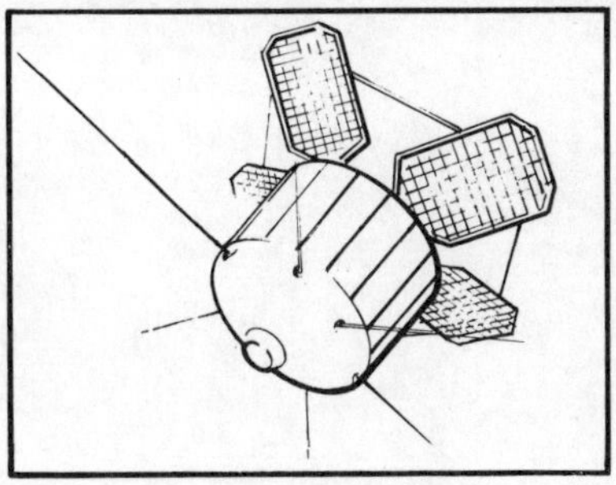

10 Report writing

After the Fittenwell meeting, a report is written to inform other members of the Board of Directors and Heads of Department of the decisions taken.

Some points to remember:

(i) An impersonal or passive form of the verb is used in preference to *we.*

It was decided that production should commence in January.
Doubts were expressed about the size of the market in Spain.
There was some disagreement about . . .

(ii) Unless the full details of the discussions are to be given, the discussion can be summarized and only the final decision recorded.

After lengthy/some/heated discussion, it was eventually/finally decided to begin production early next year.
Despite some opposition from the Italian and Spanish members, Herr Kessler's proposal was accepted.

Complete this report on the first two parts of the meeting, using one of the words or phrases below in each space.

confidence	doubts were expressed
amount of research	it was finally decided
the new X-ray equipment	it was agreed
in February	manufacturing subsidiaries
some disagreement	production capacity
difference of opinion	put into production

1 The first question to be decided was whether (1) . . . . . should be (2) . . . . . or not. Herr Kessler expressed his (3) . . . . . in the new product and although some (4) . . . . . about (5) . . . . . and the (6) . . . . . carried out, (7) . . . . . that production should start (8) . . . . . .

2 There was a considerable (9) . . . . . on the question of which of the (10) . . . . . should produce the equipment. There was (11) . . . . . about how many subsidiaries should be involved in production, but (12) . . . . . to start production in Switzerland and to review the situation after a few months.

Now write a brief paragraph on your discussion of the third point.

Tapescript for step 1

Tape section 54

KESSLER: Ladies and gentlemen, welcome to Geneva. As you know we have a number of questions to settle at this meeting. You'll all have an opportunity to express your points of view, and let me assure you that your opinions will be given the greatest consideration. On point one, may I just say that all the reports we've had in suggest that from the financial, marketing and production angle, there seem to be few problems that we cannot easily overcome. I am in no doubt whatever that our R & D team has once again provided us with a really worthwhile product. I am confident that we will be able to begin production very shortly.

MD GERMANY: If I could just come in here – um – I'm sure all you say is true, but I would have thought that it's a little too early for us to launch a new product so soon after CX12. Have we the necessary production capacity? It would require such a lot of planning that I feel we should . . .

KESSLER: Well, that really concerns our second point, but there's no doubt in my mind that there is a considerable potential market. We have carried out extensive market research, both in Europe and abroad, and the results are so positive, that we are in favour of starting production immediately. Do any of you have any strong views on the subject?

MD FRANCE: Well, from our point of view, it will certainly fulfill a need – but has sufficient research been carried out? I believe there were some set-backs during trials of the prototype.

KESSLER: Yes, that's true, but they have all been satisfactorily ironed out, and personally I don't think it would be worth delaying production any further.

Tapescript for step 3

Tape section 55

MD ITALY: Well, I accept that, but aren't there going to be problems on the technical side? I mean this new equipment has been developed entirely at the plant in Switzerland. If we are to produce it there would have to be considerable consultation.

KESSLER: Yes, indeed – there is certainly a case for limiting production to our Swiss plant. Would anyone like to comment on that?

MD SPAIN: I'm afraid I can't agree. Since we stopped production of the C219 we've had considerable spare capacity and we're counting on the new product to fill the gap – otherwise we'll almost certainly have to make a number of men redundant and that could well lead to industrial unrest – which is something we're very anxious to avoid.

MD UK: That may be true but are you confident that the Spanish market is large enough to warrant production on a large scale? I was wondering whether it wouldn't be better to concentrate on perhaps two areas just at first . . .

MD FRANCE: Yes, but on the other hand if market research has shown that there is considerable interest in the product we should take advantage of that by making it widely available.

MD GERMANY: I'd go along with that though I'm not entirely convinced that we should involve all our production plants in the project from the beginning.

MD ITALY: Just what I was thinking. It's my view that we should start production here in Switzerland and then extend to France, Germany and possibly Spain – those plants that have the spare capacity – after six months or so . . .

KESSLER: So that's settled then. Shall we move on now to our third point – the proposed UK plant?

24 Tell me why

There are 11 steps in Unit 24. You will:

- practise asking for and giving reasons
- link statements using connecting words
- write a report and make recommendations
- deal with the problem of falling profits in a public company

1 Why have sales gone down?

Within the Marketing Department at Fittenwell there is a small section which deals solely with regular customers' accounts. It is their job to investigate any significant drop in orders from such customers.

Listen to Paul Karim, Project Manager, reporting to the Sales Manager on three of his recent visits – to the Central London Hospital Purchasing Officer, the British Doctors' Council and the Ministry of Health of an African State. Note down the reasons he was given for the drop in sales.

2 Asking for reasons

When we ask the reason for something we can simply introduce our question with *why.* Here are some other ways of asking for reasons, especially when things are not going well.

How do you account for the sharp drop in sales?
What led to this state of affairs?
How is it that our competitors have announced a far higher turnover?

If we consider that there is only *one* reason we can reply in a number of ways.

Profits fell for the simple reason that sales dropped.
The reason for the drop in sales is low productivity.
The decline in production was caused by low morale among the work force.
Increased demand led to a shortage of raw materials.
We buy your products because they are the best.
We buy your products because of their high quality.

Principal(ly), main(ly) or chief(ly) are added when giving the main but not the sole reason.

We buy your products chiefly because of their high quality.
This was mainly due to foreign competition.
The principal reason was low productivity.

When there is one main reason you may also wish to speculate on additional reasons.

Bad management may have been a contributory factor.
Poor after-sales service might have had something to do with it.
One possible reason for this is insufficient investment.

3 This is the reason

Look at the notes you made while listening to Fittenwell's Project Manager reporting on his visits. Decide which of the reasons the customers gave were the principal ones, and which were less important. Then make sentences summarizing the reasons given using *chiefly because of* and *may have been contributory factors.* For example:

GM have reduced their orders chiefly because of a cut in their budget, but Asprax's marketing campaign and our production delays may have been contributory factors.

4 All is not lost

The three customers Paul Karim visited have, in part at least, found alternative sources of supply, but all had something positive to say about Fittenwell's products. He feels that they could be persuaded to increase their orders. Listen to the second part of Paul's report. For each of the three customers, note down the positive comments they made, their alternative sources of supply and Paul's recommendations.

5 Connectors

When we support one statement with another we can link the two using *and, what is more, in addition,* and, more formally, *furthermore.*

He is incompetent and, what is more, he is always late.
The quality is good and the price is reasonable.
The pay is excellent and, in addition, there are many fringe benefits.
The quality has deteriorated and, furthermore, the price has risen.

If one statement is in contrast or opposition to another we use *but, although, nevertheless, in spite of, despite (the fact that), however, even though.* Notice that *even though, although, despite (the fact that),* and *in spite of* introduce the contrasting statement; while *but, nevertheless* and *however* introduce the main one.

Although the quality is good, I feel the price is rather high.
The quality is good, but the price is rather high.
Despite the excellent pay, I cannot accept the job.
The pay is excellent. Nevertheless, I cannot accept the job.
In spite of his bad temper, he's an excellent worker.
He is very bad tempered. However, he's an excellent worker.

When one statement is made as a result or logical consequence of another we use *(and) so, therefore* or *consequently.* These last two are more formal.

He is always late, so I feel we should dismiss him.
Price seems the most important factor. Therefore I suggest we revise our pricing policy.
Mr Jones has the highest qualifications and a very impressive record, consequently I am happy to announce his appointment as our new Marketing Manager.

6 Positive thinking

Go back to your notes on the second part of Paul's report.

1 Each customer made two positive comments. Link them using *and in addition . . .*
2 Each customer has, however, found an alternative supplier. Make a sentence for each and link it to the sentences in (1) using *nevertheless . . .*
3 One of the reasons given by each customer for the decline in the orders from Fittenwell was more important than the other two (see step 3). From these principal reasons, Paul made certain recommendations to the company suggesting how Fittenwell could regain these lost orders. Link the customers' principal reasons with Paul's recommendations using *the main reason for* and *consequently.* For example:

The main reason for the drop in sales to chemists appears to be the unpleasant side effects of Vinacyn. Consequently I recommend carrying out further research on this drug.

Taken together, the sentences you have made summarize clearly the Project Manager's report on his visit: the problem areas, the positive elements and a suggested solution.

7 The tax office

In small groups, discuss the following problem. Consider possible reasons for the situation and decide which is the main one. Are there any positive aspects? What recommendations would you make? Invent any details which you feel would be useful. Finally, summarize your discussion and conclusion using Paul's report as a model, and compare your version with that of the other groups.

Place A busy department of the Inland Revenue (tax office) in a large industrial town.

People Employees: average length of service 12 months, high turnover of staff, average age 23, average take-home pay £75 per week, office frequently under-staffed.
Manager: 28 years in the department, age 56, suffers from stomach ulcer, salary £10,500 per annum.
Public: a cross-section of the population.

Background In recent years a recession has affected the area's traditional industries. Many now unemployed or on short time working. The only booming industry is entertainment. A higher than average number of pop stars live in the town's fashionable suburbs.

Problem Low morale and high absenteeism among staff; frequent complaints from the public about rudeness and inefficiency on the part of the department's employees.

8 Drill 1: Mainly due to ...

You are Export Sales Manager. Generally, results for the last twelve months were less good than the previous year. Use the cuesheet to explain last year's results. Listen to these examples.

Now then, Smith, apart from a couple of areas, results this year have been pretty poor, wouldn't you agree?
Well, the decline in sales in France was mainly due to competition from Italy, but anti-British feeling might have had something to do with it.
But in Germany we seem to have done quite well – why is this?
Well, the increase in sales in Germany was mainly due to the favourable exchange rate, but last year's advertising campaign might have had something to do with it.

Now, using the notes, go on in the same way.

Country	*Percentage change last year*	*Reasons (1)*	*Reasons (2)*
France	down 6%	competition from Italy	anti-British feeling
Germany	up 3%	favourable exchange rate	last year's advertising campaign
Italy	up 9%	devaluation of lira	our excellent new agent
Japan	down 8%	difficulty in obtaining import licences	language barrier
Scandinavia	down 5%	illness amongst our sales staff	strength of the pound
Spain	up 15%	two Government contracts	our reputation for quality products
North Africa	down 10%	unsettled political situation	arrest of our local agent
USA	down 12%	general economic recession	poor after-sales service

Drill 2: An exciting life

Listen to Natasha Kydd, a well-known journalist, being interviewed about her job.

I suppose most people would consider your life a very exciting one.
Yes, it is very exciting, and what is more it is very well paid.

And the people you meet – some of them are very wealthy.
Yes, but although they are very wealthy, they are not usually very happy.

I see. Are you sometimes in dangerous situations?
Yes, I am sometimes in dangerous situations and consequently I always carry a gun.

Now you go on in the same way. The interviewer's notes will help you (begin at number 4). You are Natasha.

1 *job*: very exciting/very well paid
2 *people*: very wealthy/not usually very happy
3 *situations*: dangerous/always carry a gun
4 *gun*: have used it/have never killed anyone
5 *president interview*: hands were shaking/dropped my tape recorder
6 *president*: was startled/continued talking quite calmly
7 *hobbies*: pilot my own helicopter/drive racing cars
8 *future plans*: am very rich/am giving up my job at the end of the year

9 Musicbox plays a sad song

Read the following article about Musicbox, a British manufacturer of hi-fi equipment.

Two years ago Musicbox was making a profit of close to £25m, had £27m of cash in the bank and was investing heavily in new plant to boost its hi-fi equipment output by up to 45 per cent. Yesterday it announced that this year's profits had slumped from £17.2m to £10.3m and the £9m cash balances at the end of last year had been transformed into a £3m overdraft. To make matters worse this sharp downturn was not due to strikes, as it was four years ago, but occurred during one of the biggest postwar spending booms. If Musicbox cannot make hefty profits under these conditions, when can it?

Musicbox, deservedly, has a reputation of being a financially strong and well-managed company. Only two years ago its finance director publicly stated that he saw no reason why the company could not continue to increase its dividends by the statutory maximum. However, Musicbox has now cut its dividends by roughly a sixth, and the shares have dropped by 15p to 164p, where they yield 9.2 per cent.

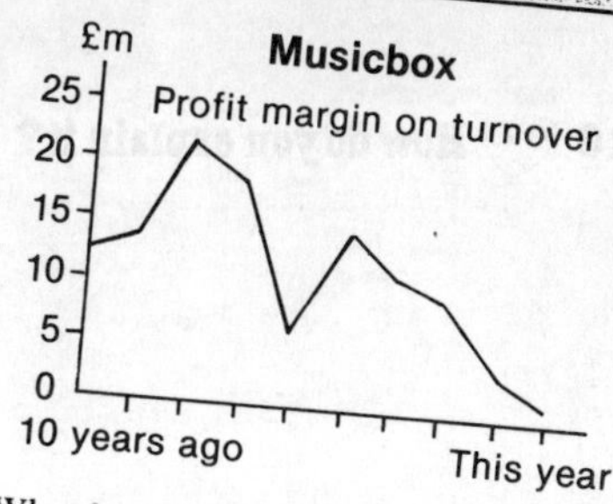

What has gone wrong is that last year Musicbox costs rose 11 per cent but its prices rose by 7 per cent, while competition from Japanese imported hi-fi equipment (roughly half the UK market) led to a further fall in market share. No other major European market has such a high import penetration. Whereas French and German producers are to some extent protected because of the local bias towards high priced quality products, here in Britain consumers seem to be much more interested in the low priced imports against which Musicbox has no hope of competing. If this trend continues Britain's hi-fi industry may well disappear.

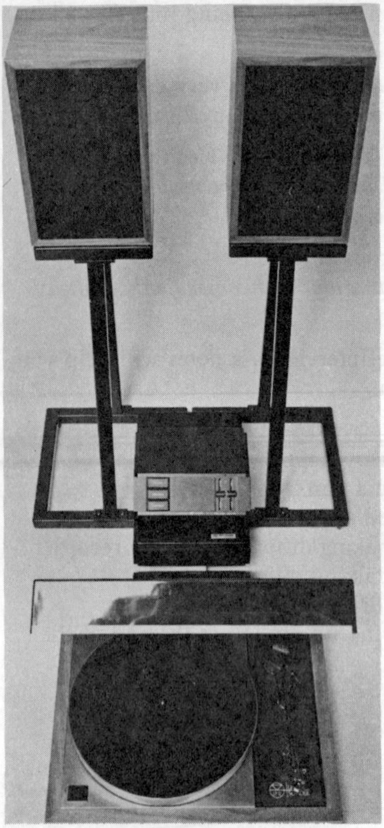

Now decide whether the following statements are true or false, according to the information in the article.

		True	*False*
1	Two years ago Musicbox had boosted output by 45%.	☐	☐
2	Musicbox cash balance had decreased from £9m last year to £3m by the end of this year.	☐	☐
3	This change in Musicbox fortunes is all the more surprising as it happened while consumer spending was at a peak.	☐	☐
4	Industrial unrest was a contributory factor in Musicbox decline.	☐	☐
5	The confident statement of the Musicbox finance director two years ago seemed justified at the time.	☐	☐
6	The main reason for the drop in Musicbox share prices was the massive cut in the dividend.	☐	☐
7	It was the disproportion between the increase in costs and the increase in prices that was the principal cause of the drop in market share.	☐	☐
8	Manufacturers in other European countries are protected against cheaper imports by locally biased import quotas.	☐	☐

10 How do you explain it?

Divide into two groups – Musicbox shareholders and Musicbox directors. The worried and angry shareholders have demanded a meeting to question the company's recent performance; the directors will try to explain and justify their poor results and offer hope for the future. One student in each group should take notes of the directors' explanations and of any suggestions for improving the company's fortunes.

Before the meeting, the directors should read the notes printed below. The shareholders will find notes printed at the end of the Unit.

Directors

Before the meeting, try to predict what questions the shareholders will ask. Prepare answers to these questions and agree on proposals for redressing the company's fortunes. For example:

—what can be done to cut costs
—plans for major modernization and streamlining of production
—closure of unprofitable sectors of the company
—marketing drive in Europe
—advertising campaign in the UK

11 Report writing

Write a brief report on the meeting (step 10). Use the report on Paul Karim's visits to customers as a model.

Tapescript for step 1

Tape section 57

SALES MANAGER: Now tell me about those three accounts that were worrying us. You went to see them all, I believe?

PAUL KARIM: Yes, well, the first one I went to see – last Friday that was – was the Central London Hospital Purchasing Officer. He just started straight off by saying that their budget had been cut by 20% this year, and obviously this was a very real constraint.

SALES MANAGER: Yes, but although their budget's been cut they still have to purchase essential equipment from somewhere, I suppose.

PAUL KARIM: Quite, so I asked him if any other factors had contributed to the fall in their order from us and he mumbled something about our delivery dates being somewhat unreliable – apparently they had to wait six weeks for delivery of two F12 microscopes, and just toward the end of our talk, he mentioned, almost as an afterthought, the fact that our list prices had risen by 12% over the last year.

SALES MANAGER: And you got the impression that this was really the critical factor?

PAUL KARIM: Yes, I'm sure it's a question of pricing rather than anything else.

SALES MANAGER: Right, now the British Doctors' Council, what did you find out there?

PAUL KARIM: Well, I spoke to a member of their advisory committee. Now he also started off by mentioning prices – all their members have apparently had strict instructions from the Ministry to prescribe the cheapest available drugs – but I didn't feel that this was really the main issue, because he immediately went on, and in fact, talked at some length, about certain unpleasant side-effects caused by Vinacyn. As you know this has always been our best-selling antibiotic and I think it's the drop in sales of Vinacyn that is the principal reason for the downturn in pharmaceutical sales.

SALES MANAGER: I see, mmm, that could be very important. Did he mention anything else?

PAUL KARIM: Well yes, he mentioned the new analgesic Medax have just brought out, which has certainly been selling well, and might have had some influence on the fall in our market share. But I'm convinced the side effects of Vinacyn is the main problem.

SALES MANAGER: Mmm, that could be a really sticky one.

PAUL KARIM: Anyway my last appointment this week was with Mr Ngoma of the Ministry of Health.

SALES MANAGER: Yes. How is it that sales to his country have dropped so sharply? Was he able to throw any light on the matter?

PAUL KARIM: Yes, well actually he was most informative. He started by giving me a brief outline of their economic problems – one possible cause of the decline seems to be their large and increasing trade deficit, which means that all foreign imports have been reduced, and drugs are no exception. Another factor is the recent expansion of their own national pharmaceutical company, Napharco, it's called. It's now able to meet a growing proportion of their needs. But what really seems to be their main worry, and I'm sure the real reason behind the drop in orders, is their great anxiety about the sales by European and American companies, of drugs which may be dangerous. You know all the publicity there has been recently about drugs banned in America or Europe, being sold under other brand names, in Asia and Africa.

SALES MANAGER: So they are simply reducing to the minimum all imports from foreign pharmaceutical companies.

PAUL KARIM: That's certainly the impression I got.

Tapescript for step 4

Tape section 58

PAUL KARIM: So you can see all three have very real problems and as a result we've lost orders, and, I'm afraid, other suppliers have benefited. For example, I hear the BDC are advising doctors to prescribe Tanacyn, a Medax antibiotic, instead of our Vinacyn, although their purchasing manager did say that in 99% of cases Vinacyn was more effective. He also complimented Fittenwell on our information service to doctors, but they are just so worried about these side-effects.

SALES MANAGER: Yes, I can understand that.

PAUL KARIM: And, of course, Mr Ngoma's Ministry are using their locally produced drugs as far as possible. However, he did emphasize that Fittenwell has an excellent reputation in his country and that compared with our main competitors, our prices are reasonable.

SALES MANAGER: Have you any idea how we could improve our position there?

PAUL KARIM: Well, I'm convinced that what's needed is a really thorough information service to counteract the adverse publicity western countries have had. Invite a group of their health officials to visit our laboratories, send the fullest reports on all our research – that kind of thing.

SALES MANAGER: Yes, that seems sensible. What about the BDC?

PAUL KARIM: Well, there I think we should do more research on the side-effects of Vinacyn. It may be that quite a minor change would eliminate them.

SALES MANAGER: It's not as simple as you seem to think, but we'll have to give it some more thought.

PAUL KARIM: Yes, well that's up to the medical department isn't it? As far as our laboratory equipment is concerned, the Hospitals' Purchasing Officer admitted that they were now buying more from Sunlab than us, in spite of what he called the 'technical superiority' of our equipment and our excellent after sales service. I don't think it should be too difficult to regain our position there, just a question of cutting our profit margin slightly.

SALES MANAGER: Just a question of cutting our profit margin! Do you realize how much time and effort has been spent already . . .

Notes for the shareholders for step 10

Before the meeting, prepare a list of questions to ask the directors. For example:

— How was it that the company suddenly slumped so far during a boom period in consumer spending?
— How can Musicbox win back its market share, both at home and abroad?
— How is it that foreign companies are so much more successful?
— What are the financial directors' proposals for the future?
— What about automation?
— How and where are they planning to cut costs?
— What about advertising/consumer service?

If satisfactory answers are not obtained, insist, rephrase questions, make suggestions, threaten to sack the whole board of directors.

The newspaper article on page 173 provides a number of points which you could raise.

25 That's the way it is

There are 10 steps in Unit 25. You will practise:

- ways of asking whether something is permitted
- prohibiting
- restricting and setting limits
- expressing regrets, recriminations and dissatisfaction

1 It's not allowed – or is it?

There has recently been adverse publicity over the discovery of serious side effects caused by two well-known drugs in Britain. Fittenwell's Head of Public Relations and two members of his department are discussing ideas for a campaign to improve the company image.

Listen to their conversation and note down whether each advertising idea is permitted, prohibited, or only permitted in certain circumstances. The ideas put forward are:

1 Adverts in medical journals
2 TV commercials
3 Cure claims
4 Doctor's recommendation
5 Refund offer

2 Is it allowed?

When enquiring about rules and regulations, we can ask:

Are you allowed to advertise medicines on TV?
Is subliminal advertising allowed?
Can we mention other companies by name in our ads?
Is it possible to say that our drugs are totally effective?

When asking for permission from an individual, we can also ask:

Do you mind if I smoke in here?
May we call on you to discuss our ideas? (formal)

If something is prohibited under the regulations or by law, reply:

It's absolutely forbidden to claim positive cures.
Offering prizes is forbidden.
You're not allowed to exploit children in advertisements.

More informally, and when the prohibition comes from the speaker, you can reply:

You can't smoke in here.
You mustn't mention the price on any account.

Often we want to tell someone that something is not allowed, but wish to avoid using the rather curt and direct forms above. We can use *not supposed,* to suggest that it is not really permitted but that exceptions to the rule are possible.

TV companies are not supposed to show more than six minutes of advertising per hour.

Written prohibitions in public places are generally very direct. The **gerund** is often used.

No parking.
Smoking prohibited.

If something is only permitted on certain conditions, we can say:

That depends on { *whether it is true or not.* / *how much you are willing to spend.* / *when you want it.* }

You can use special effects { *provided* / *as long as* } *they don't give a false impression.*

You can only advertise tobacco if you incorporate a health warning.

3 Advertising standards

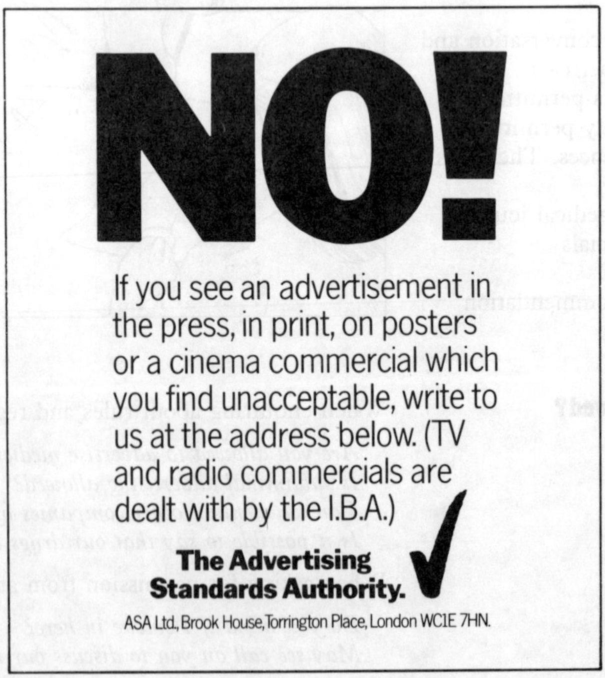

Children should not be seen leaning dangerously out of windows or over bridges, or climbing dangerous cliffs.

Advertisements should not encourage or condone defiance of the law.

No advertisement offering credit should give a telephone number without also giving the name and address of the advertiser.

Marine, etc. Broadcasting (Offences) Act 1967	Prohibits off-shore radio stations and advertisements from and for them.

An open fire in a domestic scene in an advertisement should always have a fireguard clearly visible if a child is included in the scene.

Geneva Convention Act 1957 (S.6)	Forbids unauthorised use of Red Cross or Red Crescent by, inter alia, advertisers.
Civil Aviation (Licensing) Act 1960 (S.7)	Prohibits with certain exceptions (see below) the use of aircraft and balloons for displaying advertisements.
Civil Aviation (Aerial Advertising) Regulations 1971	Permits aircraft and balloons to display an inscription identifying its owner, charterer or manufacturer.

Look at the extracts from the advertising standards applicable in the United Kingdom. This is a voluntary code subscribed to by advertisers.

After reading the extracts, use the forms in step 2 to write about advertising the following:

1 credit
2 off-shore radio
3 Red Cross
4 aircraft
5 children
6 law-breaking
7 open fires

4 Diplomat King Size

Your company is planning to launch a new cigarette on the UK market. The advertising department have so far come up with the following ideas. Discuss them in the light of the Advertising Standards regulations on page 180 and decide what form your campaign should take.

1 Buy twenty 30-second slots on commercial TV.
2 Design a series of posters showing athletes and sportsmen smoking Diplomat King Size for display on street hoardings.
3 Sponsor a sports tournament: snooker, darts, tennis, badminton.
4 Get famous personalities to endorse the cigarette: sports, film, politicians.

Appendix H Advertising of cigarettes, of the components of manufactured cigarettes and of hand-rolling tobacco

Social success

Advertisers should take particular care that their advertisements avoid encouraging people to believe that the habit of smoking, or the smoking of a particular brand, is in any way more closely associated with the rich, the successful or go-ahead than with the rest of the population.

Relaxation and concentration

Advertisements should not depict situations involving nervous strain or emotional pressure in relation to smoking.

People may be depicted in any advertisement as smoking while concentrating on a job (other than a dangerous job) or relaxing in an appropriate setting, provided that the advertisement does not claim directly or indirectly that the cigarette is a necessary aid to concentration or relaxation.

People featured in cigarette advertisements should both be and clearly be seen to be adults of 25 or over.

Claims that people are changing to a particular brand or type of cigarette are permissible, if true, provided this does not imply an increase in smoking generally.

No advertisement should appear in any publication directed wholly or mainly to young people.

Advertisements should not feature heroes of the young.

The depiction of real or fictitious individuals of obvious distinction or authority should be avoided.

Advertisements should not imply that smoking is associated with success in sport. They should not depict people participating in any active sporting pursuit or obviously about to do so or just having done so, or spectators at any organised sporting occasion.

Advertising associated with events sponsored by cigarette manufacturers is subject to separate rules.

N.B. No cigarette advertising is accepted on television.

5 The general approach of the campaign should link a successful career with Diplomat cigarettes.
6 Issue sales figures to show how popular Diplomat King Size cigarettes are compared with other brands.
7 'Spontaneous' interviews with the 'man in the street' – businessmen, housewives, young mothers – saying how smoking Diplomat King Size reduces stress and helps them cope with problems.

5 I told you so

Ambermold has just learned that it has been beaten by a rival firm in its efforts to obtain a very large and lucrative contract in the Middle East. Naturally everyone involved is feeling very disappointed.

Listen to the discussion and note down whether the following statements are true or false.

	True	*False*
1 They spent a lot of time studying the tender specifications.	☐	☐
2 They did not contact any officials from the Ministry of Industry.	☐	☐
3 They completed the tender documents in time.	☐	☐
4 They met the criteria for evaluation of the bids.	☐	☐
5 They lowered their profit margin to the minimum.	☐	☐
6 They did not realize how fierce the competition would be.	☐	☐
7 A serious error was made in costing.	☐	☐
8 They budgeted for top quality materials.	☐	☐
9 They have plenty of time to prepare the Canadian bid.	☐	☐

6 Regrets and recriminations

Past

When you regret something that happened in the past or blame someone for what has gone wrong, you can use *I wish* + **past perfect** tense.

I wish we had spent more time studying the specifications.

If only + **past perfect** is also possible.

If only we hadn't made that error in costing.

When we want to say how different the situation would have been in the past, or would be now if some other action had been taken, we use the **third conditional** form.

If we had contacted officials from the Ministry, we would/might have won the contract.

This means that in fact we *did not contact* the officials and therefore we *did not win* the contract.

If we had won the contract, the future of the company would be assured.

Here, we did not win the contract so the future of the company is not now assured.

In formal, particularly written, English *if* + **past perfect** can be replaced by *had* + subject + **past participle.**

Had you contacted officials from the Ministry, we might have won the contract.
Had we won the contract, the future of the company would be assured.

Present

When you would like a present situation to be different, you use the **past simple** or **past continuous** tense after *wish* and *if only.*

I wish I didn't have to spend so much time on paper work.
If only we had a larger budget.
I wish it wasn't raining.

These examples are saying that, in fact, I spend a lot of time on paper work and I do not enjoy it; that we have a budget which I consider too small; and that it is in fact raining now and I don't like it.

Future

Wish/if only + *would* + **infinitive** is used to express the desire for an unsatisfactory present situation to change in the future.

I wish it would stop raining.
If only they would answer our letters.

Notice that we use *hope* + *will* + **infinitive** when talking about a specific future event and are not expressing dissatisfaction with the present.

I hope the new product will be a success.

7 Problems of an advertising agency

Here are some of the problems – past, present and future – of an advertising agency. Express your dissatisfaction with each situation beginning *I wish* or *if only*:

1 We've just lost the Ambermold contract to another agency.
2 IGM are not going to renew their contract with us.
3 Our best designer left us last month.
4 Every firm seems to be cutting its advertising budget.
5 The rates for TV commercials are going up.
6 My secretary never stops complaining about how much she has to do.
7 We need bigger offices but cannot afford to move.
8 I need more time to complete the Global Motors campaign, but I don't think they'll extend their deadline.

8 Drill 1: Yes or no?

Before going on a marketing trip to Eastern Europe, Mr Grayson is enquiring about regulations that apply to visiting businessmen. Look at the notes and listen to these examples:

Now first of all, are you allowed to import a typewriter? I always like to type my own reports.
Yes, you can import a typewriter provided that you declare it to the customs authorities.

Right, then a friend of mine gave me about £20 worth of the local currency but I'm not sure if you're allowed to bring it into the country.
No, it's absolutely forbidden to bring local currency into the country.

OK. Then, when I'm there, I've heard they like to deal with all foreign trade through a central organization. Now does this mean I can't contact individual companies?
Well, you're not supposed to contact individual companies.

Now you go on. Use the notes to give the information required. (Begin at number 4.)

Regulations concerning:

1 importing a typewriter	must declare it to customs authorities
2 bringing local currency into the country	absolutely forbidden
3 contacting individual companies	not officially allowed
4 taking a camera	must declare it to customs authorities
5 taking photos	absolutely forbidden near military areas
6 changing foreign currency with private individuals	absolutely forbidden
7 having letters sent care of the British Embassy	must let them know in advance
8 importing foreign newspapers	not officially allowed

Drill 2: It wouldn't have happened if . . .

A colleague of yours is talking about various problems in the company. You feel that these could have been avoided. Listen to these examples.

Management – labour relations are really bad at the moment.
They wouldn't be bad if the Union Representative hadn't been sacked last month.

And productivity dropped by 15% last month.
It wouldn't have dropped if there hadn't been a 'flu epidemic.

Notice that if the problem is now you use *would* or *wouldn't* and the infinitive.

They wouldn't be bad.

And if the problem was in the past you use *would have* or *wouldn't have* and the past participle.

It wouldn't have dropped.

Now you respond in the same way, using the notes. (Begin at number 3.)

1 The Union Representative was sacked last month.
2 There was a 'flu epidemic.
3 We didn't spend enough money on promotions abroad.
4 Management didn't give them a pay rise.
5 The bank didn't extend their loan.
6 We didn't make a high enough profit.
7 Our delivery date was not early enough.
8 The Board of Directors didn't adopt the working party's proposals.

9 Why did it go wrong?

A marketing campaign in the UK to launch a new over-the-counter drug, 'Asbrom', a cough syrup developed by Fittenwell's research team, has not met with the success expected by Fittenwell's top management. A meeting has been called to discuss what went wrong.

Divide into two groups, the Fittenwell overseas division managers and the Fittenwell UK marketing team. Discuss the problem and decide how a similar situation could be avoided in the future.

Fittenwell UK marketing team

Your information is at the end of the Unit.

Fittenwell overseas division managers

You feel the campaign failed for the following reasons:

1 There was no TV advertising.
2 The campaign began in the summer when demand for cough syrup is low.
3 A rival company brought out a similar drug shortly before the campaign.
4 The advertisements did not emphasize the important new research Fittenwell had carried out.
5 There was no advertising in the North of England or Scotland.
6 Doctors and pharmacists were not invited to a special presentation of the new drug.
7 The price was too high.

Add to this list, and put these points to the UK marketing team.

10 A strongly worded letter

A recent, very costly advertising campaign to launch 'Kornpuff', a new brand of breakfast cereal in Britain, has proved a disaster. Write a letter from the Marketing Manager to the Brand Manager responsible for commissioning the campaign, to express the company's dissatisfaction with his performance. Point out the positive results he would have obtained if he had:

1 chosen a more imaginative advertising agency.
2 defined the target market more accurately.
3 insisted on the agency keeping to the agreed budget.

4 used more suitable media (for example, women's magazines, *not* the serious daily newspapers).

End the letter on a positive note: you hope that this experience will make him more aware of the problems and ensure the success of future campaigns.

Tapescript for step 1

Tape section 60

HEAD OF PR: Right, John. I gather you've some ideas for our PR campaign. Let's hear some of them.

FIRST ASSISTANT: Well, first we must win over the medical profession, so I thought we should launch a campaign in all the specialist medical journals – to promote our prescription drugs, antibiotics and so on.

SECOND ASSISTANT: Yes, that's a good idea.

FIRST ASSISTANT: Then TV commericals.

SECOND ASSISTANT: Just a moment, are you sure we're allowed to advertise medicines on TV?

HEAD OF PR: Oh yes, provided they are not drugs which need a prescription. You can advertise over-the-counter products.

FIRST ASSISTANT: Then I thought we could get users of our products to endorse them – 'Fittenwell's lotion cured my rheumatism in six days', for example.

HEAD OF PR: Now, hold on. It's forbidden to claim any positive cure for a disease. And we mustn't offer any drugs for illnesses which should be treated by a doctor.

FIRST ASSISTANT: Mmm. OK. What about this – a series of full page newspaper ads with the message that most doctors consider our products the best.

SECOND ASSISTANT: Mmm, that depends on whether it's true. We can only refer to doctors' preferences if our claim is supported by facts and figures.

FIRST ASSISTANT: Well, I'm sure it is. But here's another suggestion. We could offer to refund the purchase price to anyone who's dissatisfied with one of our products. It's possible to do that, isn't it?

HEAD OF PR: No, I'm afraid not. Manufacturers of medicinal products are not allowed to offer a refund in their ads.

FIRST ASSISTANT: Well, it looks as though I'll have to come up with something else. I never realized the regulations were so rigid . . .

Tapescript for step 5

Tape section 61

— I can't deny I'm very disappointed. I really thought we'd win that contract.

— Well, I'm not really all that surprised. I said at the time we were a little over-confident.

— Yes, I agree – we made a number of mistakes. I wish we'd spent a little more time studying the specifications on the tender documents. Our offer just didn't meet their requirements closely enough.

— Yes, and if we had only known how many other companies were competing for the contract we would have lowered our profit margin a little more – we could have done that quite easily.

— Yes, and I did say, we should have contacted officials from their Ministry of Industry. That's the way to do things, through personal contacts.
— So you think if we'd done that we'd have won the contract?
— Well, I think we might have done. After all we completed all the tender documents within the time limit and we certainly fulfilled all the bid requirements for the contract – financial guarantees, insurance and so on.
— Of course, the main reason I'm sure was that error we made in costing. If only we hadn't budgeted for top quality materials throughout, and allowed for 20% inflation. That really was our worst mistake.
— Yes, well, I think we've all learnt a lot from it. We've been asked to prepare another bid for the Canadian contract so let's hope we'll have better luck there. There's just one problem . . .
— What's that?
— The closing date – it's next Wednesday. I wish we had a little more time!

Fittenwell UK marketing team's information for step 9

You feel you were not altogether to blame for the failure of 'Asbrom' for the following reasons:

1 The budget was too low.
2 The UK licensing authority does not allow a drug to go on the market before it has conducted its own test.
3 TV advertising costs were too high for your budget.
4 You were not informed about the rival company's product (although Fittenwell headquarters knew about it in advance).
5 The recommended retail price was decided by headquarters, not by Fittenwell UK.
6 You were not allowed to use the Fittenwell stand at the Edinburgh Trade Fair to promote 'Asbrom'. HQ needed all the space for other products.

26 Keep the customer satisfied

There are 10 steps in Unit 26. You will practise:

- requests and offers
- the use of the gerund
- reported speech
- listening, reading and note-taking
- giving opinions
- talking about obligations and necessity
- making arrangements

1 Can we do it?

The small technical sales team at Fittenwell installs, maintains and services Fittenwell equipment in hospitals and clinics all over the world. Recent cutbacks in personnel are making their job difficult and Otto Klaus, Technical Sales Manager, is having problems meeting the requests of his overseas clients. He is now talking to two members of his department – Peter Rittman (who is responsible for the Middle East and Africa) and Claud Harz (responsible for Northern Europe and America). Peter Rittman is to visit two clients: JX Imports in Jeddah, and Hospital Supplies in Johannesburg. Claud Harz is to visit three clients: HMB in Buenos Aires, Central State Hospital in Montreal, and Medicaid in London.

Listen to part of their meeting to discuss overseas visits for the month of May, and note down the following information:

1 Dates requested by the clients.
2 Dates on which Peter Rittman and Claud Harz are not available.
3 The reasons given for 2 above.

2 The best we can do (1)

Using your notes from step 1, work out a time schedule for the two sales engineers to cover all the visits; keep as close as possible to the dates suggested by the clients, while respecting the engineers' previous arrangements.

3 The gerund

Both the gerund and the infinitive can be used as verbs and can be followed by a direct or indirect object.

It will be impossible to satisfy the customers' requirements exactly.
Meeting their requirements is going to be very difficult.
Cutting overheads has meant reducing staff levels in all departments.
I don't like making excuses to clients.

After certain verbs the gerund is always used. These verbs include *enjoy, detest, mean, mind.*

I enjoy working in this department.
I detest having complaints from customers.
This probably means working overtime.
Do you mind shutting the window?

The gerund is also used after certain expressions.

It's no use/good complaining about the situation.
I can't help thinking that it was the wrong decision.

The gerund is also used after prepositions.

We'll have difficulty in working out a schedule.
I look forward to hearing your report.

It is sometimes difficult to decide whether *to* is a preposition or part of the infinitive. If a noun can be used after *to* the gerund form of the verb must be used.

I am used to { problems like this. / dealing with problems.   *I look forward to { meeting you. / our meeting.*

Some verbs can be followed by a gerund or an infinitive according to the meaning of the sentence.

I stopped smoking two years ago.
After two hours' hard work I stopped to smoke a cigarette.

I remember meeting you last year in Paris.
I remembered to post your letter.

He regretted changing his job.
I regret to say your work is most unsatisfactory.

I like swimming.
I like to have a medical check-up every year.

They tried to find the answer to the problem.
If you feel sleepy, try going for a brisk walk, that should wake you up!

4 Letter to a friend

Put the verbs in brackets in either the gerund or the infinitive form.

Dear Bob,

I'm sorry I haven't written before. I tried (1 *get*) you at the office yesterday morning, but your secretary said she didn't want (2 *disturb*) your meeting. You seem (3 *be*) at meetings a lot. Do you really enjoy (4 *waste*) your time like that? I find it's usually not worth (5 *attend*) meetings, but it's no use (6 *say*) that to my boss. He finds it impossible to (7 *take*) even the smallest decision without (8 *consult*) everyone in the department. This means (9 *spend*) at least an hour every day (10 *attend*) boring meetings. I can't help (11 *feel*) our time could be more usefully employed. I'm just not used to (12 *work*) in this way. I sometimes regret (13 *take*) this job.

Well, I must stop (14 *complain*). I'm really writing (15 *tell*) you that I've had some difficulty in (16 *find*) a book called *Boat Maintenance* by S. Field. I know you're interested in (17 *sail*) and I remember (18 *hear*) you say you had a number of books on the subject, and wondered if you could help. I've tried (19 *ask*) various friends but no one seems (20 *know*) it.

I look forward to (21 *hear*) from you.

All the best,
John

5 Complications

Otto sent each of the technical sales department's clients a telex to say when his engineers would be arriving and to request confirmation that these dates were acceptable. He soon hears from M. Labarre, of Central State Hospital, Montreal. Note down the details of his response to the telex.

6 More trouble

Soon after, a letter arrived from Hospital Supplies, Fittenwell's major importer in Johannesburg, and a telex from their client in Jeddah. You will find the telex at the end of the Unit. The text of the letter is reproduced here.

Work with a partner and read one of these each. Then exchange your information. Remember to use the correct forms of reported speech.

Dear Mr Klaus,

I refer to your telex no. 1322 informing us that your sales engineer will be unable to call on the dates we requested. This is not the first time that this problem has arisen and while we understand the difficulties we must insist on our original dates.

We are, as you are aware, one of the major African importers of your products. However, if the standard of your after-sales service were to decline, we may be forced to reconsider our position.

We look forward to your early reply.

Yours sincerely,

Derek Piet

7 Worse to come

Otto Klaus calls another meeting to discuss these developments. Just before the meeting he hears an item of news on the radio. Make a note of what will happen at UK airports, and the dates mentioned.

8 Drill 1: There's absolutely no question . . .

Rumours are circulating about drastic cuts being made in the company. You give very positive reassurance to the Trade Union representative. Listen to these examples:

We are all extremely worried, Mr Brown. There are rumours that you're planning to make 200 redundant.
No, there's absolutely no question of making 200 redundant.

And it's said our goods are too expensive. We've heard you intend to use lower quality materials.
No, there's absolutely no question of using lower quality materials.

Now you go on in the same way.

Drill 2: There's no alternative . . .

You are due to leave this afternoon on a business trip, visiting Frankfurt, then Berlin. You have just heard that bad weather has closed down Frankfurt airport. Listen to these examples:

I'm afraid your trip to Frankfurt will have to be postponed.
Yes, it seems there's no alternative but to postpone my trip to Frankfurt.

And the meeting this evening will have to be cancelled.
Yes, it seems there's no alternative but to cancel the meeting this evening.

Now you go on in the same way.

9 The best we can do (2)

In view of the serious problems that have arisen, the sales engineers, Peter Rittman and Claud Harz, offer to rearrange their May commitments. Listen to their proposals, then write down all the factors to consider when drawing up the final schedule for the month; these include the identity of the clients, the dates requested, and the engineers' availability.

Divide into small groups. Your aim is to satisfy all your clients as far as possible, while at the same time respecting the engineers' commitments. If it is necessary for the engineers to make sacrifices, suggest a way of recompensing them for their devotion to duty.

10 We are pleased to be able to tell you . . .

Write a letter to one of the clients, informing him of the date of the engineer's visit. Make sure that the client realizes that your department has gone to considerable inconvenience to meet his requirements. Expressions which convey this are:

In view of the urgency, we have rearranged our schedule to meet your requirements.

Our engineer, Mr Rittman, has agreed to alter his holiday arrangements in order to . . .

The final sentence should show that you expect the client to agree:

We trust that these dates are convenient.

We look forward to your early confirmation of these dates.

Tapescript for step 1

Tape section 63

OTTO KLAUS: I'm afraid these cutbacks are going to mean a heavier work load for us all. Meeting the customers' requirements is going to be difficult. Let's see how things are for May. Erm, now in your sector, Peter, Middle East and Africa, things don't look too bad. We've just had two calls. JX Imports in Jeddah would like a routine service for their three clients starting on the 12th of May. They reckon you'll have no problem in getting through it all in three days. That means leaving Jeddah on the 15th.

PETER RITTMAN: Yes, but you seem to have forgotten . . .

OTTO KLAUS: And the other one is from our old friends, Hospital Supplies in Johannesburg. They've got several problems, some fairly complex, and suggest the 15th to the 21st of May – giving you almost a week there. You're used to dealing with them so that should be ample . . .

PETER RITTMAN: Sorry to disappoint you, Otto. You obviously didn't remember to make a note of my annual holiday. I'll be sunbathing in Spain from the 1st to the 15th of May.

OTTO KLAUS: Blast, yes, I remember your telling me. Well, let's look at your sector, Claud. We'll sort out the problems later. In Europe there's just one request from Medicaid London. Again for a routine service – on the 30th of May. One day will be enough, they say. Then Montreal, that's the Central State Hospital, asked for a three-day visit – an annual service check and to check the installation of the new body scanner. They'd like you to be there from the 14th to the 17th of May. And finally, HMB in Buenos Aires. Some of their clients have had trouble with our X-ray equipment and they'd like you to do a check on all their main customers at the same time. They say the 10th to the 14th would be the most suitable dates so that would fit in well with the Montreal trip.

CLAUD HARZ: Otto, I don't want to spoil your day, but you'll have to get them to change the dates. My wife's expecting a baby on the 20th of May and you agreed that I needn't do any overseas trips from the 15th to the 30th of May. She's used to being on her own but this is her first so . . .

OTTO KLAUS: Oh, my goodness. We'll have to rethink all this. It's going to be impossible to suit everyone.

Tapescript for step 5

Tape section 64

OTTO KLAUS: Technical Service.

LABARRE: Er, could I speak to Mr Klaus, please?

OTTO KLAUS: Speaking.

LABARRE: Oh good morning. This is Labarre here, Central State Hospital, Montreal. I've just received your telex about the engineer's visit.

OTTO KLAUS: Oh yes.

LABARRE: I'm afraid those dates will have to be changed. We're being inspected by people from our Department of Health in the week beginning the 18th of May, so everything must be absolutely ship-shape by then. And to make things worse, our own technical staff are likely to be on strike the 10th of May for three days so it's not much use your engineer coming then.

OTTO KLAUS: Oh, yes I see your problem, but we're rather short-staffed here and . . .

LABARRE: I'm sure you'll manage, Mr Klaus. We look forward to hearing from you. Bye now.

Tapescript for step 7

Tape section 65

. . . despite talks lasting well into the evening, the two sides have been unable to reach agreement. In a brief statement to the press at 9pm this evening, a representative of the Airport Authority said: 'We regret to inform you that talks have been suspended indefinitely.' A spokesman for the union confirmed that the strike planned for the week beginning 30th May would now certainly take place. This means a total closure of all airports in Britain. The cost is estimated . . .

Tapescript for step 9

Tape section 67

PETER RITTMAN: Look, Otto, I know you don't like having to make excuses to the customer, so if it's any help, I'll change my holiday dates. My wife's not too happy about it, well neither am I really, but it seems there's just no alternative. I've contacted the hotel and they say we can have a fortnight from the 18th of May to the 2nd of June instead of the dates we'd booked. Is this any help?

CLAUD HARZ: And the doctor says the baby's not likely to arrive early so as long as I'm back by the 20th of May I don't mind fitting in with the client's original dates.

OTTO KLAUS: That's very good of you both. I hate messing up your arrangements, though . . . and I don't think that will solve the problem entirely.

Telex for step 6

JEDDAH 12.5

REGRET DATES YOU SUGGEST UNACCEPTABLE. RELIGIOUS FESTIVAL COMMENCES HERE MAY 16 FOR 7 DAYS. MANAGING DIRECTOR IN EUROPE UNTIL MAY 10.

PLEASE DO UTMOST TO FIT IN WITH DATES REQUESTED.

BEST REGARDS

K KARIM

27 Consolidation exercises

There are seven steps in Unit 27, each one consisting of a reading (or interpretation) activity and a writing activity. These will help you revise what you have learned already.

1 Requests and offers

You are visiting Scotland on an exploratory sales visit. How would you:

1 ask your secretary to find out flight and accommodation details?
2 ask the British Embassy to provide information about relevant tax laws?
3 ask someone the time at Glasgow Airport?
4 ask the hotel receptionist if you could move to a quieter room?
5 ask your taxi driver for a receipt?

During your discussion with Alastair Lowrie of Scottish Metal Products Ltd, you realize that you need to make your product more attractive in order to sell it to him. How would you:

1 offer a discount of 12½% on your list price?
2 offer to train operators at no extra charge?
3 offer to tailor the design to SMP's exact specification?
4 offer to send an engineer to supervise installation?
5 invite Mr Lowrie to dinner at a top Glasgow restaurant?

2 A big future

Here is an extract from a booklet about Scottish industry sent to you by the British Embassy:

> Scotland can offer the businessman a wide range of exciting (1) ..... If you're thinking of setting up a manufacturing base overseas, Scotland could be worth a closer look. (2) ..... labour is readily available; land is plentiful *and* cheap; generous Government (3) ..... help cut the cost of your initial (4) ..... And new tax (5) ..... means that more of your profits can be (6) .....
>
> Scotland is just the place for a concerted sales drive. The (7) ..... in the traditional industries (shipbuilding, heavy industry and fishing) has been more than offset by the oil (8) ..... of the last decade, so there's a large market out there, just waiting to be (9) ..... And our Business Information Service can (10) ..... you with full details of any particular industrial (11) ..... you care to name. So contact us soon to find out more about Scotland, a country with a big future.

Exercise

Here are the words missing from the extract. Can you put them in the right place?

Paragraph 1	Paragraph 2
skilled	boom
legislation	sector
opportunities	exploited
grants	decline
repatriated	provide
investment	

3 Needn't have . . .

While you were in Glasgow, you gave a lecture on electroplating at the local polytechnic. Here is part of a letter to your boss about what happened.

Before I started, I offered to distribute some fact sheets about the chemical processes involved, but they already knew all about them. I explained the history of our company, not that they were very interested in that. After that I gave them details of our new machine, but most of them had already used one very much like it. So I went on to talk about R & D - unfortunately they seemed more interested in the theoretical side, so that bit wasn't very successful. Then I asked them if they wanted me to tell them about the situation in the United States and they said they already knew about all that. So I offered to show them our film; but the chairman said that wasn't necessary as everybody was well aware of our company's activities. So, instead I outlined the latest research in the field, but really, from the questions they asked, it was quite clear that they were already very well-informed. So, all in all, visiting the Polytechnic was rather a waste of time.

Exercise

Now make sentences using *didn't need to* or *needn't have* for each of the phrases underlined.

Note that the phrase *didn't need to* shows that it wasn't necessary, so the speaker didn't do it, while *needn't have* shows that the speaker did it and found out afterwards that it hadn't been necessary.

4 A decline in sales

Sales of your electroplating equipment have been rather low for some time. You have investigated the situation and have come up with the following reasons:

World-wide economic recession
High value of domestic currency
Low rates of commission to agents
Availability of cheap versions from Korea and Taiwan*
Reliability problems with some machines
Fall in amount of electroplating generally*
Long delivery periods

The asterisk (*) indicates *Very important reason*

Exercise

Write a paragraph setting out the reasons for the decline. Try to use some of the expressions you learned in Unit 24.

5 Allowed, prohibited, restricted

You are setting up an electroplating factory in a South American country. You want to know if certain things are allowed or not. This is what you have found out:

	Allowed	*Prohibited*	*Condition*
Importing parts for assembly	☑	☐	inform Ministry of Industry
Repatriating profits	☑	☐	pay 10% local tax
Using factory 24 hours a day, 7 days a week	☐	☑	—
Employing Europeans as supervisors and engineers	☑	☐	20% must be local people
Using dangerous chemicals in production process	☑	☐	workers have protective clothing
Taking over local companies	☑	☐	your company must first be established for 5 years
Employing people under 16	☐	☑	—

Exercise

Write sentences summarizing this information. Use these phrases where appropriate:

It's absolutely forbidden to . . .
You're not allowed to . . .
You can . . . provided that . . .
You can . . . as long as . . .
You can only . . . if . . .

6 Our success

Here is part of the lecture you gave at Glasgow Polytechnic.

Our company (1 *start*) in the electroplating business fifteen years ago. Prior to that we (2 *be*) dealers in various types of equipment. Since that time we (3 *develop*) 30 plating machines of various kinds and (4 *become*) one of the leading manufacturers in Europe.

Our success (5 *be*) largely due to the emphasis we (6 *place*) over the years on R & D. We (7 *set up*) this Department ten years ago and (8 *recruit*) the best engineers, chemists and physicists we (9 *can*) find. In 1980 we (10 *win*) an award for our contribution to exports. This was the first time in our company's history that we (11 *receive*) such an award and it (12 *help*) us to break into new markets.

Exercise

Put the verbs into the correct tense: simple past, present perfect or past perfect.

7 Wishes

You have recently had a hard time at work. You made some unwise decisions and are now having to live with the consequences. Also there are certain daily irritations:

Opening the factory in South America was a big mistake.
Appointing a marketing consultant was the wrong thing to do.
The MD insists on a complete set of statistics every week.
Allowing 25% discount on the German order was certainly the wrong decision.
The Italian agent keeps sending telexes about next year's catalogue.
Asking Bill to translate the report into French was a mistake.
James arrives late every single day.

Exercise

Make sentences starting with 'I wish'. Use *I wish*+past perfect if you are regretting a past action; *I wish*+*would* if you are irritated with the present situation.

Glossary

Words are defined according to the context in which they appear in this book.

Numbers in brackets refer to the Units from which the words are taken.

absenteeism (22) staying away from work without a good reason
to abstain (23) not to register a vote
abstention (23) non-registered vote
access (20) opportunity to approach or use
accommodation (16) place to stay or live (e.g. house, flat or hotel)
account (3) arrangement to receive invoices for goods supplied every month
administration (5) direction or management of a company
adverse (25) negative (adj.)
advertisement (2) public notice aimed at selling goods or services
after-sales service (24) agreement by supplier to repair as necessary goods sold to a customer for an agreed period
agenda (12) list of points for discussion at a meeting
agent (1) representative of a company in another part of the country or overseas
to allocate (6) to divide and share out
annual (1) every year (adj.)
applicant (7) a person wanting to be considered for a job
appointment (21) an agreement to meet someone at a specific time for a discussion
assembly (1) putting together prefabricated parts of a machine or other product in a factory
asset (19) natural resource which has potential cash value
attributes (14) personal qualities
authorities (7) official bodies (e.g. Government departments)
available (2) can be used or obtained

ball bearings (1) system of rolling balls in a metal casing used to reduce friction between two pieces of metal
bid (25) detailed offer to supply goods or services
bilingual (14) able to speak two languages equally well
body scanner (26) machine which locates any medical abnormalities in the body
boom (24) high point of business activity
boundary fence (10) barrier around the edge of a factory site
brand name (3) registered name of a product used in all advertising
breakdown (8) failure (of a machine)
to bring forward (26) to rearrange a meeting or appointment for an earlier date
brochure (1) small book or pamphlet giving details of goods or services
to budget (2) to make financial calculations for a period in the future
building society (15) organization which lends money to people buying their own homes

campaign (6) a planned series of activities with a specific objective (e.g. increasing sales)
to cancel (9) to go back on an agreement; to make something invalid (e.g. to cancel an order or a cheque)
candidate (14) a person who is interviewed for a job
capacity (23) total amount of production possible
capital (15) money used to start a business or to provide income through investment
carrier (13) company arranging transport of goods from supplier to customer
cashflow (8) movement of money to, from and within a company
catalogue (2) a list of a company's products, including specifications, order numbers and prices
check-in (3) reporting your arrival at the airport in advance of your flight
client (14) person who pays a professional for help, advice or other service
commitments (26) promises to do certain things
committee (22) a group of people who meet to discuss a particular aspect of a company's activities
competitive (11) being able to supply goods or services more cheaply and on better terms than another supplier
competitor (11) company supplying similar service or product
complaint (13) statement of dissatisfaction with goods or services
components (1) parts needed for a manufacturing process

conference (1) international (or national) meeting in which people working in the same field or industrial sector exchange ideas and information
consignment (9) a number of goods sent together to a customer
constraint (26) something limiting one's freedom of action
consultancy (14) professional advice service
consultation (23) meeting to obtain professional advice
consumer (24) person who buys goods or uses services
consumption (10) total amount used or bought
contract (2) formal agreement between people or companies
controversy (22) public argument and disagreement
to convince (12) to make a person believe something is true
coup (19) sudden take-over of power
to credit (13) to add to the credit balance of an account
credit card (7) plastic card used to obtain goods and services (payment is made later direct to the credit card company)
credit note (13) document issued when goods are returned showing that the supplier owes the customer a certain amount of money
curriculum vitae (14) a list of personal details, including job experience, prepared by a job applicant
customer (7) person or company buying goods or services
cutback (26) reduction in spending or production

damage (5) bad condition of property resulting from accident, fire, etc.
data processing (5) computer controlled system of storing and using information
to debit (13) to add to the debit (negative) side of an account
degree (14) university qualification
delegate (2) person representing a company or political group at a conference
delivery (3) taking goods to a buyer's address
demand (1) desire by people or companies to buy particular products or services
departure (3) leaving, taking off (of a plane)
devaluation (24) reduction in value of a currency in comparison with other currencies
dimension (4) measurement of length, width, depth or height
discount (2) special percentage reduction in price
discrepancy (17) small difference between sets of financial calculations
to distribute (1) to send out goods to shops, agents, etc., for sale to the public
diversification (6) moving into new, related areas of business activity
dividend (24) money paid to shareholders from company profits according to the number of shares held
documents (7) official papers
downturn (24) fall or reduction

economical (17) using energy or money efficiently
to economize (16) to save money by reducing spending
employee (1) person working for a company and receiving a salary or wage
to endorse (25) to allow your name to be used to advertise a product
equipment (1) machinery, etc. needed for all aspects of production
essential (24) absolutely necessary
estimate (8) provisional calculation (e.g. of price) sent to a potential customer
exchange rate (20) price fixed on international money markets or currencies in terms of other currencies
executive (1) manager responsible for an aspect of company policy
expansion (21) increase in size, staffing and activity of a company
expatriate (20) UK citizen working and living abroad
expenditure (12) total spending
expense (16) cost
experience (7) practical knowledge gained by working in a particular field
extractor fan (10) machine which removes hot, dirty air from a building

feasibility study (23) investigation to find out if a proposed project is possible and/or profitable
file (21) case, folder or box holding information (e.g. correspondence) about a particular customer or product
flight (3) journey by plane
floodlighting (10) lighting system for a large, open space (e.g. factory site, football pitch)
fluctuation (15) small change (e.g. in price) up and down
to found (1) to establish a company or institution
funds (1) resources in the form of money
furniture (16) all movable articles in a home (e.g. tables, chairs, desks)

gilt-edged securities (15) stock exchange investment considered safe
goodwill (16) company's good image and reputation for quality, reliability, value, etc.
government stock (15) bonds, shares, etc., issued by the Government to raise money
grant (22) money given by Government or other institution to companies or individuals to finance a particular project
guarantee (3) legal promise that goods supplied are in good order

headquarters (1) head office of a company
to hire (15) to borrow something for a limited period against payment
hoarding (25) place on a building or by the roadside for a large advertising poster

import licence (7) official permission to import goods
to incorporate (25) to include
inefficient (23) not working quickly or accurately
inflation (6) annual percentage increase in prices

installation (8) setting up equipment or machine ready for use
insurance (5) agreement that a sum of money will be paid in case of accident, loss, death, etc.
interest (7) money paid for the use of money
in transit (8) during transport of goods
to investigate (5) to find out reasons, to examine the background, etc.
investment (1) putting money into a project, bank, etc., with the hope of income or profit later

joint venture (6) project carried out together with a partner

leaflet (15) piece of paper with advertising or information about a product, service or event
lease (22) agreement to rent property for a fixed period
lecture (2) speech on technical or academic subject by an expert to a group
legal (14) concerned with the law
liability (9) legal responsibility
local authority bond (15) stock issued by town or local area to raise money
location (1) place where factory, office, etc., is sited
loss (5) damage to insured article
lucrative (9) extremely profitable

mail shot (1) letter sent to potential customers to publicize goods or services
maintenance (17) keeping a machine in good working order
manpower (17) number of people working in a factory, office, etc.
to manufacture (1) to make or prodcue in a factory
marketing (1) making potential customers aware of a company's goods or services
market research (23) investigating potential market for a product or service using questionnaires, etc.
media (25) public and commercial news organizations (e.g. TV, radio, the press)
memo (1) (also *memorandum*) letter sent to a person or a department within the same company
minutes (18) official record of a meeting
monopoly (19) control by one company (or Government department) of all aspects of the provision of a particular commodity or service
multinational (1) large organization which has companies in more than one country

to nationalize (19) to take into public ownership
National Savings Certificate (15) investment bond issued by the Government to the general public
negotiation (1) detailed discussion about prices, terms and conditions
net (3) amount payable; exact amount after all reductions, such as discounts, have been deducted
night-shift (13) team working on production at night

output (24) total amount produced
over-the-counter (25) available without doctor's prescription
overtime (14) extra working hours paid at higher rate

to patent (1) to register a product or service to obtain legal protection against copies by competitors
payroll (1) number of people employed directly by a company
personnel (7) staff working for a company (also department) concerned with the appointment and well-being of staff
petty cash (21) small amount of cash held by company to repay employees' small expenses (e.g. taxi fares, meals)
to phase out (26) to take away gradually
policy (5) document which sets out risks which are covered by an insurance company
portfolio (15) a collection of shares owned by an investor (or group of investors)
premises (5) group of buildings, a factory or offices where a company carries on its business
press release (6) information given to newspapers and TV about products and services
priority (19) place in a list according to importance
to promote (25) to bring to the attention of the public
property (15) general term for buildings, offices or a factory
proposal (12) formal suggestion
prototype (18) experimental model of a machine used for tesing
publicity (25) making people aware of a product or service
public relations (12) company department which makes sure that the company's public image is favourable
publisher (2) company which arranges the printing and selling of books, newspapers or magazines
to purchase (3) to buy

qualifications (1) certificates or diplomas from official institutions (e.g. schools, universities) relevant to a particular job
quality control (1) checking the standards of finished goods
questionnaire (1) a list of questions designed to find out public opinion on a particular subject
quotation (3) offer to supply goods or services at a certain price, under certain terms and conditions

recession (1) a period of reduced economic activity
recommendation (12) statement in favour of project, etc., giving reasons
recreation (22) amusement; way of spending free time
to recruit (7) to advertise for, interview and appoint new staff
red tape (19) troublesome rules and procedures which delay business
redundant (10) unemployed because the company does not have enough work
refund (25) credit given when damaged or wrongly ordered goods are returned to the supplier
regulations (7) legal rules and requirements
reliability (1) high quality of a machine; not breaking down or needing frequent repairs or maintenance

rent (16) money paid for use of flat or house
repatriation (20) sending back (money) to home country
reputation (20) opinion held by others about a company, product or service
reservation (3) booking of a ticket, hotel room, etc.
roller bearings (1) friction-reducing systems with metal rollers in an outer casing
routine (26) regular arrangements of daily life, production, office procedure, etc.

salary (19) money paid monthly to staff of a company
to sample (1) to take a percentage of finished goods for quality control testing
seminar (20) small group of people meeting to discuss a particular subject (usually theoretical or academic)
settlement (5) an agreement at the end of negotiations (especially on a question of insurance)
share (15) a part of the ownership of a company
ship-shape (26) in good order
short-staffed (26) not having enough staff for the amount of work to be done
to simplify (16) to make easier
site (1) location of a factory
slot (25) advertising spot on TV
sophisticated (12) complex and up-to-date
specification (10) list of technical details of a machine, etc.
sponsor (25) company which supports arts or sports event financially, partly for advertising purposes
statement (13) document showing details of financial transactions during a given period (e.g. between customer and supplier; bank and customer)
statistics (6) collected numbers representing facts or other information
stock (3) goods or supplies held for immediate use
stockbroker (15) person who buys and sells shares, especially at the Stock Exchange
stock control (12) system of monitoring level of stocks held at any one time
stock market (15) place where stocks and shares in public companies are bought and sold
subliminal (25) at a level of the mind at which the conscious senses are unaware
suburbs (16) residential area on the edge of a town or city
to supervise (8) to watch over a section of workers or office staff
supplier (3) company selling goods to another company
survey (12) investigation of a particular subject, market, etc.
to suspend (26) to stop for a period of time

take-over (1) the purchase of one company by another
team spirit (16) the feeling that the success of the group is more important than the individual
telex (2) message sent by post office lines with teleprinter
tender (19) statement of price one would charge to provide goods or services (tenders are submitted by a number of companies and then opened and compared at an agreed time)
trade deficit (24) negative balance of imports of a country against exports
trade journal (6) newspaper or magazine with news about a particular industrial or professional sector
translation (7) version of a text in another language
travellers' cheque (11) cheque bought in home country for later exchange in foreign country to obtain services, goods or local currency
trend (6) general direction
troubleshooter (22) person employed specifically to solve technical and other problems
turnover (1) volume of goods sold annually
TV commercial (25) short spot on TV used to make the public aware of products and services

unanimous (23) supported by all present (or all those voting)
unemployed (22) without a job
unit trust (15) company which controls investments of different types

VAT (7) Value Added Tax
venture (1) project or scheme
visa (11) official permission to enter a foreign country (often stamped in the passport)
visual aid (17) picture, map, film, etc., used as back-up for presentation

warehouse (5) place where finished goods are stored
workload (17) amount of work to be done
workshop (1) informal group learning and discussion session